Cambridge School Shakespeare

OTHELLO

Edited by Jane Coles

Series editors: Richard Andrews and Vicki Wienand

Founding editor: Rex Gibson

CAMBRIDGE
UNIVERSITY PRESS

CAMBRIDGE
UNIVERSITY PRESS

University Printing House, Cambridge CB2 8BS, United Kingdom

One Liberty Plaza, 20th Floor, New York, NY 10006, USA

477 Williamstown Road, Port Melbourne, VIC 3207, Australia

314–321, 3rd Floor, Plot 3, Splendor Forum, Jasola District Centre, New Delhi – 110025, India

79 Anson Road, #06–04/06, Singapore 079906

Cambridge University Press is part of the University of Cambridge.

It furthers the University's mission by disseminating knowledge in the pursuit of education, learning and research at the highest international levels of excellence.

www.cambridge.org
Information on this title: www.cambridge.org/9781107615595

Commentary and notes © Cambridge University Press 1992, 2014
Text © Cambridge University Press 1984, 2014

First published 1992
Second edition 2005
Third edition 2014

20 19 18 17 16 15 14 13 12 11

Printed in Italy by Rotolito S.p.A.

A catalogue record for this publication is available from the British Library

ISBN 978-1-107-61559-5 Paperback

....

Cover image: Ludlow Festival 2010, © Donald Cooper/Photostage

Contents

**Cambridge School
Shakespeare**

Introduction

This *Othello* is part of the **Cambridge School Shakespeare** series. Like every other play in the series, it has been specially prepared to help all students in schools and colleges.

The **Cambridge School Shakespeare** *Othello* aims to be different. It invites you to lift the words from the page and to bring the play to life in your classroom, hall or drama studio. Through enjoyable and focused activities, you will increase your understanding of the play. Actors have created their different interpretations of the play over the centuries. Similarly, you are invited to make up your own mind about *Othello*, rather than having someone else's interpretation handed down to you.

Cambridge School Shakespeare does not offer you a cut-down or simplified version of the play. This is Shakespeare's language, filled with imaginative possibilities. You will find on every left-hand page: a summary of the action, an explanation of unfamiliar words, and a choice of activities on Shakespeare's stagecraft, characters, themes and language.

Between each act and in the pages at the end of the play, you will find notes, illustrations and activities. These will help to encourage reflection after every act and give you insights into the background and context of the play as a whole.

This edition will be of value to you whether you are studying for an examination, reading for pleasure or thinking of putting on the play to entertain others. You can work on the activities on your own or in groups. Many of the activities suggest a particular group size, but don't be afraid to make up larger or smaller groups to suit your own purposes. Please don't think you have to do every activity: choose those that will help you most.

Although you are invited to treat *Othello* as a play, you don't need special dramatic or theatrical skills to do the activities. By choosing your activities, and by exploring and experimenting, you can make your own interpretations of Shakespeare's language, characters and stories.

Whatever you do, remember that Shakespeare wrote his plays to be acted, watched and enjoyed.

Rex Gibson
Founding editor

This new edition contains more photographs, more diversity and more supporting material than previous editions, whilst remaining true to Rex's original vision. Specifically, it contains more activities and commentary on stagecraft and writing about Shakespeare, to reflect contemporary interest. The glossary has been enlarged too. Finally, this edition aims to reflect the best teaching and learning possible, and to represent not only Shakespeare through the ages, but also the relevance and excitement of Shakespeare today.

Richard Andrews and Vicki Wienand
Series editors

This edition of *Othello* uses the text of the play established by Norman Sanders in **The New Cambridge Shakespeare**.

Othello tells the story of a black army general who has secretly married the white daughter of a leading politician. Will their marriage survive in the face of racism, jealousy and a struggle for power?

v

▲ Othello has no idea that his trusted ensign (standard-bearer), Iago, is plotting against him. Iago says he is angry that Othello has promoted his younger colleague Cassio to the rank of lieutenant instead of him, but we never know exactly why Iago hates Othello so much.

▶ Iago enlists the help of a local gentleman, Roderigo, to stir up trouble for Othello and Desdemona. They tell Desdemona's father about the secret marriage, and spread racist lies.

▲ Meanwhile, a Turkish fleet threatens the island of Cyprus, and Othello is sent to command the Venetian forces.

▶ Othello is hailed as a 'noble and valiant general!' A terrible storm scatters and destroys the Turkish invasion fleet, and Othello lands safely in Cyprus.

Othello is reunited with Desdemona, and he takes up official duties as commander of the occupying forces in Cyprus.

Othello is unaware that Iago is watching their every move. He plans to destroy Othello by suggesting that Desdemona is having an affair with the handsome Cassio.

Iago tricks Cassio into getting drunk at a barracks party. After Cassio is involved in a drunken brawl, Othello dismisses him from office and promotes Iago in his place.

Meanwhile, Iago tells his wife Emilia to steal Desdemona's handkerchief – an antique love token given to her as a wedding gift by Othello. Iago later places it in Cassio's lodgings, as supposed evidence of Desdemona's adultery.

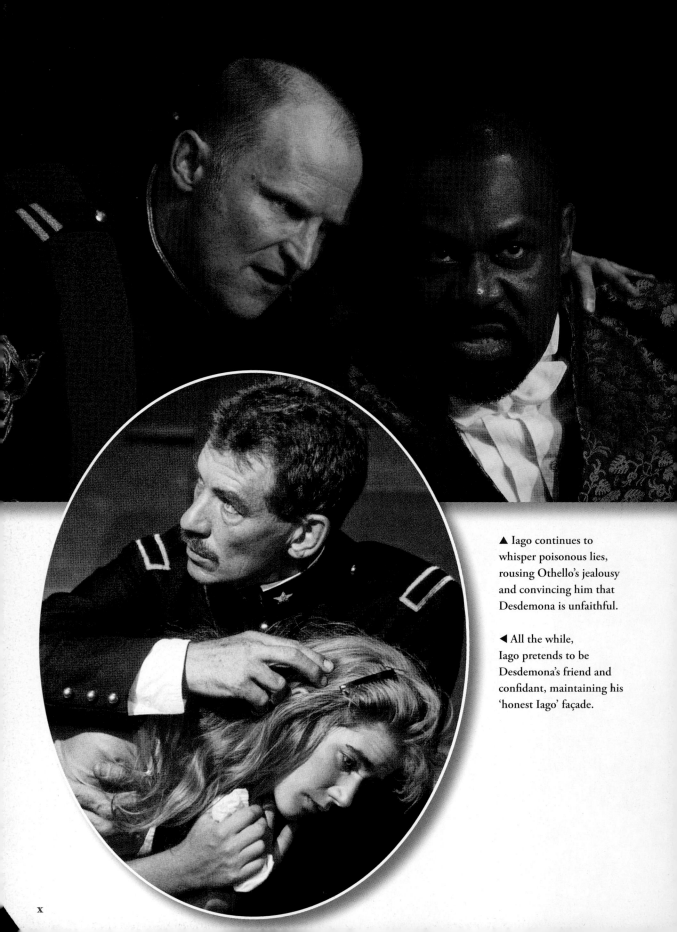

▲ Iago continues to whisper poisonous lies, rousing Othello's jealousy and convincing him that Desdemona is unfaithful.

◄ All the while, Iago pretends to be Desdemona's friend and confidant, maintaining his 'honest Iago' façade.

▶ Eventually, Iago's lies and tricks move Othello to a jealous rage: 'jealousy: / It is the green-eyed monster which doth mock / The meat it feeds on'.

▼ Othello attacks Desdemona, refusing to listen to reason.

▲ Only after he has killed Desdemona does Othello discover the truth about her innocence. Grief-stricken and full of remorse, Othello kills himself. Iago is arrested.

List of characters

OTHELLO A black army general in the service of the Duke of Venice
DESDEMONA Othello's wife, daughter of Brabantio
IAGO Othello's ensign (standard-bearer)
EMILIA Iago's wife, companion to Desdemona
CASSIO Othello's lieutenant
BIANCA in love with Cassio

DUKE OF VENICE
BRABANTIO A Venetian senator, father of Desdemona
RODERIGO A Venetian gentleman, in love with Desdemona
GRATIANO Brabantio's brother
LODOVICO Brabantio's relative

MONTANO Governor of Cyprus

Senators of Venice
Gentlemen of Cyprus

CLOWN Servant to Othello

Herald
Messenger
Musicians, soldiers, attendants, servants
Sailor

The action of the play takes place in Venice and Cyprus

Two men are in the middle of an argument. Roderigo accuses Iago of cheating him. Iago is angry about failing to gain the promotion that has gone instead to Michael Cassio.

Stagecraft

A dramatic opening (in pairs)

In the theatres of Shakespeare's time, there was no electric lighting and no stage curtain. The playwright had to signal the start of the play by means of a dramatic opening scene. Here, the noisy audience would be silenced by two men in the middle of a heated argument, accompanied by much swearing.

a   Read this opening conversation (lines 1–34) aloud. Try reading it in several different ways and decide which sounds best. Can you bring out differences between the two characters? Discuss which words in the script give you clues as to how they should be spoken. For example, look carefully at the use of pronouns: in Shakespeare's day, 'thou' indicated familiarity, or suggested that the speaker was addressing someone socially inferior; 'you' was a more polite or respectful form of address.

b   Movie and theatre directors have chosen various ways to begin the play. Think about how you might want to set the scene – for example, how could you suggest to an audience that this opening scene takes place in Venice? Consider the ways the actors might enter the stage or screen, and what sound and lighting effects might imply a street at night.

c   The play opens halfway through an argument. Make up what you think Iago and Roderigo have been saying before the play begins. Improvise the full argument, making sure that your dialogue ends on the first line of the play.

d   Imagine you are preparing to direct a performance of *Othello*. Start a Director's Journal and record your ideas (advice for actors, costume sketches, set designs) as you read through the play.

'Sblood by God's blood (a swear word)

Abhor me you may hate me

In personal suit personally requested

Off-capped to him paid him their respects (by taking off their hats)

bombast circumstance fancy excuse

epithets of war military jargon

Non-suits my mediators rejects proposals made by my supporters

Certes certainly

arithmetician theorist (i.e. has studied the theory of war)

Florentine person from Florence

squadron small group of soldiers

devision strategic placing of soldiers

togèd consuls senators wearing the robes of peace

had the election was chosen

1   Michael Cassio – why does Iago dislike him?

Iago explains why he believes he has not been promoted to the rank of lieutenant (lines 8–27).

- Look carefully at the way Iago describes Cassio (lines 19–26) and pick out four key phrases that suggest why Iago is jealous of him. Compare your phrases with those of other students. How many do you have in common?

Othello, the Moor of Venice

Act 1 Scene 1
Venice   A street at night

Enter RODERIGO *and* IAGO.

RODERIGO	Tush, never tell me, I take it much unkindly
	That thou, Iago, who hast had my purse
	As if the strings were thine shouldst know of this.
IAGO	'Sblood, but you will not hear me.
	If ever I did dream of such a matter,
	Abhor me.
RODERIGO	Thou told'st me thou didst hold him in thy hate.
IAGO	Despise me if I do not: three great ones of the city,
	In personal suit to make me his lieutenant,
	Off-capped to him; and by the faith of man,
	I know my price, I am worth no worse a place.
	But he, as loving his own pride and purposes,
	Evades them with a bombast circumstance,
	Horribly stuffed with epithets of war,
	And in conclusion,
	Non-suits my mediators. For 'Certes', says he,
	'I have already chosen my officer.'
	And what was he?
	Forsooth, a great arithmetician,
	One Michael Cassio, a Florentine,
	A fellow almost damned in a fair wife,
	That never set a squadron in the field,
	Nor the devision of a battle knows
	More than a spinster, unless the bookish theoric,
	Wherein the togèd consuls can propose
	As masterly as he. Mere prattle without practice
	Is all his soldiership. But he, sir, had the election,

Line numbers: 5, 10, 15, 20, 25

Iago continues to complain about 'the Moor' and the system of promotion. He says he pretends to be a faithful officer, but follows Othello only to serve his own purposes.

Characters

First impressions of Iago (in small groups)

a Read the script opposite aloud several times, sharing out the lines between all members of the group (hand over to the next person at each full stop, question mark or exclamation mark).

b On a large, plain piece of paper, write 'Iago' in the centre (see the diagram below). In the script, look for the key statements that Iago makes about himself. What words reveal something about his character or motivation? Write these quotations on the second layer of the diagram. On the outer layer, explain in your own words what you believe each quotation tells us about him.

c When you have finished, join together with other groups and compare your sheets. Explain how and why you chose your particular quotations.

d Pool your ideas to produce one final diagram for display on your classroom wall.

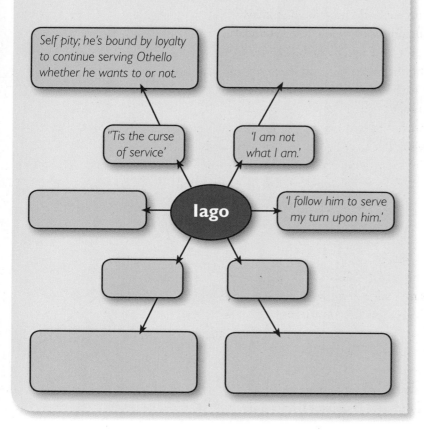

Self pity; he's bound by loyalty to continue serving Othello whether he wants to or not.

''Tis the curse of service'

'I am not what I am.'

Iago

'I follow him to serve my turn upon him.'

lee'd pacified (sailing terminology)
counter-caster accountant

Moorship 'Moor' indicates someone from North Africa
ancient ensign, standard-bearer
Preferment promotion
letter academic qualifications
affection favouritism
old gradation conventional promotion through the ranks
affined bound

obsequious bondage crawling service
provender food and drink
cashiered dismissed from service
trimmed … duty pretending to be loyal

complement extern outward show
daws jackdaws

	And I, of whom his eyes had seen the proof	
	At Rhodes, at Cyprus, and on other grounds	
	Christian and heathen, must be lee'd and calmed	30
	By debitor and creditor; this counter-caster,	
	He, in good time, must his lieutenant be,	
	And I, God bless the mark, his Moorship's ancient.	
RODERIGO	By heaven, I rather would have been his hangman.	
IAGO	Why, there's no remedy. 'Tis the curse of service;	35
	Preferment goes by letter and affection,	
	Not by the old gradation, where each second	
	Stood heir to the first. Now sir, be judge yourself	
	Whether I in any just term am affined	
	To love the Moor.	
RODERIGO	I would not follow him then.	40
IAGO	O sir, content you.	
	I follow him to serve my turn upon him.	
	We cannot all be masters, nor all masters	
	Cannot be truly followed. You shall mark	
	Many a duteous and knee-crooking knave,	45
	That doting on his own obsequious bondage,	
	Wears out his time much like his master's ass	
	For nought but provender, and when he's old, cashiered.	
	Whip me such honest knaves. Others there are	
	Who, trimmed in forms and visages of duty,	50
	Keep yet their hearts attending on themselves,	
	And throwing but shows of service on their lords,	
	Do well thrive by them; and when they have lined their coats,	
	Do themselves homage. These fellows have some soul,	
	And such a one do I profess myself.	55
	For, sir,	
	It is as sure as you are Roderigo,	
	Were I the Moor, I would not be Iago;	
	In following him, I follow but myself.	
	Heaven is my judge, not I for love and duty,	60
	But seeming so for my peculiar end.	
	For when my outward action doth demonstrate	
	The native act and figure of my heart	
	In complement extern, 'tis not long after	
	But I will wear my heart upon my sleeve	65
	For daws to peck at. I am not what I am.	

Iago suggests a way of taking revenge against Othello. They shout in the street outside Brabantio's house, and tell him the news that he has been 'robbed'.

Stagecraft

'BRABANTIO [appears] above at a window' (in pairs)

Below is a photograph of Shakespeare's Globe in London, which was built towards the end of the twentieth century as a replica of the theatre in which Shakespeare's company worked in Elizabethan and Jacobean times. Notice that the theatre has a deep 'thrust' stage, with two exits at the back and a balcony above.

- Talk together about how you would stage lines 68–93, first on the stage of Shakespeare's Globe and then in a modern acting space (for example, in a drama studio). Think about the use of lighting and consider any props that seem appropriate.
- As an extension to this activity, talk together about what you think might be the main challenges of directing a play on the stage at Shakespeare's Globe.

owe own

timorous frightening or fearful

Zounds 'by Christ's wounds' (a swear word)

tupping mating or copulating with
snorting snoring
devil (in old church paintings, devils were commonly portrayed as black)
grandsire grandfather

RODERIGO   What a full fortune does the thick-lips owe,
           If he can carry it thus!

IAGO   Call up her father:
           Rouse him, make after him, poison his delight,
           Proclaim him in the street, incense her kinsmen,   70
           And though he in a fertile climate dwell,
           Plague him with flies: though that his joy be joy,
           Yet throw such chances of vexation on't
           As it may lose some colour.

RODERIGO   Here is her father's house; I'll call aloud.   75

IAGO   Do, with like timorous accent and dire yell,
           As when, by night and negligence, the fire
           Is spied in populous cities.

RODERIGO   What ho, Brabantio! Signior Brabantio, ho!

IAGO   Awake! What ho, Brabantio! Thieves, thieves!   80
           Look to your house, your daughter, and your bags!
           Thieves, thieves!

           BRABANTIO [appears] above at a window.

BRABANTIO What is the reason of this terrible summons?
           What is the matter there?

RODERIGO   Signior, is all your family within?   85

IAGO   Are your doors locked?

BRABANTIO   Why, wherefore ask you this?

IAGO   Zounds, sir, you're robbed; for shame, put on your gown;
           Your heart is burst; you have lost half your soul;
           Even now, now, very now, an old black ram
           Is tupping your white ewe. Arise, arise;   90
           Awake the snorting citizens with the bell,
           Or else the devil will make a grandsire of you.
           Arise, I say!

Brabantio suspects that the two men are drunk. He learns Roderigo's name, but not Iago's. Iago tells Brabantio that Desdemona and Othello are having sexual intercourse and that his descendants will be mere animals.

Language in the play
Verse and prose (in pairs)

Brabantio and Roderigo speak in **blank verse** (a poetic style of writing that does not rhyme). Each line usually has five main beats or stresses. But when Iago interjects at line 109, the script switches to prose. Read the information about verse and prose in 'The language of *Othello*' on page 230, then suggest why Shakespeare has Iago speak in prose here. Consider:

- the different social status of the three characters
- what each of the men is saying
- the context of the scene as a whole.

1 Freeze the action (in threes)

There are three men on stage when Brabantio asks the question 'What profane wretch art thou?'

- Decide where each man is positioned at this point. Who is visible to whom? Then create a tableau (a freeze-frame) of this moment. Think carefully about facial expressions and ways of standing/crouching. Other groups should try to guess who is who in your frozen picture.

2 Who is Roderigo?

When Roderigo introduces himself (line 96), Brabantio is not pleased to see him ('The worser welcome'). He reminds Roderigo that on a previous occasion he ordered him to stay away from his house and his daughter (lines 97–9).

- What might have happened in the past to cause this reaction from Brabantio? Carefully read lines 96–105 and prepare a short improvised drama in modern English, depicting the incident that led to Roderigo being banned from the house.

▶ **What gestures might Brabantio use to express his displeasure?**

charged ordered

distempering draughts alcohol
malicious bravery drunken behaviour
start disturb

place position

grange country residence

Barbary horse North African breed of horse
coursers racehorses
jennets small Spanish breed of horse
germans relatives
profane foul-mouthed
making ... two backs having sexual intercourse

BRABANTIO	What, have you lost your wits?
RODERIGO	Most reverend signior, do you know my voice?
BRABANTIO	Not I; what are you? 95
RODERIGO	My name is Roderigo.
BRABANTIO	The worser welcome;
	I have charged thee not to haunt about my doors;
	In honest plainness thou hast heard me say
	My daughter is not for thee. And now in madness,
	Being full of supper and distempering draughts, 100
	Upon malicious bravery dost thou come
	To start my quiet.
RODERIGO	Sir, sir, sir –
BRABANTIO	But thou must needs be sure
	My spirit and my place have in them power
	To make this bitter to thee.
RODERIGO	Patience, good sir. 105
BRABANTIO	What tell'st thou me of robbing? This is Venice;
	My house is not a grange.
RODERIGO	Most grave Brabantio,
	In simple and pure soul I come to you.
IAGO	Zounds, sir; you are one of those that will not serve God if the
	devil bid you. Because we come to do you service and you think 110
	we are ruffians, you'll have your daughter covered with a Barbary
	horse, you'll have your nephews neigh to you, you'll have
	coursers for cousins, and jennets for germans.
BRABANTIO	What profane wretch art thou?
IAGO	I am one, sir, that comes to tell you your daughter and the Moor 115
	are now making the beast with two backs.
BRABANTIO	Thou art a villain.
IAGO	You are a senator.

Roderigo tells Brabantio that Desdemona has run away to live with Othello. Brabantio leaves to check if the story is true, saying he has already dreamt of such a thing happening.

1 'a gross revolt' (in small groups)

Roderigo tells Brabantio that Desdemona has run away from home to get married without her father's permission. Several of Shakespeare's plays include young people rebelling against their parents' wishes (most famously *Romeo and Juliet*). Generally speaking, in the comedies they are eventually forgiven, while in the tragedies the situation ends in disaster.

- Talk together about stories you have read, and movies or television shows you have seen, that include a similar plot element. How is the family split resolved in those storylines?

2 The chain of being (by yourself)

In medieval England, people believed that God assigned all humans a specific place in society. This meant that people had to accept whatever social status they were born into; it also meant that young people were expected to obey their parents without question. By Shakespeare's time, however, this belief was being challenged.

- Carry out some research of your own into this 'chain of being'. Write some notes about the way in which an Elizabethan audience might view Desdemona's decision to run away and marry without her father's knowledge. How might those views differ from modern perspectives on the issue?

Language in the play
Roderigo's references (in pairs)

In lines 119–39, Roderigo refers to Desdemona in positive terms ('fair'), whereas he uses derogatory language to speak about Othello ('gross clasps', line 125).

- **a** List all the words or phrases Roderigo uses in the script opposite to refer to Desdemona and Othello. Write down what these words and phrases mean.

- **b** We have not yet met Desdemona or Othello. Talk together about the way the audience's expectations are being shaped at this point. Record your ideas and then review them when you reach the end of Act 1.

answer be called to account for

odd-even just after midnight
dull watch late hour

lascivious lustful

saucy insolent

stranger foreigner

Strike on the tinder make a light
taper candle

gall hurt
cast dismiss
loud reason strong support from the Senate

BRABANTIO   This thou shalt answer; I know thee, Roderigo.
RODERIGO   Sir, I will answer anything. But I beseech you
            If't be your pleasure and most wise consent   120
            (As partly I find it is) that your fair daughter,
            At this odd-even and dull watch o'the night,
            Transported with no worse nor better guard,
            But with a knave of common hire, a gondolier,
            To the gross clasps of a lascivious Moor: 125
            If this be known to you, and your allowance,
            We then have done you bold and saucy wrongs.
            But if you know not this, my manners tell me,
            We have your wrong rebuke. Do not believe
            That from the sense of all civility   130
            I thus would play and trifle with your reverence.
            Your daughter, if you have not given her leave,
            I say again, hath made a gross revolt,
            Tying her duty, beauty, wit, and fortunes
            In an extravagant and wheeling stranger   135
            Of here and everywhere. Straight satisfy yourself.
            If she be in her chamber or your house,
            Let loose on me the justice of the state
            For thus deluding you.
BRABANTIO   Strike on the tinder, ho!
            Give me a taper; call up all my people.   140
            This accident is not unlike my dream;
            Belief of it oppresses me already.
            Light, I say, light!   *Exit*
IAGO   Farewell, for I must leave you.
            It seems not meet nor wholesome to my place
            To be produced, as if I stay I shall,   145
            Against the Moor. For I do know the state,
            However this may gall him with some check,
            Cannot with safety cast him; for he's embarked
            With such loud reason to the Cyprus wars,

Iago slips away, not wishing to be identified as a trouble-maker. Brabantio discovers his daughter is indeed missing. He goes off with Roderigo to seek assistance from neighbours and the police.

Characters
'the Moor' (in small groups)

Throughout the whole of this first scene no one has used Othello's name, although all three men have referred to him several times.

a   Collect all the terms used to describe Othello in Scene 1. Copy the table below and add to it to record your findings. Decide what aspect of Othello is being highlighted in each instance – is it a complimentary term or an insulting one? In each case, note down what these descriptive terms tell you about the speaker.

Term used	Aspect of Othello	Spoken by?	What does it say about the speaker?
'the Moor' (line 40)	His ethnicity or 'race'	Iago	He's trying to take away Othello's individuality.
'the thick-lips' (line 67)	His physical features (stereotype)		He is being racist and purposely insulting.
'stranger' (line 135)	He was not born in Venice	Roderigo	

b   When you have completed your table, compare your ideas with those of other groups.

Write about it
Describing Othello

- Using the information you gathered for the activity above, write a paragraph analysing the language by which Othello has been introduced during Scene 1.
- Write a second paragraph, suggesting why a dramatist might want to delay the entrance of the main character until the audience has heard a significant amount about him from other characters in the play.

fathom capability

life livelihood, occupation
flag outward appearance

Sagittary (the name of an inn)

despisèd time time of great dishonour

charms spells, love potions
property nature

discover him reveal where he is

deserve your pains reward you for your trouble

Which even now stands in act, that, for their souls, 150
Another of his fathom they have none
To lead their business; in which regard,
Though I do hate him as I do hell's pains,
Yet, for necessity of present life,
I must show out a flag and sign of love, 155
Which is indeed but sign. That you shall surely find him,
Lead to the Sagittary the raisèd search,
And there will I be with him. So farewell. *Exit*

Enter Brabantio in his nightgown, and SERVANTS *with torches.*

BRABANTIO It is too true an evil. Gone she is,
And what's to come of my despisèd time 160
Is nought but bitterness. Now Roderigo,
Where didst thou see her? O unhappy girl!
With the Moor, say'st thou? Who would be a father?
How didst thou know 'twas she? O she deceives me
Past thought! What said she to you? Get more tapers, 165
Raise all my kindred. Are they married, think you?
RODERIGO Truly I think they are.
BRABANTIO O heaven! How got she out? O treason of the blood!
Fathers, from hence trust not your daughters' minds
By what you see them act. Is there not charms 170
By which the property of youth and maidhood
May be abused? Have you not read, Roderigo,
Of some such thing?
RODERIGO   Yes, sir, I have indeed.
BRABANTIO Call up my brother. O that you had had her!
Some one way, some another. Do you know 175
Where we may apprehend her and the Moor?
RODERIGO I think I can discover him, if you please
To get good guard and go along with me.
BRABANTIO Pray you lead on. At every house I'll call;
I may command at most. Get weapons, ho! 180
And raise some special officers of night:
On, good Roderigo; I'll deserve your pains. *Exeunt*

Iago, pretending to be Othello's faithful supporter, warns Othello that Brabantio will attempt to break up the marriage. Othello is confident that his service to Venice and his noble descent will make all well.

1 Iago's version (in pairs)

In lines 6–10, Iago tells of the conversation he had with Roderigo.

- Talk together about how this version compares with what was actually said in the previous scene. You could draw up two columns on a sheet of paper. In the first column, write down the key items of information given here by Iago; in the second column record how it was presented in Scene 1.

Write about it

Opinions of Othello (by yourself)

We have heard a lot about Othello from other characters. Now we meet him for the first time, in the second scene of the play.

- Look closely at Othello's lines 17–28. Think about what he says and the way he says it. Does your impression of Othello differ now from the opinion you had formed based on the words of Iago, Roderigo and Brabantio in Scene 1? Write a paragraph analysing the language of Othello's first full speech in the play, and explaining what it suggests to you as a viewer or reader.

Stagecraft

'Enter OTHELLO' (in small groups)

a If you were directing a production of the play, what effect would you want to create with Othello's entrance? In Trevor Nunn's 1990 Royal Shakespeare Company (RSC) production, the imposing figure of Othello (played by opera singer Willard White) was framed in a doorway illuminated by brilliant light. He was dressed in smart military uniform. In Janet Suzman's 1987 Market Theatre of Johannesburg production, the physically slight figure of John Kani (playing Othello) was leaning against a wall, dressed in a flowing white shirt and brushing a rose against his lips. What impression do you think each of these directors was trying to make?

b Create a tableau of the stage direction 'Enter OTHELLO, IAGO and ATTENDANTS with torches'. Compare your ideas with other groups and talk about the effects of each tableau.

stuff essence
contrived premeditated
I lack ... service sometimes I'm too nice for my own good
yerked stabbed

fast firmly, properly
magnifico nobleman (Brabantio)

give him cable allow him

signiory the Venetian government

provulgate make public
siege rank
demerits worth

unhousèd unrestrained
circumscription restriction
confine constraint
For the sea's worth for all the treasure in the sea

14

Act 1 Scene 2
Venice   Outside the Sagittary

Enter OTHELLO, IAGO *and* ATTENDANTS *with torches.*

IAGO   Though in the trade of war I have slain men,
              Yet do I hold it very stuff o'the conscience
              To do no contrived murder. I lack iniquity
              Sometimes to do me service. Nine or ten times
              I had thought to have yerked him here, under the ribs.   5

OTHELLO   'Tis better as it is.

IAGO   Nay, but he prated,
              And spoke such scurvy and provoking terms
              Against your honour,
              That, with the little godliness I have,
              I did full hard forbear him. But I pray, sir,   10
              Are you fast married? For be sure of this,
              That the magnifico is much beloved,
              And hath in his effect a voice potential
              As double as the duke's. He will divorce you,
              Or put upon you what restraint and grievance   15
              The law, with all his might to enforce it on,
              Will give him cable.

OTHELLO   Let him do his spite;
              My services which I have done the signiory
              Shall out-tongue his complaints. 'Tis yet to know –
              Which, when I know that boasting is an honour,   20
              I shall provulgate – I fetch my life and being
              From men of royal siege, and my demerits
              May speak unbonneted to as proud a fortune
              As this that I have reached. For know, Iago,
              But that I love the gentle Desdemona,   25
              I would not my unhousèd free condition
              Put into circumscription and confine
              For the sea's worth. But look what lights come yond!

Cassio arrives on an urgent mission from the Duke to find Othello. He reports that war is imminent and the Senate urgently needs Othello. Iago tells Cassio of Othello's marriage.

Themes

Appearance and reality: two-faced Janus (in pairs)

Why is it significant that Iago swears 'By Janus'?

- Stand back to back. One partner reads Iago's words in lines 1–53 aloud, pausing at the end of each sentence. The other partner speaks in each pause, saying what Iago's real thoughts might be.

1 Greetings (in large groups)

Two separate search parties come looking for Othello in lines 34–61 – one on official war business, the other pursuing a personal grievance.

- Work out how each search party might enter and how they would greet Othello and Iago. Freeze each scene at the moment of greeting, making it clear from the way the characters are looking or standing who they are and what their intentions are. Perform your tableaux for the rest of the class to guess who is who.

raisèd awakened and indignant

parts natural gifts
manifest me rightly be justly evident
Janus (a Roman god with a face on both sides of his head; January is named after him, as it faces back to winter and forward to summer)

haste-post-haste urgent

divine guess

sequent one after the other

▼ Can you work out who is who in this image?

boarded a land carrack taken a treasure ship by an act of piracy
lawful prize legal capture

IAGO	Those are the raisèd father and his friends;
	You were best go in.
OTHELLO	Not I; I must be found. 30
	My parts, my title, and my perfect soul
	Shall manifest me rightly. Is it they?
IAGO	By Janus, I think no.

Enter CASSIO, *with* OFFICERS *and torches.*

OTHELLO	The servants of the duke and my lieutenant!
	The goodness of the night upon you, friends. 35
	What is the news?
CASSIO	The duke does greet you, general,
	And he requires your haste-post-haste appearance
	Even on the instant.
OTHELLO	What is the matter, think you?
CASSIO	Something from Cyprus, as I may divine.
	It is a business of some heat. The galleys 40
	Have sent a dozen sequent messengers
	This very night at one another's heels;
	And many of the consuls, raised and met,
	Are at the duke's already. You have been hotly called for,
	When, being not at your lodging to be found, 45
	The senate hath sent about three several quests
	To search you out.
OTHELLO	'Tis well I am found by you.
	I will but spend a word here in the house,
	And go with you. [*Exit*]
CASSIO	Ancient, what makes he here?
IAGO	Faith, he tonight hath boarded a land carrack; 50
	If it prove lawful prize, he's made for ever.
CASSIO	I do not understand.
IAGO	He's married.
CASSIO	To who?

[*Enter Othello.*]

IAGO	Marry, to – Come, captain, will you go?
OTHELLO	Have with you.
CASSIO	Here comes another troop to seek for you.

Stagecraft

Direct Othello and Brabantio (in pairs)

a If you were directing a production of *Othello*, what advice would you give to the two actors playing Othello and Brabantio at line 57 ('Down with him, thief!') and lines 59–61 (from 'Keep up your bright swords')? Experiment with ways of saying the lines. For example, should Othello sound:

- defensive
- angry and frustrated
- calm
- authoritative and in control
- scared?

Show your version to the rest of the class, then explain how you reached your decisions.

b Look at the production photographs below and on page 16. How do these productions differ in their visual presentation of Othello? Are either of them how you imagine Othello to look? If not, why not? Can you suggest another way to present Othello (perhaps think of a particular actor who might suit the part)?

Keep up put away

refer me … sense appeal to common sense

guardage guardianship, safety of her home

gross in sense quite obvious

disputed on legally challenged

abuser of the world corruptor of Venetian society
arts inhibited black magic
out of warrant against the law

of my inclining my supporters

Enter BRABANTIO, RODERIGO *and* OFFICERS *with lights and weapons.*

IAGO	It is Brabantio; general, be advised,	55
	He comes to bad intent.	
OTHELLO	Holla, stand there!	
RODERIGO	Signior, it is the Moor.	
BRABANTIO	Down with him, thief!	
IAGO	You, Roderigo? Come, sir, I am for you.	
OTHELLO	Keep up your bright swords, for the dew will rust them.	
	Good signior, you shall more command with years	60
	Than with your weapons.	
BRABANTIO	O thou foul thief, where hast thou stowed my daughter?	
	Damned as thou art, thou hast enchanted her,	
	For I'll refer me to all things of sense,	
	If she in chains of magic were not bound,	65
	Whether a maid so tender, fair, and happy,	
	So opposite to marriage that she shunned	
	The wealthy curlèd darlings of our nation,	
	Would ever have, t'incur a general mock,	
	Run from her guardage to the sooty bosom	70
	Of such a thing as thou – to fear, not to delight.	
	Judge me the world, if 'tis not gross in sense	
	That thou hast practised on her with foul charms,	
	Abused her delicate youth with drugs or minerals	
	That weakens motion. I'll have't disputed on;	75
	'Tis probable and palpable to thinking.	
	I therefore apprehend and do attach thee	
	For an abuser of the world, a practiser	
	Of arts inhibited and out of warrant.	
	Lay hold upon him. If he do resist,	80
	Subdue him at his peril.	
OTHELLO	Hold your hands,	
	Both you of my inclining and the rest.	
	Were it my cue to fight, I should have known it	
	Without a prompter. Where will you that I go	
	To answer this your charge?	
BRABANTIO	To prison, till fit time	85
	Of law and course of direct session	
	Call thee to answer.	

19

Brabantio is certain that the Duke will decide in his favour. In the next scene, the Duke and Venetian senators are considering news of the Turkish threats of war on Cyprus, a Venetian colony.

1 Setting Scene 3 – the Council Chamber

Scene 3 marks a change from private – even secret – matters to public affairs of state.

- If you were directing this scene on stage, what kind of room would you have it take place in? Consider how you would show the change of location from the previous street scene, using a bare minimum of props or sound effects. Remember that in most modern productions, scene-changing is very swift and one scene flows quickly into the next. You could sketch out a stage set and add printed images found on an Internet search.

▼ A contemporary illustration of the Duke of Venice.

present urgent

idle trivial
brothers of the state
fellow senators

Bondslaves slaves

composition agreement
credit credibility
disproportioned inconsistent

jump not ... accompt
do not agree precisely

bearing up sailing towards

20

OTHELLO What if I do obey?
How may the duke be therewith satisfied,
Whose messengers are here about my side
Upon some present business of the state   90
To bring me to him?
OFFICER 'Tis true, most worthy signior;
The duke's in council, and your noble self
I am sure is sent for.
BRABANTIO How? The duke in council?
In this time of the night? Bring him away;
Mine's not an idle cause. The duke himself,   95
Or any of my brothers of the state,
Cannot but feel this wrong as 'twere their own;
For if such actions may have passage free,
Bondslaves and pagans shall our statesmen be.

Exeunt

Act 1 Scene 3
Venice   The Council Chamber

Enter DUKE *and* SENATORS, *set at a table with lights, and*
ATTENDANTS.

DUKE There is no composition in these news
That gives them credit.
1 SENATOR Indeed they are disproportioned.
My letters say a hundred and seven galleys.
DUKE And mine, a hundred and forty.
2 SENATOR And mine, two hundred;
But though they jump not on a just accompt –   5
As in these cases where the aim reports
'Tis oft with difference – yet do they all confirm
A Turkish fleet, and bearing up to Cyprus.

1 The Mediterranean – the commercial empire of Venice

In the sixteenth century, Venice was a thriving commercial centre. It was also the dominant colonial force in the Mediterranean. Powerful merchants protected their commercial empire with military strength, including mercenary forces. Cyprus was particularly valued as a colony because it was a profitable source of sugar and cotton.

- Read the script opposite, using the map below – which shows the extent of the Ottoman (Turkish) Empire – to help your understanding of the reports of the Turkish invasion plans in lines 14–46.

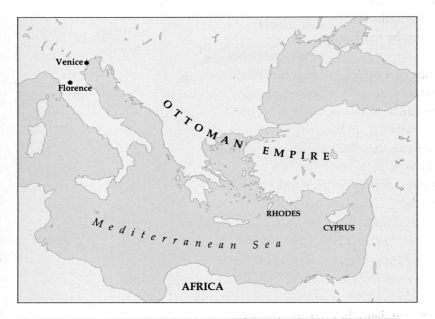

Write about it

Declaration of war

Read up to line 49. The Duke and Senators conclude that the Turkish fleet is heading for Cyprus and give orders for Othello to lead the Venetian counter-attack.

- Write the formal statement published by the Duke's press office. Briefly explain the case for war against the Turks, and outline the strategic decisions made by the Senate.

secure me feel confident

approve accept

In fearful sense as a cause for alarm

galleys warships

assay test

pageant show, diversion

in false gaze looking the wrong way

more facile question bear it an easier target to attack

brace readiness

wake bustle about

wage risk

in all confidence we can confidently say

DUKE	Nay, it is possible enough to judgement:
	I do not so secure me in the error,	10
	But the main article I do approve
	In fearful sense.
SAILOR	(*Within*) What ho! What ho! What ho!
OFFICER	A messenger from the galleys.

Enter a SAILOR.

DUKE	Now, what's the business?
SAILOR	The Turkish preparation makes for Rhodes;
	So was I bid report here to the state	15
	By Signior Angelo.
DUKE	How say you by this change?
1 SENATOR	This cannot be,
	By no assay of reason. 'Tis a pageant
	To keep us in false gaze. When we consider
	The importancy of Cyprus to the Turk,	20
	And let ourselves again but understand
	That as it more concerns the Turk than Rhodes,
	So may he with more facile question bear it,
	For that it stands not in such warlike brace,
	But altogether lacks the abilities	25
	That Rhodes is dressed in. If we make thought of this,
	We must not think the Turk is so unskilful
	To leave that latest which concerns him first,
	Neglecting an attempt of ease and gain
	To wake and wage a danger profitless.	30
DUKE	Nay, in all confidence he's not for Rhodes.
OFFICER	Here is more news.

A messenger from Montano, the governor of Cyprus, brings more news: the Turkish fleet, reinforced, sails towards Cyprus. Discussion of war tactics is interrupted by Brabantio's and Othello's arrival.

1 What is the Turkish fleet doing? (in pairs)

Read the messenger's words at lines 33–42 and the Duke's response at line 43. Look back at the map on page 22 and see if you can work out the Turkish war strategy. Remind yourself why Cyprus was important to both the Venetians and to the Turks.

2 Valiant Othello – the statue! (in pairs)

It has long been common practice to erect statues to commemorate military leaders who have performed 'great' deeds.

- One person becomes the sculptor, the other the 'raw material'. Create your own statue to commemorate 'Valiant Othello'. Then pose your partner into a second sculpture with the title 'foul thief' (Brabantio uses these words to greet Othello in Scene 2, line 62). How different are your two sculptures based on these descriptions?

3 Public affairs and private anxiety (in small groups)

Brabantio wants to make a formal complaint about Othello to the Duke of Venice and the Venetian Senate. Unfortunately, he raises his complaint just at the moment when the Senate is dealing with urgent matters of state. In lines 52–8, Brabantio tries to convey the extent of his grief, and ends up using the **imagery** of a flood-gate to do it (see p. 231).

- Discuss how appropriate you think it is for Brabantio to take his complaint to the Senate at this moment. If you were the Duke or a Senator, would you consider this to be a public or a personal matter?

Ottomites Turks (from the Ottoman Empire)
injointed linked up

restem … backward course switch back to their original course

servitor servant
free duty respect

straight immediately

engluts engulfs, overwhelms

▼ Is Brabantio being selfish in demanding the attention of the Senate for this personal issue during a time of war?

Enter a MESSENGER.

MESSENGER	The Ottomites, reverend and gracious,
	Steering with due course toward the isle of Rhodes
	Have there injointed with an after fleet.	35
1 SENATOR	Ay, so I thought. How many, as you guess?
MESSENGER	Of thirty sail, and now they do restem
	Their backward course, bearing with frank appearance
	Their purposes toward Cyprus. Signior Montano,
	Your trusty and most valiant servitor,	40
	With his free duty recommends you thus,
	And prays you to believe him.
DUKE	'Tis certain then for Cyprus.
	Marcus Luccicos, is not he in town?
1 SENATOR	He's now in Florence.
DUKE	Write from us to him	45
	Post-post-haste dispatch.
1 SENATOR	Here comes Brabantio and the valiant Moor.

Enter BRABANTIO, OTHELLO, CASSIO, IAGO, RODERIGO *and*
OFFICERS.

DUKE	Valiant Othello we must straight employ you
	Against the general enemy Ottoman.
	[*To Brabantio*] I did not see you: welcome, gentle signior;	50
	We lacked your counsel and your help tonight.
BRABANTIO	So did I yours. Good your grace, pardon me:
	Neither my place nor aught I heard of business
	Hath raised me from my bed, nor doth the general care
	Take hold on me; for my particular grief	55
	Is of so flood-gate and o'erbearing nature
	That it engluts and swallows other sorrows
	And yet is still itself.

Brabantio publicly accuses Othello of abducting and seducing his daughter. Othello offers to explain what has really happened.

Write about it
Brabantio's story

Legends and stories play an important part in *Othello*. Here, in lines 59–64, Brabantio composes his own version of his daughter's flight. In the form of a sinister-feeling myth, write at least three paragraphs telling the story of:

- how Desdemona was charmed
- how she was stolen
- how she was 'abused'.

Language in the play
'Rude am I in my speech' (in groups of four to six)

a Read through Othello's speech in lines 76–94, with each person handing over to the next at a punctuation mark.

b Go through the speech again, this time reading round the group in different styles or moods. Experiment with the sound of the speech until you can agree on the style that best fits the words.

c Talk together about whether you think Othello is 'rude' (clumsy) in his speech. Find examples of his language to support your views, considering terms of address, vocabulary, style and tone. (As you read on, look particularly at Othello's speech from line 127 onwards, and think about how it contrasts with Iago's construction of Othello.)

1 'Here is the man' (in sevens)

At one precise moment (line 71), there are at least seven characters on the stage.

- Work out who they all are and discuss how each might react to the events that are unfolding.
- Present this moment as a tableau to the rest of the class and have them guess who is who.
- Once everyone has been correctly identified, class members can ask certain characters to step forward out of the tableau to reveal what their thoughts are at that moment.

of mountebanks from dubious dealers

deficient simple-minded
Sans without

beguiled ... of herself put a charm on your daughter
bloody book of law laws including the death penalty
After your own sense however you want
our proper son my own son

potent powerful

tane taken

head and front whole extent

pith strength
nine moons wasted nine months ago
field battlefield

conjuration spells

DUKE	Why, what's the matter?
BRABANTIO	My daughter! O, my daughter!
SENATORS	Dead?
BRABANTIO	Ay, to me.

She is abused, stol'n from me, and corrupted 60
By spells and medicines bought of mountebanks;
For nature so preposterously to err,
Being not deficient, blind, or lame of sense,
Sans witchcraft could not.

DUKE Whoe'er he be that in this foul proceeding 65
Hath thus beguiled your daughter of herself,
And you of her, the bloody book of law
You shall yourself read in the bitter letter
After your own sense, yea, though our proper son
Stood in your action.

BRABANTIO Humbly I thank your grace. 70
Here is the man: this Moor, whom now it seems
Your special mandate for the state affairs
Hath hither brought.

ALL We are very sorry for't.

DUKE [*To Othello*] What in your own part can you say to this?

BRABANTIO Nothing, but this is so. 75

OTHELLO Most potent, grave, and reverend signiors,
My very noble and approved good masters,
That I have tane away this old man's daughter,
It is most true; true I have married her;
The very head and front of my offending 80
Hath this extent, no more. Rude am I in my speech
And little blessed with the soft phrase of peace,
For since these arms of mine had seven years' pith
Till now some nine moons wasted, they have used
Their dearest action in the tented field; 85
And little of this great world can I speak
More than pertains to feats of broil and battle;
And therefore little shall I grace my cause
In speaking for myself. Yet, by your gracious patience,
I will a round unvarnished tale deliver 90
Of my whole course of love: what drugs, what charms,
What conjuration and what mighty magic –
For such proceedings I am charged withal –
I won his daughter.

Brabantio again accuses Othello of drugging his daughter. The Duke asks for proof. Othello suggests that Desdemona is sent for to give her side of the story. Iago goes to fetch her.

1 Perfection in a woman?

a According to Brabantio, his daughter is a perfect mixture of womanly virtues. Read his lines 94–8 and note down the aspects he seems to admire in a woman.

b Carry out some research into the position of women in Shakespeare's day. How are the views in Brabantio's speech consistent with or different from the common views of the time?

c Write a paragraph giving your own opinion of Brabantio's views. Make sure you refer explicitly to his words in your writing, and use embedded quotations.

2 'Against all rules of nature' (in small groups)

a Discuss whether you think that today's society is more tolerant of so-called 'mixed-race' marriages. What do you think your family's reaction would be if you were in a similar situation? Think of any countries where other circumstances (for example, politics or religion) might make certain relationships illicit. Compare your views with other groups in your class.

b As your study of *Othello* progresses, look out for items of news (local, national or international) that involve 'mixed-race' relationships. Consider how the matter is reported. For example, commentators famously made reference to *Othello* during the 1995 trial of O.J. Simpson, an African-American sports star accused of murdering his white wife.

3 The case against Othello (in pairs)

With all the talk of criminal acts and sentencing in the script opposite, it is almost as if Othello is on trial. What exactly is the case against him?

a Take a large sheet of paper and draw two columns, headed 'Accusations' and 'Defence'. In the first column, list all the accusations Brabantio makes against Othello, using words and phrases from the script. Read on up to line 158 and add Othello's main points of defence to the chart. Who do you believe – Brabantio or Othello? Why?

b If you were directing the play, how might you increase or decrease the audience's sympathy for Brabantio's view?

---

motion emotion, desires

credit reputation

blood sexual passion,
dram potion
conjured to this effect
created for this purpose
vouch assert

thin habits outward appearances
poor likelihoods
weak possibilities
modern seeming common beliefs

BRABANTIO	A maiden never bold;	
	Of spirit so still and quiet that her motion	95
	Blushed at herself; and she, in spite of nature,	
	Of years, of country, credit, everything,	
	To fall in love with what she feared to look on?	
	It is a judgement maimed and most imperfect	
	That will confess perfection so could err	100
	Against all rules of nature, and must be driven	
	To find out practices of cunning hell	
	Why this should be. I therefore vouch again	
	That with some mixtures powerful o'er the blood	
	Or with some dram conjured to this effect	105
	He wrought upon her.	
DUKE	To vouch this is no proof	
	Without more wider and more overt test	
	Than these thin habits and poor likelihoods	
	Of modern seeming do prefer against him.	
1 SENATOR	But, Othello, speak:	110
	Did you by indirect and forcèd courses	
	Subdue and poison this young maid's affections?	
	Or came it by request and such fair question	
	As soul to soul affordeth?	
OTHELLO	I do beseech you	
	Send for the lady to the Sagittary	115
	And let her speak of me before her father.	
	If you do find me foul in her report,	
	The trust, the office I do hold of you,	
	Not only take away, but let your sentence	
	Even fall upon my life.	
DUKE	Fetch Desdemona hither.	120
OTHELLO	Ancient, conduct them: you best know the place.	
	[*Exit Iago with two or three Attendants*]	
	And till she come, as truly as to heaven	
	I do confess the vices of my blood,	
	So justly to your grave ears I'll present	
	How I did thrive in this fair lady's love,	125
	And she in mine.	
DUKE	Say it, Othello.	

Othello tells how he was introduced to Brabantio's household. He recounts how his relationship with Desdemona began when he entertained her with the story of his life.

1 Othello's life story (whole class)

- As a class, read through the summary Othello gives of his life in lines 131–44, and list the incidents and strange sights that Othello describes.
- Split into small groups. Each group chooses one of Othello's descriptions from the list and prepares a short mime based on his words.
- Afterwards, come back together as a class and show your collective version of Othello's life story in order.

2 Two contrasting stories (in pairs)

Othello's account of his courtship of Desdemona gives a very different picture of their relationship from that told by Brabantio.

a Storyboard two scenes between Othello and Desdemona: one taken from Brabantio's version of events (lines 59–64 and 94–106) and the other illustrating how Othello claims the courtship occurred (lines 144–69).

b Discuss which version you think is true, based on your impressions of the characters of Brabantio and Othello so far. What evidence from the script do you have to support your position?

Language in the play
Othello's 'soft phrase of peace'

Othello claims to be a soldier who is 'little blessed with the soft phrase of peace' (line 82). Now you have read Othello's explanation of his conduct with Desdemona, what do you think?

- Write a paragraph describing the way Othello speaks in this section of the play. Add this to the other notes on language that you have made so far. As you read on, you will find further activities on Othello's language; you can add to your description as you discover more. Always try to include quotations from the script to support your viewpoint.

chances events
moving accidents thrilling adventures
by flood and field on sea and on land

antres caves
idle desolate

Anthropophagi man-eaters, cannibals

pliant favourable

dilate tell in full

intentively altogether

OTHELLO   Her father loved me, oft invited me,
          Still questioned me the story of my life
          From year to year – the battles, sieges, fortunes
          That I have passed.   130
          I ran it through, even from my boyish days
          To the very moment that he bade me tell it;
          Wherein I spake of most disastrous chances,
          Of moving accidents by flood and field,
          Of hair-breadth scapes i'th'imminent deadly breach,   135
          Of being taken by the insolent foe
          And sold to slavery; of my redemption thence,
          And with it all my travels' history:
          Wherein of antres vast and deserts idle,
          Rough quarries, rocks, and hills whose heads touch heaven,   140
          It was my hint to speak – such was the process:
          And of the cannibals that each other eat,
          The Anthropophagi, and men whose heads
          Do grow beneath their shoulders. This to hear
          Would Desdemona seriously incline;   145
          But still the house affairs would draw her thence,
          Which ever as she could with haste dispatch
          She'd come again, and with a greedy ear
          Devour up my discourse; which I observing
          Took once a pliant hour and found good means   150
          To draw from her a prayer of earnest heart
          That I would all my pilgrimage dilate
          Whereof by parcels she had something heard,
          But not intentively. I did consent,
          And often did beguile her of her tears   155
          When I did speak of some distressful stroke
          That my youth suffered. My story being done,
          She gave me for my pains a world of sighs:

Othello completes the story of his courtship just as Desdemona arrives. Brabantio demands to know where her duty lies, and she answers him diplomatically, but makes it clear that she now obeys Othello before her father.

1 'She loved me for the dangers I had passed'
(in small groups)

a Improvise a short scene, using line 166 as the title, in which Othello recounts some of his dangerous adventures. Othello should narrate the tale, while others in the group act out or mime the scenes described. Experiment with different styles of presentation, both serious and comic. Afterwards, discuss whether you think this is a solid foundation for a marriage.

b What is Desdemona looking for in a man? Imagine that she has placed an advertisement in the 'lonely hearts' column of a magazine or on a dating website. Write her ad. As an extension to this activity, you could write Othello's reply to the ad.

Characters

'*Enter* DESDEMONA' (in large groups)

There are six or seven main characters on stage at this moment, as well as a number of Senators.

a Work out who each of these characters is, and then decide where everyone would be positioned on stage when Desdemona enters the scene. Freeze the action at this moment in such a way as to make it clear who's who.

b Consider the different ways in which Desdemona might make her entrance. Secretly? Defiantly? Respectfully? What is her status in this space and how might you show this in your tableau? How do other characters look at her – and what does this reveal about their individual attitudes? Try a number of versions of Desdemona's entrance and choose which one you feel is best.

c Act out lines 173–87, paying particular attention to Desdemona's movement around the stage. For example, she speaks of her 'divided duty' (line 179) to her father and to her husband. To whom does she address those lines? Does she kneel to her father, then move over to her husband? Does she speak directly to the Duke at any point? Try acting out this section in several ways. Once you have agreed on the best way of directing and acting it, share your production with the rest of the class.

passing exceedingly

witness give evidence about

take up ... at the best make the best of a bad job

Light fall
hither here

education upbringing
learn me teach me

hitherto up to now

challenge claim

She swore, in faith, 'twas strange, 'twas passing strange,
'Twas pitiful, 'twas wondrous pitiful;   160
She wished she had not heard it, yet she wished
That heaven had made her such a man. She thanked me,
And bade me, if I had a friend that loved her,
I should but teach him how to tell my story,
And that would woo her. Upon this hint I spake: 165
She loved me for the dangers I had passed,
And I loved her that she did pity them.
This only is the witchcraft I have used.
Here comes the lady: let her witness it.

Enter DESDEMONA, *Iago and Attendants.*

DUKE   I think this tale would win my daughter too.   170
                Good Brabantio, take up this mangled matter at the best:
                Men do their broken weapons rather use
                Than their bare hands.

BRABANTIO   I pray you hear her speak.
                If she confess that she was half the wooer,
                Destruction on my head if my bad blame   175
                Light on the man! Come hither, gentle mistress;
                Do you perceive in all this noble company
                Where most you owe obedience?

DESDEMONA   My noble father,
                I do perceive here a divided duty:
                To you I am bound for life and education;   180
                My life and education both do learn me
                How to respect you. You are lord of all my duty;
                I am hitherto your daughter. But here's my husband;
                And so much duty as my mother showed
                To you, preferring you before her father,   185
                So much I challenge that I may profess
                Due to the Moor my lord.

33

Brabantio grudgingly gives up his accusations against Othello. The Duke attempts to cheer him up, but Brabantio refuses comfort. The Duke appoints Othello to supreme charge of the defence of Cyprus.

1 Brabantio as a father (in pairs)

Read Brabantio's lines 187–96 and 208–18. He wishes Desdemona was adopted, rather than his own flesh and blood. He says that he is forced to give his daughter to Othello because Othello already possesses her, and that he is giving away something very precious to him. Brabantio is glad that he has no more children because he would be tempted to hobble them (like a horse) to stop them running away.

a Which of Brabantio's words do you find the most moving or shocking (if any)? Discuss your reactions with your partner.

b To what extent is Brabantio's attitude the same or different from that of a father in your own time and culture? Write a contemporary version of Brabantio's speech – what might a strict father say nowadays?

2 Rhyming proverbs and clichés (in threes)

Read aloud the Duke's words (lines 200–7) to hear what his speech sounds like. He offers a series of clichés and proverbs (along the lines of 'every cloud has a silver lining') as consolation to Brabantio for the loss of his daughter. He also speaks in **rhyming couplets** (two lines of the same length, with rhyming endings).

a Pick out the three distinct pieces of advice that the Duke offers Brabantio. Choose one each and express it in your own words.

b What effect do these words have? How sincere do you think the Duke is? Discuss subject matter, tone and style of delivery.

c One person takes the role of the Duke, one Desdemona and one Othello. In these roles, write two or three lines expressing what your character is thinking at this point in the play.

3 Back to business – in prose

At line 219, the Duke stops speaking in verse when he begins to discuss affairs of state. Some critics argue that the reason for the switch from verse to prose is that the Duke urgently wishes to move on to what he considers to be more important matters, rather than Brabantio's private affairs.

• If you were directing this scene, how would you mark this change on stage (for example, through tone of voice, movement or the position of the characters)? Write a list of key points in your Director's Journal. What indication is there of Othello's value to the Duke and his Senators?

God bu'y! God be with you! (goodbye)

get beget

that with all my heart the one I wholeheartedly loved

clogs blocks of wood tied to horses' legs to stop them escaping

lay a sentence offer a few words of advice

grise step on a staircase

The robbed someone who has been robbed

bootless useless

He bears ... he hears it is easy to listen to platitudes if you are not suffering as badly as I am

gall bitterness

piercèd through the ear (i.e. by words)

slubber spoil

boisterous violent

BRABANTIO	God bu'y! I have done.

Please it your grace, on to the state affairs.
I had rather to adopt a child than get it.
Come hither, Moor: 190
I here do give thee that with all my heart
Which, but thou hast already, with all my heart
I would keep from thee. For your sake, jewel,
I am glad at soul I have no other child,
For thy escape would teach me tyranny 195
To hang clogs on them. I have done, my lord.

DUKE   Let me speak like yourself and lay a sentence
Which as a grise or step may help these lovers
Into your favour.
When remedies are past the griefs are ended 200
By seeing the worst which late on hopes depended.
To mourn a mischief that is past and gone
Is the next way to draw new mischief on.
What cannot be preserved when fortune takes,
Patience her injury a mockery makes. 205
The robbed that smiles steals something from the thief;
He robs himself that spends a bootless grief.

BRABANTIO   So let the Turk of Cyprus us beguile,
We lose it not so long as we can smile;
He bears the sentence well that nothing bears 210
But the free comfort which from thence he hears;
But he bears both the sentence and the sorrow
That to pay grief must of poor patience borrow.
These sentences, to sugar or to gall,
Being strong on both sides, are equivocal. 215
But words are words; I never yet did hear
That the bruisèd heart was piercèd through the ear.
Beseech you now, to the affairs of the state.

DUKE   The Turk with a most mighty preparation makes for Cyprus.
Othello, the fortitude of the place is best known to you; and 220
though we have there a substitute of most allowed sufficiency,
yet opinion, a more sovereign mistress of effects, throws a
more safer voice on you. You must therefore be content to
slubber the gloss of your new fortunes with this more stubborn
and boisterous expedition. 225

Othello promises to depart immediately for Cyprus, asking only that Desdemona be provided for. Neither Brabantio nor Desdemona wishes her to return to her father's house. Desdemona asks if she might accompany Othello.

Characters

'A maiden never bold'?

Remember, Desdemona's father said of her:

> A maiden never bold;
> Of spirit so still and quiet that her motion
> Blushed at herself

Act 1 Scene 3, lines 94–6

a How well does her father really know her? Read all Desdemona's lines in the script opposite. Identify the things she says that appear to challenge both her father's description of her and the convention that a wife should not accompany her husband to war.

b Write two paragraphs outlining your thoughts about the presentation of Desdemona as a dramatic role. Provide evidence to support your ideas, including quotations from the script.

Themes

Appearance and reality

One of the themes that runs through the whole play is that of appearance and reality, including the difference between expected and actual behaviour. Iago pretends to be Othello's loyal ensign while plotting behind his back. Desdemona has appeared to be a dutiful daughter while marrying Othello without her father's knowledge.

- In pairs, discuss Desdemona's comment at line 248: 'I saw Othello's visage in his mind'. What do you think she means by this? What assumption might many Venetians make when they see Othello's face? Can you suggest reasons why she feels it important to make such a point at this moment?

thrice-driven bed of down
feather bed of the finest quality
agnise acknowledge

disposition arrangements
exhibition financial support
besort servants
As levels with her breeding
as is fit for someone in her position

prosperous favourable
charter permission
simpleness innocence

downright violence
open rebellion

quality nature
visage face

OTHELLO   The tyrant custom, most grave senators,
Hath made the flinty and steel couch of war
My thrice-driven bed of down. I do agnise
A natural and prompt alacrity
I find in hardness, and do undertake   230
These present wars against the Ottomites.
Most humbly, therefore, bending to your state,
I crave fit disposition for my wife,
Due reference of place and exhibition
With such accommodation and besort   235
As levels with her breeding.

DUKE   If you please,
Be't at her father's.

BRABANTIO   I'll not have it so.

OTHELLO   Nor I.

DESDEMONA   Nor I; I would not there reside
To put my father in impatient thoughts
By being in his eye. Most gracious duke,   240
To my unfolding lend your prosperous ear
And let me find a charter in your voice
T'assist my simpleness.

DUKE   What would you, Desdemona?

DESDEMONA   That I did love the Moor to live with him,
My downright violence and storm of fortunes   245
May trumpet to the world. My heart's subdued
Even to the very quality of my lord.
I saw Othello's visage in his mind
And to his honours and his valiant parts
Did I my soul and fortunes consecrate.   250
So that, dear lords, if I be left behind
A moth of peace, and he go to the war,
The rites for which I love him are bereft me,
And I a heavy interim shall support
By his dear absence. Let me go with him.   255

1 'Let housewives make a skillet of my helm'

Othello assures the Senators that he is too mature to be swayed by sexual appetite or distracted by Desdemona's presence during a military campaign. In lines 262–70, he uses two images to emphasise this: first, that of Cupid (the god of love) blindfolding him; second, his helmet converted to a cooking pot (skillet).

- Locate the exact words in the script, then create a visual representation of both images.

2 Dramatic irony (in small groups)

Othello says of Iago: 'A man he is of honesty and trust' (line 280). This is an example of **dramatic irony**, when the audience knows more than a character on stage. Dramatic conflict arises out of the fact that this character is unconsciously relying upon crucial information that is untrue.

- You will come across numerous other examples of dramatic irony as you read or watch *Othello*. Make a note of this example in your Director's Journal, and continue to add to this list as you read on.

Themes

Honesty, trust and loyalty (in pairs)

Brabantio's parting words are a warning to Othello that Desdemona is untrustworthy (line 289). Othello swears that he would stake his life on Desdemona's loyalty (line 290).

- On a large sheet of paper, try ways of mapping out which characters have been explicitly described as trustworthy (and by whom), matched by those characters who have been described as untrustworthy or dishonest (and by whom). If you doubt any of these opinions, highlight these on your map and explain why.

Language in the play

Black versus white

The Duke comments: 'If virtue no delighted beauty lack, / Your son-in-law is far more fair than black' (lines 285–6).

- What does this suggest to you about the Duke's attitude to Othello as a black man?

voice consent

scant neglect

seel close up

disports sexual pleasures
skillet cooking pot
helm helmet
indign unworthy
Make head against attack
estimation reputation

import concern

OTHELLO	Let her have your voice.
	Vouch with me, heaven, I therefore beg it not
	To please the palate of my appetite,
	Nor to comply with heat the young affects
	In my distinct and proper satisfaction,
	But to be free and bounteous to her mind.
	And heaven defend your good souls that you think
	I will your serious and great business scant
	For she is with me. No, when light-winged toys
	Of feathered Cupid seel with wanton dullness
	My speculative and officed instruments,
	That my disports corrupt and taint my business,
	Let housewives make a skillet of my helm,
	And all indign and base adversities
	Make head against my estimation!
DUKE	Be it as you shall privately determine,
	Either for her stay or going. Th'affair cries haste,
	And speed must answer it. You must hence tonight.
DESDEMONA	Tonight, my lord?
DUKE	This night.
OTHELLO	With all my heart.
DUKE	At nine i'the morning, here we'll meet again.
	Othello, leave some officer behind
	And he shall our commission bring to you
	With such things else of quality and respect
	As doth import you.
OTHELLO	So please your grace, my ancient:
	A man he is of honesty and trust.
	To his conveyance I assign my wife,
	With what else needful your good grace shall think
	To be sent after me.
DUKE	Let it be so.
	Good night to everyone. [*To Brabantio*] And noble signior,
	If virtue no delighted beauty lack,
	Your son-in-law is far more fair than black.
1 SENATOR	Adieu, brave Moor; use Desdemona well.
BRABANTIO	Look to her, Moor, if thou hast eyes to see:
	She has deceived her father and may thee.
OTHELLO	My life upon her faith!
	Exeunt [*Duke, Brabantio, Cassio, Senators and Attendants*]

Line numbers: 260, 265, 270, 275, 280, 285

Othello charges Iago to look after Desdemona. Roderigo is despondent, but Iago scorns his love-sickness and argues that will and reason govern men's appetites.

1 Contrasting characters (in threes)

Read the exchange between Iago and Roderigo, then try different ways of acting it out. The third member of your group should be the director. Try to distinguish between the two characters in your presentation – for example, Roderigo complains of being mortally love-sick, but Iago scorns such feelings. Remember also that Roderigo is a 'gentleman', while Iago is a professional soldier. Try reading the dialogue in a variety of styles (serious, funny, threatening) and at different paces. Which one sounds best?

Language in the play

Iago's garden imagery (in pairs)

Writers use imagery (see p. 231) to help create a picture or association in the reader's or listener's mind.

a How successful is Iago at creating a picture for you in lines 313–24. Does the imagery make his point clearer?

b Talk about whether you agree with Iago's view that 'our wills are gardeners' where emotions are concerned, and that love (or what Roderigo claims to be love) is 'a sect or scion'. Can love be controlled by reason? One of you argues that it can, the other that it cannot. Whose case is stronger?

Themes

The role of women: sexist language

Some readers find the way Iago describes women to be highly offensive. Examples are derogatory terms like 'guinea-hen' (a prostitute) and his exclamation of 'A fig!', which was a contemptuous remark usually accompanied by a rude gesture (thrusting the thumb between the first and second fingers).

a Write down at least two bullet points explaining why you think Iago uses sexist language.

b Consider how sexist language is used to oppress women today. In your experience, how is sexist language received. Is it always challenged? Prepare notes to support a three-minute presentation to the class.

incontinently immediately

hyssop, thyme aromatic herbs
gender type

corrigible authority ability to control

poise counterbalance
preposterous unnatural
carnal stings sexual urges
unbitted unbridled, unrestrained
sect or scion cutting or graft (a small piece of a larger whole)

                    Honest Iago,   290
          My Desdemona must I leave to thee;
          I prithee, let thy wife attend on her,
          And bring her after in the best advantage.
          Come, Desdemona, I have but an hour
          Of love, of worldly matters and direction   295
          To spend with thee. We must obey the time.

                              Exeunt Othello and Desdemona

RODERIGO   Iago.
IAGO   What say'st thou, noble heart?
RODERIGO   What will I do, think'st thou?
IAGO   Why, go to bed and sleep.   300
RODERIGO   I will incontinently drown myself.
IAGO   If thou dost, I shall never love thee after. Why, thou silly
           gentleman?
RODERIGO   It is silliness to live, when to live is torment: and then we
           have a prescription to die, when death is our physician.   305
IAGO   O villainous! I have looked upon the world for four times seven
           years, and since I could distinguish betwixt a benefit and an
           injury, I never found a man that knew how to love himself. Ere
           I would say I would drown myself for the love of a guinea-hen,
           I would change my humanity with a baboon.   310
RODERIGO   What should I do? I confess it is my shame to be so fond,
           but it is not in my virtue to amend it.
IAGO   Virtue? A fig! 'Tis in ourselves that we are thus or thus. Our
           bodies are our gardens, to the which our wills are gardeners. So
           that if we will plant nettles or sow lettuce, set hyssop and weed   315
           up thyme, supply it with one gender of herbs or distract it
           with many, either to have it sterile with idleness or manured with
           industry, why the power and corrigible authority of this lies in
           our wills. If the balance of our lives had not one scale of reason
           to poise another of sensuality, the blood and baseness of our   320
           natures would conduct us to most preposterous conclusions. But
           we have reason to cool our raging motions, our carnal stings,
           our unbitted lusts; whereof I take this, that you call love, to be
           a sect or scion.
RODERIGO   It cannot be.   325

Iago continues to persuade Roderigo that Desdemona and Othello will soon tire of one another. He tells of his hatred for Othello and urges Roderigo to join him in seeking revenge.

Language in the play
More verse and prose (in small groups)

a The dialogue in lines 297–364 is all written in prose. Discuss why Shakespeare might have chosen prose rather than verse here. Think about the situation, the content of Iago's words, and the fact that he urges Roderigo *ten times* to arrange to have a plentiful supply of cash at his disposal.

b Look back through Act 1 and locate all the occasions on which characters speak in prose. Write down the reference (the scene and line numbers) and briefly summarise what is being said and by whom. Then suggest a possible reason why Shakespeare used prose in each case.

▼ What does this photograph suggest about the relationship between Iago and Roderigo?

perdurable long-lasting
stead help

sequestration separation

locusts fruits of the carob tree
acerb bitter
coloquintida bitter apple

compassing achieving
fast true

hearted sincere
conjunctive allied

delivered given birth to
Traverse! about turn

IAGO It is merely a lust of the blood and a permission of the will. Come, be a man. Drown thyself? Drown cats and blind puppies. I have professed me thy friend, and I confess me knit to thy deserving with cables of perdurable toughness. I could never better stead thee than now. Put money in thy purse. Follow thou these wars; defeat thy favour with an usurped beard. I say, put money in thy purse. It cannot be that Desdemona should long continue her love to the Moor – put money in thy purse – nor he his to her. It was a violent commencement, and thou shalt see an answerable sequestration – put but money in thy purse. These Moors are changeable in their wills – fill thy purse with money. The food that to him now is as luscious as locusts shall be to him shortly as acerb as the coloquintida. She must change for youth; when she is sated with his body she will find the error of her choice. Therefore put money in thy purse. If thou wilt needs damn thyself, do it a more delicate way than drowning. Make all the money thou canst. If sanctimony and a frail vow betwixt an erring barbarian and a super-subtle Venetian be not too hard for my wits and all the tribe of hell, thou shalt enjoy her – therefore make money. A pox of drowning thyself! It is clean out of the way. Seek thou rather to be hanged in compassing thy joy than to be drowned and go without her.

RODERIGO Wilt thou be fast to my hopes, if I depend on the issue?

IAGO Thou art sure of me. Go make money. I have told thee often, and I retell thee again and again, I hate the Moor. My cause is hearted: thine hath no less reason. Let us be conjunctive in our revenge against him. If thou canst cuckold him, thou dost thyself a pleasure, me a sport. There are many events in the womb of time which will be delivered. Traverse! Go, provide thy money. We will have more of this tomorrow. Adieu.

RODERIGO Where shall we meet i'the morning?

IAGO At my lodging.

RODERIGO I'll be with thee betimes.

IAGO Go to; farewell. Do you hear, Roderigo?

RODERIGO What say you?

IAGO No more of drowning, do you hear?

RODERIGO I am changed.

IAGO Go to; farewell. Put money enough in your purse.

RODERIGO I'll sell all my land.   *Exit*

330

335

340

345

350

355

360

Alone, Iago reveals that he suspects his wife has been unfaithful with Othello. He begins to make plans to ruin Othello's marriage and to seek revenge on Cassio, by making Othello believe Cassio and Desdemona are lovers.

Stagecraft

Iago's soliloquy (in pairs)

The **soliloquy** is a dramatic convention in which a character who is alone on stage speaks his or her thoughts aloud. In Shakespeare's theatre, the speech was probably delivered from the front of the stage directly to the audience. Usually, a soliloquy reveals a character's motives or state of mind at that point in the play.

This is the first time that Iago has been alone on stage, and the first time the audience hears his version of events. Three ways in which a director could present this speech are:

- directed towards the audience
- as if Iago is talking to himself
- as a voice-over, while the actor looks pensive and lost in thought.

All three methods have been used in movie and television versions of Shakespeare's plays.

a Read the speech in each of the three ways listed above. For each method, consider:

- how the actor would speak the lines
- what movements would be required
- in what ways you would want the audience to react
- how it affects your interpretation of Iago's character. Is he sly, evil or manipulative? Does it draw the audience into colluding and sympathising with Iago?

b Make notes on the impact of each version as you try it out. Get together with two other pairs, present one different interpretation to one another and discuss which is most effective and why.

profane abuse

snipe a long-beaked bird (here a derogatory term)

But only

abroad generally

done my office done my job (i.e. slept with my wife)

holds me well thinks highly of me

proper handsome

plume up my will have a bit of fun, or glorify myself

abuse Othello's ear tell Othello lies

framed made

engendered formed, created

IAGO   Thus do I ever make my fool my purse;   365
For I mine own gained knowledge should profane
If I would time expend with such a snipe
But for my sport and profit. I hate the Moor,
And it is thought abroad that 'twixt my sheets
He's done my office. I know not if't be true   370
Yet I, for mere suspicion in that kind,
Will do as if for surety. He holds me well:
The better shall my purpose work on him.
Cassio's a proper man: let me see now;
To get his place and to plume up my will   375
In double knavery. How? How? Let's see.
After some time, to abuse Othello's ear
That he is too familiar with his wife;
He hath a person and a smooth dispose
To be suspected, framed to make women false.   380
The Moor is of a free and open nature,
That thinks men honest that but seem to be so,
And will as tenderly be led by the nose
As asses are.
I have't. It is engendered. Hell and night   385
Must bring this monstrous birth to the world's light.   *Exit*

Looking back at Act 1
Activities for groups or individuals

1 Cast the play

Imagine you are a movie director about to shoot a new version of *Othello*. Read through the list of characters on page 1, noting down all those who have appeared in Act 1. Decide which well-known actors you would cast in each part. In each case, explain why you have chosen them – what makes them suited to the part?

2 Disputed stories

In Act 1 Scene 3, it is clear that Brabantio believes his daughter has been charmed by Othello – unnaturally lured away from her family by 'witchcraft'. The version of events that Othello offers is that Desdemona was simply enchanted by his heroic stories, which are a mixture of travellers' tales and action-man adventures. Desdemona does not reveal what actually happened during her courtship, but suggests to her father that she is in control of the situation. Re-read this scene, then write four short pieces:

- Brabantio makes a formal written complaint to the Senate, disputing the Duke's ruling.
- Roderigo writes a witness statement in support of Brabantio's complaint (above). How much is really based on his first-hand experience?
- Othello writes a letter to the Duke, thanking him for his support and looking forward to representing the state of Venice in the forthcoming war with Turkey.
- Desdemona writes to her father, describing the events leading up to her marriage to Othello. She explains how she feels after hearing her father's abusive words in front of the Senate.

3 Emerging themes

- 'Thus do I ever make my fool my purse' (Act 1 Scene 3, line 365)
- 'The robbed that smiles steals something from the thief' (Act 1 Scene 3, line 206)
- 'I am not what I am.' (Act 1 Scene 1, line 66)

- 'I must show out a flag and sign of love' (Act 1 Scene 1, line 155)
- 'trust not your daughters' minds / By what you see them act.' (Act 1 Scene 1, lines 169–70)
- 'She loved me for the dangers I had passed' (Act 1 Scene 3, Line 166)

In small groups, choose three of the quotations listed above. Talk together about the meanings of the lines, and the ideas that link them together. Devise a short improvisation, set in a modern context, in which you include your three quotations. Share this with the rest of the class and hold a wider discussion about the themes that seem to be emerging.

4 Iago's language

When talking candidly to Roderigo about Othello, Iago's language is peppered with references to different kinds of animals (e.g. Act 1 Scene 1, lines 87–116). When giving his opinions about love, he draws on garden images (Act 1 Scene 3, lines 313–55). When talking about women, he employs offensive language (Act 1 Scene 3, lines 306–47).

- Re-read the lines mentioned above and discuss with a partner the impression you have of Iago from the way he speaks at these moments. Next, locate some other moments in Act 1 when Iago talks more guardedly. Who is he speaking to and what is the context? How is his language different?

5 Venice: public and private tensions

Why does Shakespeare set Act 1 in Venice? One answer is that the original story that inspired *Othello* was set in Venice and Cyprus and that he simply copied it – but that's not the only possibility. In order to fully understand *Othello*, it is important to know something about sixteenth-century Venice and its social and economic significance in Europe.

In Act 1, Venetian law and order is seen to operate quickly and efficiently. Iago's troublemaking is easily dealt with, as is the Turkish threat to Venetian stability. In Act 2, the setting shifts to a disputed outpost on the edges of Venetian rule. Our introduction to Cyprus is a violent storm, where the natural boundaries between sea and sky are blurred.

- Before you read on, use the information on Venice and Venetian culture on page 237 to write several paragraphs on the tensions between 'private' and 'public' interests in the play so far. You could take each of the main characters in turn and write about their personal interests, discussing whether these conflict with their public duty.

The Doge's Palace in St Mark's Square in Venice still stands today as a testimony to the city's powerful past.

Montano and two gentlemen discuss the terrible storm. A third gentleman brings news that the Turkish fleet has been destroyed. He reports that Cassio's ship has safely docked, but that Othello is still at sea.

Stagecraft

Staging a storm (in pairs)

As with most Elizabethan drama, there are no original stage directions for this scene specifying where it takes place ('Cyprus A quayside' has been added by later editors). Playwrights gave clues in the dialogue to convey to an audience who the characters were and where a scene was set.

a Read lines 1–29 opposite and pick out any words or phrases that provide clues as to:

- where this scene is set
- what has happened since we last saw Othello and the others depart for war with Turkey
- who these characters are.

b In your Director's Journal, write notes on how you would stage the script opposite, including:

- directions you would give the actors
- props or specific items of clothing you might use
- lighting you would like
- any sound effects you might employ.

1 The storm – symbolic significance? (whole class)

In the original story by Giraldi Cinthio, from which Shakespeare took his ideas for *Othello*, there is no storm at all. Yet we have here a whole page of dialogue devoted to a description of it. You will also find that as the scene continues, most of the characters mention the storm several times. Presumably Shakespeare felt that a storm at this point would have some dramatic or thematic use; it certainly echoes the ominous mood established by Iago's couplet at the end of Act 1. Some commentators suggest that the storm also has a symbolic function (as the calm before the storm, or as stormy emotions, and so on).

- Can you think of other possible symbolic functions of the storm? Discuss any ideas you have about its purpose at this point in the play. As you read the rest of this scene, keep in mind this stormy opening, and think about its effect on what follows.

high-wrought flood angry sea

Descry make out, see

ruffianed raged
ribs of oak (of a boat)
hold the mortise hold their joints together
segregation dispersal
banning forbidding
chidden billow waves hurled back
with high and monstrous mane like a wild beast
Bear, Pole constellation of stars (Ursa Major), and the Pole Star
enchafèd flood enraged sea

embayed protected in a bay

designment halts enterprise is crippled
sufferance damage

Veronesa Italian ship

in full commission assuming military authority

48

Act 2 Scene 1
Cyprus   A quayside

Enter MONTANO *and two* GENTLEMEN.

MONTANO   What from the cape can you discern at sea?

1 GENTLEMAN   Nothing at all; it is a high-wrought flood.
I cannot 'twixt the heaven and the main
Descry a sail.

MONTANO   Methinks the wind does speak aloud at land,   5
A fuller blast ne'er shook our battlements.
If it hath ruffianed so upon the sea,
What ribs of oak, when mountains melt on them,
Can hold the mortise? What shall we hear of this?

2 GENTLEMAN   A segregation of the Turkish fleet: 10
For do but stand upon the banning shore,
The chidden billow seems to pelt the clouds;
The wind-shaked surge, with high and monstrous mane,
Seems to cast water on the burning Bear
And quench the guards of th'ever-fixèd Pole.   15
I never did like molestation view
On the enchafèd flood.

MONTANO   If that the Turkish fleet
Be not ensheltered and embayed, they are drowned:
It is impossible they bear it out.

Enter a third GENTLEMAN.

3 GENTLEMAN   News, lads! Our wars are done: 20
The desperate tempest hath so banged the Turks
That their designment halts. A noble ship of Venice
Hath seen a grievous wrack and sufferance
On most part of their fleet.

MONTANO   How? Is this true?

3 GENTLEMAN   The ship is here put in,   25
A Veronesa; Michael Cassio,
Lieutenant to the warlike Moor Othello,
Is come on shore; the Moor himself at sea,
And is in full commission here for Cyprus.

MONTANO   I am glad on't; 'tis a worthy governor.   30

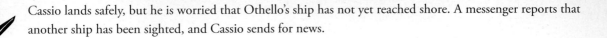

Cassio lands safely, but he is worried that Othello's ship has not yet reached shore. A messenger reports that another ship has been sighted, and Cassio sends for news.

1 A delayed entrance (in pairs)

In the first 171 lines of Scene 1, several characters ask the question 'Is Othello alive or dead?'

* Locate these points in the script. Talk together about what you think is the dramatic purpose of this delay before Othello's triumphant entrance, fresh from the storm. You may find it helpful to think about how Othello's entrance in Act 1 was also delayed.

Characters
More views of Othello

Lines 1–59 contain several references to Othello.

* Find them in the script and list them on a piece of paper. For each quotation, decide whether it is a positive or a negative reference to Othello. Are the comments about Othello's professional or personal attributes? Consider the people making the comments, and what views each person might represent.
* Present your findings in the format of a chart or table, and compare this with the chart you drew up on page 12.

Write about it
Front page news (in small groups)

Imagine you are a news team reporting on the destruction of the Turkish fleet and on Othello's expected triumphant return. Compile the front page of your newspaper. It might contain:

* news of the routing of the Turkish fleet (see lines 10–23)
* a description of the storm (either as part of the main news story or as a separate weather report)
* reports of the fears for Othello's safety
* a profile of Othello, including a report on his recent marriage and interviews with witnesses/colleagues/friends.

Produce a large-format front page for your classroom wall and compare it with other groups' versions. As an additional challenge, one group could choose to write a version of events from either a Turkish or a Cypriot point of view. (A Venetian paper would be very supportive of Othello and his exploits, whereas a Cypriot or Turkish newspaper might view the events differently.)

---

main sea
aerial blue sky
An indistinct regard indistinguishable
arrivance arrivals

approve speak well of

bark ship
pilot navigator on board the ship
allowance reputation
surfeited to death excessive
in bold cure healthy

3 GENTLEMAN   But this same Cassio, though he speak of comfort
Touching the Turkish loss, yet he looks sadly
And prays the Moor be safe; for they were parted
With foul and violent tempest.

MONTANO   Pray heaven he be;
For I have served him, and the man commands   35
Like a full soldier. Let's to the seaside, ho!
As well to see the vessel that's come in
As to throw out our eyes for brave Othello,
Even till we make the main and th'aerial blue
An indistinct regard.

3 GENTLEMAN   Come, let's do so;   40
For every minute is expectancy
Of more arrivance.

Enter CASSIO.

CASSIO   Thanks, you the valiant of this warlike isle
That so approve the Moor. O, let the heavens
Give him defence against the elements,   45
For I have lost him on a dangerous sea.

MONTANO   Is he well shipped?

CASSIO   His bark is stoutly timbered, and his pilot
Of very expert and approved allowance;
Therefore my hopes, not surfeited to death,   50
Stand in bold cure.
                [*A shout*] *within, 'A sail, a sail, a sail!'*

Enter a MESSENGER.

CASSIO   What noise?

MESSENGER   The town is empty; on the brow o'the sea
Stand ranks of people and they cry, 'A sail!'

CASSIO   My hopes do shape him for the governor.   55
                A shot [*is heard within*].

2 GENTLEMAN   They do discharge their shot of courtesy;
Our friends at least.

CASSIO   I pray you, sir, go forth,
And give us truth who 'tis that is arrived.

2 GENTLEMAN   I shall.   *Exit*

Cassio describes to Montano the virtues of Desdemona. Iago is reported to have come ashore. Desdemona, Iago, Emilia and Roderigo are greeted by Cassio, but there is still no news of Othello.

1 Cassio's descriptions of Desdemona (in pairs)

Cassio refers to Desdemona in several different ways. For example, the 'riches of the ship' is how he describes her as she comes ashore.

a Pick out four descriptions of Desdemona from the script opposite and write them down. Comment on the kind of language used (such as comparison or exaggeration) and the effect you think it has.

b Iago and Brabantio have already compared Desdemona to treasure (in Act 1 Scene 1, line 88 and Act 1 Scene 2, line 62). Discuss the significance of linking Desdemona with treasure. What does this use of language reveal about attitudes to women in Othello's society? Are similar terms used today? If so, how they are received?

Characters

Impressions of Cassio

a What advice would you give an actor playing Cassio? Go through the script opposite and decide how you would like each of his speeches to be delivered.

b Look back at Act 1 Scene 1, lines 19–27, and Act 1 Scene 3, lines 374–80, and then make a list of the qualities you think Cassio possesses. Does the production photograph of Cassio below match your expectations of what this character looks like? If not, find an image that more closely represents your impression of Cassio.

---

wived married

paragons excels
blazoning praising
essential vesture perfect beauty
ingener designer

enscarped drawn up into ridges
guiltless keel unwary ship

footing landing
se'nnight week

let her have your knees kneel to her

Enwheel encircle

MONTANO	But, good lieutenant, is your general wived?	60
CASSIO	Most fortunately: he hath achieved a maid	
	That paragons description and wild fame;	
	One that excels the quirks of blazoning pens	
	And in th'essential vesture of creation	
	Does tire the ingener.	

Enter Second Gentleman.

	How now? Who's put in?	65
2 GENTLEMAN	'Tis one Iago, ancient to the general.	
CASSIO	He's had most favourable and happy speed:	
	Tempests themselves, high seas, and howling winds,	
	The guttered rocks and congregated sands,	
	Traitors enscarped to clog the guiltless keel,	70
	As having sense of beauty do omit	
	Their mortal natures, letting go safely by	
	The divine Desdemona.	
MONTANO	What is she?	
CASSIO	She that I spake of, our great captain's captain,	
	Left in the conduct of the bold Iago,	75
	Whose footing here anticipates our thoughts	
	A se'nnight's speed. Great Jove Othello guard	
	And swell his sail with thine own powerful breath,	
	That he may bless this bay with his tall ship,	
	Make love's quick pants in Desdemona's arms,	80
	Give renewed fire to our extinced spirits,	
	And bring all Cyprus comfort.	

Enter DESDEMONA, IAGO, EMILIA *and* RODERIGO.

	O, behold,	
	The riches of the ship is come on shore!	
	You men of Cyprus, let her have your knees.	
	Hail to thee, lady! And the grace of heaven,	85
	Before, behind thee, and on every hand,	
	Enwheel thee round.	
DESDEMONA	I thank you, valiant Cassio.	
	What tidings can you tell me of my lord?	
CASSIO	He is not yet arrived; nor know I aught	
	But that he's well, and will be shortly here.	90

While waiting for news of Othello's ship, Iago, Emilia and Desdemona pass the time in conversation. Iago makes provocative comments about wives and women.

Stagecraft

Cassio's kiss – dramatic possibilities (in threes)

Cassio has greeted Desdemona with a flourish and a bow (lines 84–5). Now he kisses Emilia – but he apologises first to Iago for his 'bold show of courtesy', justifying his actions on the grounds of good 'breeding' and 'manners'. This can be a dramatically fascinating moment on stage, open to a wide range of acting possibilities.

a Discuss some of these possibilities and then decide which of the following interpretations of Cassio's behaviour you most agree with:

- He's a naturally courteous man.
- Aware of Iago's jealous nature, he is being deliberately provocative.
- He's trying to be nice to everyone at a difficult moment.
- He's not very confident in social situations.
- He's deliberately patronising Emilia (she's just a common soldier's wife).
- Another interpretation (give details).

b Consider ways of acting out this moment. For example, is Cassio's kiss a courteous peck, or is he taking liberties? How does Emilia react? Is she embarrassed? Flattered? Irritated?

c What about Iago? In Trevor Nunn's 1990 production, Iago is clearly jealous. He swiftly moves across to take hold of Emilia, as if reclaiming his property. Decide how you would like Iago to react. In what tone of voice does he say lines 100–2?

1 Friendly banter or pointed comments?
(in small groups)

- Read lines 100–60. How should this part of the scene be played? Is it light-hearted banter, the only tension being that of Desdemona awaiting news that her husband is safe? Or is there bitterness and tension arising out of Iago's comments about women in general and his wife in particular? (Some commentators have suggested that there is an underlying class conflict between the courtly, educated Cassio and the uneducated, lower-class Iago).
- Discuss whether you think this is an episode of friendly chatter, or one tinged with misogyny (hatred of women), domestic strife and class-based tension.

gall annoy

still always
have list want
puts her tongue … heart holds her tongue
chides with thinking keeps her thoughts to herself
pictures silent
bells noisy
players deceivers

or else I am a Turk (the Turks were the enemy at the time)
You shall not write my praise don't describe me like that

assay try
There's one has someone

54

DESDEMONA	O, but I fear – how lost you company?
CASSIO	The great contention of the sea and skies
	Parted our fellowship.

[A shout] within, 'A sail, a sail!' [A shot is heard.]

But hark, a sail!

2 GENTLEMAN	They give their greeting to the citadel:	
	This likewise is a friend.	
CASSIO	See for the news.	95

[Exit Second Gentleman]

Good ancient, you are welcome. [*To Emilia*] Welcome, mistress.
Let it not gall your patience, good Iago,
That I extend my manners. 'Tis my breeding
That gives me this bold show of courtesy.

[He kisses Emilia.]

IAGO	Sir, would she give you so much of her lips	100
	As of her tongue she oft bestows on me	
	You would have enough.	
DESDEMONA	Alas, she has no speech.	
IAGO	In faith, too much:	
	I find it still when I have list to sleep.	
	Marry, before your ladyship, I grant	105
	She puts her tongue a little in her heart	
	And chides with thinking.	
EMILIA	You've little cause to say so.	
IAGO	Come on, come on; you are pictures out of doors, bells in your parlours, wild-cats in your kitchens, saints in your injuries, devils being offended, players in your housewifery, and housewives in your beds.	110
DESDEMONA	O fie upon thee, slanderer!	
IAGO	Nay, it is true, or else I am a Turk:	
	You rise to play and go to bed to work.	
EMILIA	You shall not write my praise.	
IAGO	No, let me not.	115
DESDEMONA	What wouldst thou write of me, if thou shouldst praise me?	
IAGO	O, gentle lady, do not put me to't,	
	For I am nothing if not critical.	
DESDEMONA	Come on, assay. There's one gone to the harbour?	
IAGO	Ay, madam.	120

Desdemona reveals that she is joining in the conversation to take her mind off waiting for Othello. Iago continues to joke about women.

Language in the play
Puns, paradoxes and epigrams (in pairs)

Shakespeare's audiences were amused and fascinated by all types of language play. Find examples of each of the following:

- **Puns** These are words that sound the same but have quite different meanings. Puns were a highly fashionable form of wordplay in Shakespeare's time. In *Romeo and Juliet*, Mercutio, fatally stabbed, makes a pun: 'Ask for me tomorrow, and you shall find me a grave man.' Here, Iago puns on the words 'white' (meaning colour, wit or cleverness) and 'wight' (an old word for person or lover). The words 'fair' and 'black' are used repeatedly in this play. They are used to denote the physical colouring of Desdemona and Othello, but they also carry certain connotations (associations), which Iago is keen to exploit.
- **Epigrams** Also very popular with Shakespeare's audiences, an epigram is a concise, witty poem that often ends on a surprising turn of thought. Sardonic generalisations were commonly put into the mouths of down-to-earth, 'honest' characters.
- **Paradoxes** A kind of riddle, paradoxes contain ideas that are self-contradictory.

▼ Identify who is who in this production photograph. What line from the script opposite do you think is being spoken at this moment?

beguile ... I am disguise my real feelings

pate head
birdlime sticky substance to catch birds
frieze woollen cloth
muse goddess of poetry

black with dark hair and complexion

witty wise
white fair lover

folly foolishness (with a suggestion of sexual promiscuity)
fond foolish
foul ugly

One that ... itself a good woman that even malice would praise

wight person, lover

chronicle small beer keep household accounts

profane and liberal rude and immoral

DESDEMONA [*Aside*] I am not merry, but I do beguile
The thing I am by seeming otherwise –
Come, how wouldst thou praise me?

IAGO I am about it, but indeed my invention
Comes from my pate as birdlime does from frieze – 125
It plucks out brains and all. But my muse labours,
And thus she is delivered:
'If she be fair and wise, fairness and wit,
The one's for use, the other useth it.'

DESDEMONA Well praised! How if she be black and witty? 130

IAGO 'If she be black, and thereto have a wit,
She'll find a white that shall her blackness fit.'

DESDEMONA Worse and worse.

EMILIA How if fair and foolish?

IAGO 'She never yet was foolish that was fair,
For even her folly helped her to an heir.' 135

DESDEMONA These are old fond paradoxes to make fools laugh
i'th'alehouse. What miserable praise hast thou for her that's foul
and foolish?

IAGO 'There's none so foul and foolish thereunto,
But does foul pranks which fair and wise ones do.' 140

DESDEMONA O heavy ignorance! Thou praisest the worst best. But
what praise couldst thou bestow on a deserving woman indeed? One
that in the authority of her merit did justly put on the vouch of
very malice itself?

IAGO 'She that was ever fair, and never proud, 145
Had tongue at will, and yet was never loud;
Never lacked gold, and yet went never gay;
Fled from her wish, and yet said "Now I may";
She that being angered, her revenge being nigh,
Bade her wrong stay, and her displeasure fly; 150
She that in wisdom never was so frail
To change the cod's head for the salmon's tail;
She that could think and ne'er disclose her mind,
See suitors following and not look behind;
She was a wight, if ever such wight were –' 155

DESDEMONA To do what?

IAGO 'To suckle fools and chronicle small beer.'

DESDEMONA O, most lame and impotent conclusion! Do not learn of
him, Emilia, though he be thy husband. How say you, Cassio, is
he not a most profane and liberal counsellor? 160

Iago revels in Cassio's attention to Desdemona, seeing in it a way in which he can ruin Cassio. Othello arrives safely. He and Desdemona greet each other, speaking of happiness and love.

1 'an excellent courtesy!' (in threes)

Iago uses a dramatic device called an **aside** here, speaking in such a way that the audience can hear him but the other characters on stage cannot. Elizabethan and Jacobean playwrights used asides to share characters' thoughts or intentions without revealing secrets to other characters.

- Act out Iago's aside (lines 163–71), matching the movements of Cassio and Desdemona to Iago's commentary. Where should Iago stand, and how should he say the words? Iago uses several images in his speech: a spider's web, a snare ('gyve') and, lastly, tubes for inserting enemas ('clyster-pipes')!

2 Another kiss (in small groups)

a How would you have Othello and Desdemona kiss? In Oliver Parker's 1995 movie version, it was an intensely passionate embrace, the lovers oblivious of the public gaze. In Trevor Nunn's 1990 Royal Shakespeare Company production, it was restrained and revealed little of the couple's private life. This picture shows another version of the same moment.

b Discuss how you would differentiate between the three different kisses contained in this scene so far (one is mentioned in Iago's aside). Then show them in tableau form and ask the rest of the class to identify each one. Don't forget to include Iago – consider his position, actions, facial expressions and so on.

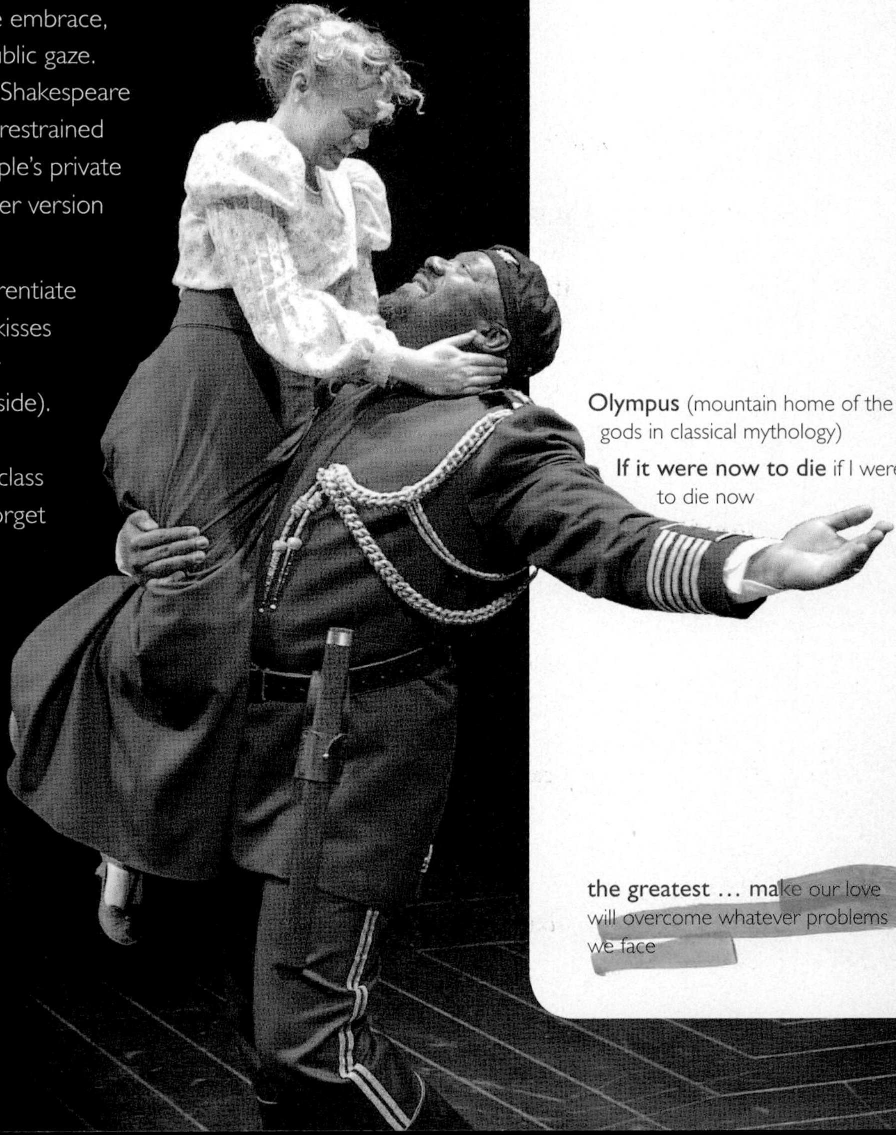

home plainly

relish him … scholar he is more skilful as a soldier than as a scholar

well said well done

gyve snare

kissed your three fingers a courtly gesture between men and women

clyster-pipes tubes for inserting enemas

Olympus (mountain home of the gods in classical mythology)

If it were now to die if I were to die now

the greatest … make our love will overcome whatever problems we face

CASSIO   He speaks home, madam; you may relish him more in the soldier than in the scholar.

IAGO   [*Aside*] He takes her by the palm. Ay, well said; whisper. With as little a web as this will I ensnare as great a fly as Cassio. Ay, smile upon her, do. I will gyve thee in thine own courtship. You say true, 'tis so indeed. If such tricks as these strip you out of your lieutenantry, it had been better you had not kissed your three fingers so oft, which now again you are most apt to play the sir in. Very good, well kissed, an excellent courtesy! 'Tis so indeed. Yet again your fingers to your lips? Would they were clyster-pipes for your sake! 165

170

Trumpets within.

The Moor! I know his trumpet.

CASSIO   'Tis truly so.

DESDEMONA   Let's meet him and receive him.

CASSIO   Lo, where he comes!

Enter OTHELLO *and* ATTENDANTS.

OTHELLO   O, my fair warrior!

DESDEMONA   My dear Othello!

OTHELLO   It gives me wonder great as my content 175
To see you here before me. O, my soul's joy,
If after every tempest come such calms,
May the winds blow till they have wakened death,
And let the labouring bark climb hills of seas,
Olympus-high, and duck again as low 180
As hell's from heaven. If it were now to die,
'Twere now to be most happy; for I fear
My soul hath her content so absolute
That not another comfort like to this
Succeeds in unknown fate.

DESDEMONA   The heavens forbid 185
But that our loves and comforts should increase,
Even as our days do grow.

OTHELLO   Amen to that, sweet powers!
I cannot speak enough of this content;
It stops me here; it is too much of joy.

They kiss.

And this, and this, the greatest discords be 190
That e'er our hearts shall make.

Othello and Desdemona go off together, leaving Iago alone with Roderigo. Iago tells him that Desdemona is in love with Cassio, because she must necessarily tire of Othello.

Language in the play
Imagery of music and food (in small groups)

'Making sweet music together': Iago's comment (line 191) that Othello and his wife 'are well tuned' is followed by his vow to 'set down the pegs' (to slacken the strings of an instrument). The **metaphor** (see p. 231) uses the harmony of music to indicate the harmony of Othello's marriage, and Iago's intention to disrupt it. Iago's speech in lines 212–28 contains more metaphors – references to food, eating and appetite.

* Read through the speeches and pick out as many examples as you can find of these metaphors. Discuss what Iago is talking about and what his language reveals about his attitude to women, love and affection.

Write about it
Ship's log (by yourself)

Write Othello's ship's log for his journey to Cyprus. You might include some of the following:

* thoughts on setting out
* plans to defend Cyprus
* any encounters with the Turkish ships
* thoughts about Desdemona
* a description of the storm
* fears for Desdemona's safety
* feelings on reaching harbour safely.

1 Iago's argument – how convincing? (in pairs)

According to Iago, Othello is defective in 'loveliness in favour, sympathy in years, manners and beauties'. He assures Roderigo that Desdemona will quickly tire of her husband ('When the blood is made dull with the act of sport') and that she is only attracted to his 'bragging' and 'fantastical lies'.

* Read lines 212–35 to each other, taking turns to read small sections. On what evidence is Iago basing his view of their relationship? How does Iago try to convince Roderigo that he is right? Start a file noting the attempts Iago has made to manipulate people and events so far. Add to this as you continue reading.

---

well tuned like properly tuned instruments playing in harmony

set down ... music slacken the strings so that the music is out of tune

well desired well received

I dote I'm not making sense

disembark my coffers unload my luggage

master captain of the ship

list me listen to me

directly certainly

Lay thy finger thus put your finger to your lips (ssshh!)

prating chattering

pregnant and unforced position obvious and natural assumption

voluble smooth-tongued

conscionable conscientious

compassing achieving

salt lecherous

IAGO   [*Aside*]   O, you are well tuned now!
             But I'll set down the pegs that make this music,
             As honest as I am.

OTHELLO   Come, let us to the castle.
             News, friends; our wars are done; the Turks are drowned.
             How does my old acquaintance of this isle?   195
             Honey, you shall be well desired in Cyprus;
             I have found great love amongst them. O my sweet,
             I prattle out of fashion and I dote
             In mine own comforts. I prithee, good Iago,
             Go to the bay and disembark my coffers;   200
             Bring thou the master to the citadel;
             He is a good one, and his worthiness
             Does challenge much respect. Come, Desdemona,
             Once more well met at Cyprus!

                                Exeunt [all except Iago and Roderigo]

IAGO   [*To a departing Attendant*] Do thou meet me presently at the   205
             harbour. [*To Roderigo*] Come hither. If thou be'st valiant – as
             they say base men being in love have then a nobility in their
             natures more than is native to them – list me. The lieutenant
             tonight watches on the court of guard. First, I must tell thee this:
             Desdemona is directly in love with him.   210

RODERIGO   With him? Why, 'tis not possible!

IAGO   Lay thy finger thus, and let thy soul be instructed. Mark me
             with what violence she first loved the Moor but for bragging and
             telling her fantastical lies. And will she love him still for prating?
             Let not thy discreet heart think it. Her eye must be fed. And   215
             what delight shall she have to look on the devil? When the blood
             is made dull with the act of sport, there should be, again to
             inflame it and to give satiety a fresh appetite, loveliness in
             favour, sympathy in years, manners and beauties: all which the
             Moor is defective in. Now for want of these required conveniences, 220
             her delicate tenderness will find itself abused, begin to heave the
             gorge, disrelish and abhor the Moor. Very nature will instruct
             her in it, and compel her to some second choice. Now, sir, this
             granted – as it is a most pregnant and unforced position – who
             stands so eminent in the degree of this fortune as Cassio does? – a   225
             knave very voluble; no further conscionable than in putting on
             the mere form of civil and humane seeming for the better
             compassing of his salt and most hidden loose affection.

Iago assures Roderigo that Desdemona has tired of Othello, and has her eye on other men. Iago tells his plan. He urges Roderigo to provoke Cassio to anger that night. The resulting riot will ruin Cassio's prospects.

1 'a slipper and subtle knave' (in pairs)

Read Iago's description of Cassio in lines 229–35. Pick out features that you agree are an accurate portrait of this character, and those that you think are deliberately false.

Characters

Roderigo (in pairs)

a In discussion, sum up what you have learned about Roderigo from the play so far.

b Read lines 205–67. Roderigo seems remarkably gullible. His protests about Iago's descriptions suggest he is besotted with Desdemona, yet he quickly agrees to Iago's plan. One person takes the part of Roderigo and the other steps into role as director. Advise Roderigo how he might react as Iago speaks lines 248–65, and the way he should interject at lines 236, 242, 254 and 263.

▶ Choose lines from the script opposite that might provide a suitable caption for this image of Iago (left) and Roderigo.

slipper slippery
stamp and counterfeit make a forgery of

green immature
pestilent complete knave completely poisonous rogue

blest condition heavenly innocence

fig's end rubbish

paddle with fondle
mark notice

incorporate bodily

watch keep guard
I'll lay't upon you I'll give you responsibility

tainting sneering at
minister provide

in choler when angry

qualification pacifying

I warrant thee I promise you
necessaries luggage

Why none; why none – a slipper and subtle knave, a finder
out of occasions, that has an eye can stamp and counterfeit
advantages, though true advantage never present itself; a
devilish knave! Besides, the knave is handsome, young, and hath
all those requisites in him that folly and green minds look after.
A pestilent complete knave; and the woman hath found him
already.

RODERIGO I cannot believe that in her; she's full of most blest
condition.

IAGO Blest fig's end! The wine she drinks is made of grapes. If she
had been blest she would never have loved the Moor. Blest
pudding! Didst thou not see her paddle with the palm of his
hand? Didst not mark that?

RODERIGO Yes, that I did; but that was but courtesy.

IAGO Lechery, by this hand: an index and obscure prologue to the
history of lust and foul thoughts. They met so near with their lips
that their breaths embraced together – villainous thoughts,
Roderigo! When these mutualities so marshal the way, hard
at hand comes the master and main exercise, the incorporate
conclusion. Pish! But, sir, be you ruled by me. I have brought
you from Venice; watch you tonight; for the command, I'll lay't
upon you. Cassio knows you not; I'll not be far from you. Do you
find some occasion to anger Cassio, either by speaking too loud or
tainting his discipline, or from what other course you please,
which the time shall more favourably minister.

RODERIGO Well.

IAGO Sir, he's rash and very sudden in choler, and haply with his
truncheon may strike at you: provoke him that he may; for even
out of that will I cause these of Cyprus to mutiny, whose
qualification shall come into no true taste again but by the
displanting of Cassio. So shall you have a shorter journey to your
desires by the means I shall then have to prefer them, and the
impediment most profitably removed without the which there
were no expectation of our prosperity.

RODERIGO I will do this, if you can bring it to any opportunity.

IAGO I warrant thee. Meet me by and by at the citadel. I must fetch
his necessaries ashore. Farewell.

RODERIGO Adieu.   *Exit*

Iago again says that he is seeking revenge because he suspects that Othello has slept with Emilia. He plans to use Roderigo to ensure the downfall of Cassio, whom he also suspects has made love to Emilia.

Stagecraft

Direct the actor

- Read lines 267–93 and identify all the words associated with love. Then pick out words to do with sex. Explain to an actor playing Iago what the character appears to be saying in this speech. How might Iago deliver key words such as 'love', 'the Moor', 'Michael Cassio', 'revenge')?
- In your Director's Journal, summarise your thoughts by writing out two or three paragraphs of advice for your Iago. (It will help if you are able to watch two different versions of this soliloquy in performance so you can consider the differences in movement, setting and props.)

Characters

Hot-seat Iago (whole class)

What questions would you really like to ask Iago? A volunteer steps into role as Iago and the class questions him. Your questions might include:

- Why do you hate Othello so much?
- What did you think about Desdemona's decision to marry Othello?
- Do you enjoy being in the army?
- Do you love your wife?

The person playing Iago should base his or her answers on the script. Take turns as Iago in the hot-seat.

howbeit even though

absolute pure
peradventure perhaps
accountant accountable
diet feed
leaped into my seat made love to my wife
mineral drug
inwards innards, guts

trace follow after (hunting term)
stand the putting on continues to do what I say
on the hip at my mercy (hunting metaphor)
rank garb foul manner
with my night-cap in my bed
egregiously extraordinarily, outstandingly
practising upon plotting against

64

IAGO   That Cassio loves her, I do well believe't;
That she loves him, 'tis apt and of great credit.
The Moor, howbeit that I endure him not,
Is of a constant, loving, noble nature;   270
And I dare think he'll prove to Desdemona
A most dear husband. Now, I do love her too,
Not out of absolute lust – though peradventure
I stand accountant for as great a sin –
But partly led to diet my revenge,   275
For that I do suspect the lusty Moor
Hath leaped into my seat, the thought whereof
Doth like a poisonous mineral gnaw my inwards;
And nothing can or shall content my soul
Till I am evened with him, wife for wife;   280
Or failing so, yet that I put the Moor
At least into a jealousy so strong
That judgement cannot cure. Which thing to do,
If this poor trash of Venice, whom I trace
For his quick hunting, stand the putting on,   285
I'll have our Michael Cassio on the hip,
Abuse him to the Moor in the rank garb –
For I fear Cassio with my night-cap too –
Make the Moor thank me, love me, and reward me,
For making him egregiously an ass,   290
And practising upon his peace and quiet
Even to madness. 'Tis here, but yet confused;
Knavery's plain face is never seen till used.   *Exit*

A Herald publicly announces celebrations to mark the destruction of the Turkish fleet. These festivities also honour Othello's wedding. Scene 3 opens with Othello asking Cassio to inspect the guard at night.

1 The proclamation (in small groups)

a Read the Herald's proclamation aloud. Talk together about whether you would cut this or keep it in if you were directing a performance of the play. Give your reasons.

b Decide how Scene 2 might be performed. Directly to the audience? Spoken to a crowd on stage, with the Herald mingling in the audience? Or in some other dramatically effective way?

c Imagine three or four ordinary Cypriot workers pausing from their labours to listen to the proclamation. Improvise their reactions to each section of the speech.

d Suggest how the proclamation characterises both Othello's public role and his private role.

certain reliable
mere perdition total destruction
triumph public celebration

offices kitchens, food stores
full liberty of free

Stagecraft

A change of atmosphere

Othello and Desdemona have had to endure the drama of appearing in front of the Senate, the tension of war and a terrifying storm at sea.

• Consider how these two characters make their entrance at this point in the play, when they are looking forward to the celebrations acknowledging their marriage. How might you show a change of atmosphere on stage? Consider: costumes (is Othello still in uniform?); lighting; music, sound effects and background noise; scenery and props. Add your ideas to your Director's Journal.

stop restraint
out-sport discretion celebrate to excess

---

2 'Iago is most honest'

a The obvious piece of dramatic irony (see p. 38) in line 6 of Scene 3 comes soon after Iago's vow in Scene 1 to drive Othello 'Even to madness'. What effect do you think Othello's comment would have on an audience in the theatre?

b If this were a pantomime, such a misguided comment by the hero would invite the audience to shout out to warn him! Write down what you would say to Othello at this moment if you had the chance to step out of the audience and onto the stage with the characters.

with your earliest at your earliest convenience

Act 2 Scene 2
Cyprus   A street

Enter Othello's HERALD *with a proclamation.*

HERALD   It is Othello's pleasure, our noble and valiant general, that upon certain tidings now arrived importing the mere perdition of the Turkish fleet, every man put himself into triumph: some to dance, some to make bonfires, each man to what sport and revels his addiction leads him; for besides these beneficial news, it is   5
the celebration of his nuptial. So much was his pleasure should be proclaimed. All offices are open, and there is full liberty of feasting from this present hour of five till the bell have told eleven. Heaven bless the isle of Cyprus and our noble general Othello!   *Exit*   10

Act 2 Scene 3
Cyprus   A room in the castle

Enter OTHELLO, DESDEMONA, CASSIO *and* ATTENDANTS.

OTHELLO   Good Michael, look you to the guard tonight.
Let's teach ourselves that honourable stop,
Not to out-sport discretion.

CASSIO   Iago hath direction what to do;
But notwithstanding with my personal eye   5
Will I look to't.

OTHELLO   Iago is most honest.
Michael, good night; tomorrow with your earliest
Let me have speech with you – Come, my dear love,
The purchase made, the fruits are to ensue;
That profit's yet to come 'tween me and you.   10
Good night.

Exeunt Othello, Desdemona [and Attendants]

Iago persuades Cassio to join in the celebrations with various male friends. Cassio reveals he has a poor head for alcohol, and declines to drink further. Iago plans to make Cassio drunk and quarrelsome.

Characters

Men's talk (in pairs)

a Read the dialogue between Iago and Cassio. What differences can you detect between the two speakers in their attitudes towards women in general and Desdemona in particular?

b Act out the dialogue up to line 39 in such a way as to highlight any significant differences between the two men and the nature of their remarks. Experiment with playing Cassio in more than one way. For example, do you think that he is ill at ease with the way Iago directs the conversation?

c After you have experimented with speaking the lines, talk together about how Iago takes control of the dialogue. Do this by considering each interchange between the two men. For example, Cassio begins by stressing 'we must to the watch', implying that they must ensure quiet and restraint among the public while Othello and Desdemona consummate their love. How does Iago avoid that order?

Not this hour not for another hour

cast dismissed

Jove (king of the gods, known for his sexual prowess)

game sexual tricks

parley summons, invitation

alarum call to arms, summons

stoup jug

fain like to

craftily qualified carefully diluted
innovation disturbance

caroused gulped down, quaffed
Potations pottle-deep many mugs or tankards of drink

Enter IAGO.

CASSIO	Welcome, Iago; we must to the watch.
IAGO	Not this hour, lieutenant; 'tis not yet ten o'th'clock. Our general cast us thus early for the love of his Desdemona; who let us not therefore blame: he hath not yet made wanton the night with her, and she is sport for Jove.
CASSIO	She's a most exquisite lady.
IAGO	And I'll warrant her full of game.
CASSIO	Indeed she is a most fresh and delicate creature.
IAGO	What an eye she has! Methinks it sounds a parley to provocation.
CASSIO	An inviting eye, and yet methinks right modest.
IAGO	And when she speaks, is it not an alarum to love?
CASSIO	She is indeed perfection.
IAGO	Well, happiness to their sheets! Come, lieutenant, I have a stoup of wine, and here without are a brace of Cyprus gallants, that would fain have a measure to the health of the black Othello.
CASSIO	Not tonight, good Iago; I have very poor and unhappy brains for drinking. I could well wish courtesy would invent some other custom of entertainment.
IAGO	O, they are our friends – but one cup; I'll drink for you.
CASSIO	I have drunk but one cup tonight, and that was craftily qualified too; and behold what innovation it makes here. I am unfortunate in the infirmity and dare not task my weakness with any more.
IAGO	What, man! 'Tis a night of revels; the gallants desire it.
CASSIO	Where are they?
IAGO	Here at the door; I pray you call them in.
CASSIO	I'll do't, but it dislikes me. *Exit*
IAGO	If I can fasten but one cup upon him,

Line numbers: 15, 20, 25, 30, 35, 40, 45

IAGO
    If I can fasten but one cup upon him,
    With that which he hath drunk tonight already,
    He'll be as full of quarrel and offence
    As my young mistress' dog. Now my sick fool Roderigo,
    Whom love hath turned almost the wrong side out,
    To Desdemona hath tonight caroused
    Potations pottle-deep, and he's to watch.

1 'My boat sails freely' (in pairs)

Iago's metaphor 'My boat sails freely, both with wind and stream' (line 55) echoes earlier imagery.

- Work out what Iago means by this image, and talk together about whether you think it is appropriate. Make sure you can give reasons for your decision.

Characters

Iago: a man of many parts

Iago (third on the left in the photograph below) is a man of many parts, able to switch roles with great ease depending on who he is talking to and what he wants to achieve. In this 'party scene', he demonstrates a sociable side, and comes across as someone who is fun to be with.

- Make a list of other parts or roles Iago has played so far.

swelling arrogant

That hold ... distance quick to protect their honour

flustered confused

rouse drink

cannikin drinking can, tankard

potent in potting heavy drinkers

with facility easily
sweats not finds it no effort
Almain German
pottle tankard

Three lads of Cyprus, noble swelling spirits,
That hold their honours in a wary distance,
The very elements of this warlike isle,
Have I tonight flustered with flowing cups; 50
And they watch too. Now, 'mongst this flock of drunkards,
Am I to put our Cassio in some action
That may offend the isle. But here they come.

Enter Cassio, MONTANO *and* GENTLEMEN.

If consequence do but approve my dream,
My boat sails freely, both with wind and stream. 55

CASSIO   'Fore God, they have given me a rouse already.

MONTANO   Good faith, a little one; not past a pint, as I am a soldier.

IAGO   Some wine, ho!
           [*Sings*]
               And let me the cannikin clink, clink,
               And let me the cannikin clink; 60
                   A soldier's a man,
                   O, man's life's but a span,
               Why then, let a soldier drink.
           Some wine, boys!

CASSIO   'Fore God, an excellent song. 65

IAGO   I learned it in England, where indeed they are most potent in
           potting. Your Dane, your German, and your swag-bellied
           Hollander – drink, ho! – are nothing to your English.

CASSIO   Is your Englishman so exquisite in his drinking?

IAGO   Why, he drinks you with facility your Dane dead drunk; he sweats 70
           not to overthrow your Almain; he gives your Hollander a vomit
           ere the next pottle can be filled.

CASSIO   To the health of our general!

MONTANO   I am for it, lieutenant, and I'll do you justice.

The party continues and Cassio becomes drunk very quickly. He goes off to take his turn on guard, and Iago comments on his dangerous 'vice': his weakness for alcohol.

1 Party photograph (in groups of four to six)

Take line 97 – 'Do not think, gentlemen, I am drunk' – and imagine freezing the action on stage. The photograph below shows one version of this moment, in the middle of what is clearly quite a wild barracks party. In what other ways might this moment be presented? Create a tableau, with each person in the group making it clear from the way they are positioned whom they represent. The rest of the class guesses who is who.

crown a coin

lown rogue

degree status

2 Acting the drunk (in pairs)

a   Acting a drunk is one of the most difficult tasks for any actor. But in lines 85–102, Shakespeare provides a script for Cassio that really does catch the rhythms of drunken speech. Take parts and read the lines, using any actions you think appropriate.

b   Cassio has let Othello down by behaving unprofessionally. He also declares his social superiority when he asserts that 'the lieutenant is to be saved before the ancient'. Talk together about whether you think Cassio is displaying a less attractive side of his character here.

platform gun ramparts
set the watch mount the guard
stand by be the equal of

just equinox exact equivalent or counterbalance

odd time chance moment
shake destroy

IAGO   O sweet England!   75
         [*Sings*]

            King Stephen was and a worthy peer,
               His breeches cost him but a crown;
            He held them sixpence all too dear,
               With that he called the tailor lown.

            He was a wight of high renown,   80
               And thou art but of low degree;
            'Tis pride that pulls the country down;
               Then take thine auld cloak about thee.

     Some wine, ho!

CASSIO   'Fore God, this is a more exquisite song than the other.   85

IAGO   Will you hear't again?

CASSIO   No, for I hold him to be unworthy of his place that does those things. Well, God's above all, and there be souls must be saved, and there be souls must not be saved.

IAGO   It's true, good lieutenant.   90

CASSIO   For mine own part – no offence to the general, nor any man of quality – I hope to be saved.

IAGO   And so do I too, lieutenant.

CASSIO   Ay, but by your leave, not before me; the lieutenant is to be saved before the ancient. Let's have no more of this; let's to our   95 affairs. God forgive us our sins! Gentlemen, let's look to our business. Do not think, gentlemen, I am drunk; this is my ancient, this is my right hand, and this is my left hand. I am not drunk now, I can stand well enough, and I speak well enough.

ALL   Excellent well.   100

CASSIO   Why, very well then; you must not think then that I am drunk.   *Exit*

MONTANO   To the platform, masters. Come, let's set the watch.

IAGO   You see this fellow that is gone before,
            He is a soldier fit to stand by Caesar   105
            And give direction. And do but see his vice –
            'Tis to his virtue a just equinox,
            The one as long as th'other. 'Tis pity of him.
            I fear the trust Othello puts him in,
            On some odd time of his infirmity,   110
            Will shake this island.

Montano thinks that Othello should be told of Cassio's weakness for drink. Iago sends Roderigo after Cassio, and the two re-enter fighting. Montano tries to stop Cassio striking Roderigo.

Themes

Appearance versus reality; honesty and dishonesty

Iago continues to paint a very negative picture of Cassio, alleging that his 'vice' of drunkenness occurs every night. Montano is concerned that Othello should be advised of Cassio's 'evils', because Othello's good nature sees only 'virtue' in his lieutenant.

a Write two paragraphs explaining how this exchange between Montano and Iago contributes to the theme of appearance versus reality.

b Note down at least two other examples where there has been a significant difference between appearance and reality in the play so far.

Characters

Honest Iago? (in fours)

At line 124, Montano suggests that it would be 'an honest action' for Iago to tell Othello about Cassio's drink problem.

a This is not the first time that the word 'honest' has been used in connection with Iago. Flick back through the play and find other examples where the word 'honest' has been applied to this character. Note down the line references and the speakers, then compare your findings with those of other groups.

b Two group members take parts as Montano and Iago and act out lines 121–7, pausing at the end of key phrases or sentences. The other two become Montano and Iago's 'inner thoughts', voicing exactly what is in each character's mind during this short exchange.

1 What did Roderigo do? (in pairs)

So, what happened outside? What *did* Roderigo do or say to annoy Cassio so much?

- Consider what you know about both men. For example, Roderigo is a civilian and Cassio is an army officer; also, Roderigo is jealous of Othello's marriage to Desdemona, whilst Cassio appears to be fiercely loyal to Othello. Taking lines 130–1 as a clue, improvise the incident.

the horologe a double set twice round the clock

put in mind told

hazard risk
ingraft deep-rooted

twiggen bottle bottle encased in wicker-work

mazzard head, skull

MONTANO	But is he often thus?
IAGO	'Tis evermore the prologue to his sleep:
	He'll watch the horologe a double set,
	If drink rock not his cradle.
MONTANO	It were well
	The general were put in mind of it. 115
	Perhaps he sees it not, or his good nature
	Prizes the virtue that appears in Cassio
	And looks not on his evils: is not this true?

Enter RODERIGO.

IAGO	[*Aside to Roderigo*] How now, Roderigo?
	I pray you after the lieutenant, go. 120

Exit Roderigo

MONTANO	And 'tis great pity that the noble Moor
	Should hazard such a place as his own second
	With one of an ingraft infirmity;
	It were an honest action to say so
	To the Moor.
IAGO	Not I, for this fair island: 125
	I do love Cassio well, and would do much
	To cure him of this evil.

[*A cry of*] '*Help, help!*' *within.*

But hark! what noise?

Enter Cassio, pursuing Roderigo.

CASSIO	Zounds, you rogue, you rascal!
MONTANO	What's the matter, lieutenant?
CASSIO	A knave teach me my duty! I'll beat the knave into a 130 twiggen bottle.
RODERIGO	Beat me?
CASSIO	Dost thou prate, rogue?

[*He strikes Roderigo.*]

MONTANO	Nay, good lieutenant, I pray you, sir, hold your hand.
CASSIO	Let me go, sir; or I'll knock you o'er the mazzard. 135
MONTANO	Come, come, you're drunk.

Cassio, incensed by Montano's accusation of drunkenness, fights him. The alarm is sounded. Othello enters to restore order and demand an explanation. Iago denies he knows who began the brawl.

1 The fight (in small groups)

Create a slow-motion, silent version of this scene from line 128 ('*Enter Cassio, pursuing Roderigo*') to line 150 ('From whence ariseth this?') Make each character recognisable and clearly define each stage of the action. Start and end your presentation with a tableau. Remember, your movements must be slow, controlled, safe and easy to follow.

Themes

Honesty and dishonesty (in pairs)

At line 158, Iago is once again described as 'honest'. Design a diagram of all the uses of 'honest' in the script so far. Leave room for further additions to the list – you'll find many more as this scene progresses. Continue adding to your diagram as you read the rest of the play.

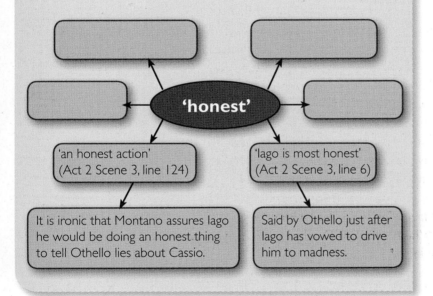

'honest'

'an honest action'
(Act 2 Scene 3, line 124)

'Iago is most honest'
(Act 2 Scene 3, line 6)

It is ironic that Montano assures Iago he would be doing an honest thing to tell Othello lies about Cassio.

Said by Othello just after Iago has vowed to drive him to madness.

Write about it

Iago's language

In lines 160–8, find three or four expressions that Iago knows will appeal to Othello. Write two paragraphs explaining how Iago chooses his words to suit his listeners, giving precise examples from the script opposite.

cry a mutiny tell everyone there is a riot

Diabolo the devil
rise riot

carve for his own rage stab someone in anger
Holds his soul light doesn't value his life
propriety peaceful state
love loyalty

quarter friendship

tilting striking
speak explain
peevish odds senseless quarrel

CASSIO   Drunk?

They fight.

IAGO   [*Aside to Roderigo*] Away I say, go out and cry a mutiny.

[*Exit Roderigo*]

Nay, good lieutenant; God's will, gentlemen!
Help ho! Lieutenant, sir! Montano, sir!   140
Help, masters, here's a goodly watch indeed!

A bell rings.

Who's that which rings the bell? Diabolo, ho!
The town will rise. God's will, lieutenant, hold!
You will be shamed forever.

Enter Othello, and GENTLEMEN *with weapons.*

OTHELLO   What is the matter here?

MONTANO   Zounds, I bleed still.   145
I am hurt to th'death.

OTHELLO   Hold for your lives!

IAGO   Hold ho, lieutenant, sir; Montano, gentlemen,
Have you forgot all place of sense and duty?
Hold! the general speaks to you; hold, for shame!

OTHELLO   Why, how now, ho! From whence ariseth this?   150
Are we turned Turks, and to ourselves do that
Which heaven hath forbid the Ottomites?
For Christian shame, put by this barbarous brawl.
He that stirs next to carve for his own rage
Holds his soul light: he dies upon his motion.   155
Silence that dreadful bell: it frights the isle
From her propriety. What is the matter, masters?
Honest Iago, that looks dead with grieving,
Speak. Who began this? On thy love, I charge thee.

IAGO   I do not know. Friends all but now, even now,   160
In quarter and in terms like bride and groom,
Divesting them for bed; and then but now –
As if some planet had unwitted men –
Swords out and tilting one at other's breasts
In opposition bloody. I cannot speak   165
Any beginning to this peevish odds:
And would in action glorious I had lost
Those legs that brought me to a part of it.

Othello tries to discover who started the fight. Cassio gives no explanation. Montano pleads self-defence, and says that Iago knows as much as he does. Othello orders Iago to speak.

1 Cassio's silence (in pairs)

At the start of this scene, Othello twice called Cassio 'Michael'. Here, once again, he uses Cassio's first name as he asks him to explain. This denotes a friendship and trust that will soon be lost. Why, when questioned, does Cassio choose to say nothing?

- Do you think that is the right course of action? If not, what should he have said? Discuss in pairs, then spend about five minutes writing down a possible reply for Cassio.

Language in the play

Black and white

Othello becomes impatient and indicates that he is on the verge of losing his temper with the brawlers. At line 187, he exclaims: 'passion having my best judgement collied, / Assays to lead the way.' He is saying that his rage is about to overtake his better ('best') judgement. The word 'collied' is usually defined as 'blackened', with its links with the word 'coal' ('collier', 'colliery').

- Why is black/white imagery appropriate in this play? What other examples of black and white in **binary opposition** have we heard so far? (Binary opposition is a term used in literary criticism to describe a pair of related terms or ideas that have opposite meanings.)

Characters

Iago the actor (in pairs)

At lines 201–3, Iago pretends he would rather have his own tongue cut out than make any allegation against Cassio (thus revealing the identity of the guilty person).

- How should the actor playing Iago say these lines? Should he slightly overplay the moment (for example, by adopting a tone of mock innocence for the audience to enjoy)? Or do you think he should underplay the words?
- With your partner, try acting out Iago's lines in two or three different ways. Share your most successful version with the class.

---

are thus forgot have forgotten yourself like this

stillness sobriety

censure judgement

something now offends me it is rather painful for me

self-charity self-defence

safer guides reason
collied blackened
Assays attempts

foul rout uncivilised brawl
approved found guilty

partially affined taking sides
leagued in office intimidated because of his inferior rank

78

OTHELLO	How comes it, Michael, you are thus forgot?
CASSIO	I pray you pardon me, I cannot speak. 170
OTHELLO	Worthy Montano, you were wont be civil:

OTHELLO How comes it, Michael, you are thus forgot?
CASSIO I pray you pardon me, I cannot speak.   170
OTHELLO Worthy Montano, you were wont be civil:
The gravity and stillness of your youth
The world hath noted; and your name is great
In mouths of wisest censure. What's the matter
That you unlace your reputation thus,   175
And spend your rich opinion for the name
Of a night-brawler? Give me answer to it.
MONTANO Worthy Othello, I am hurt to danger;
Your officer Iago can inform you –
While I spare speech, which something now offends me –   180
Of all that I do know; nor know I aught
By me that's said or done amiss this night,
Unless self-charity be sometimes a vice,
And to defend ourselves it be a sin
When violence assails us.
OTHELLO   Now by heaven   185
My blood begins my safer guides to rule,
And passion having my best judgement collied,
Assays to lead the way. Zounds, if I stir,
Or do but lift this arm, the best of you
Shall sink in my rebuke. Give me to know   190
How this foul rout began, who set it on,
And he that is approved in this offence,
Though he had twinned with me, both at a birth,
Shall lose me. What, in a town of war,
Yet wild, the people's hearts brimful of fear,   195
To manage private and domestic quarrel,
In night, and on the court and guard of safety?
'Tis monstrous. Iago, who began't?
MONTANO If partially affined or leagued in office,
Thou dost deliver more or less than truth,   200
Thou art no soldier.
IAGO   Touch me not so near.
I had rather have this tongue cut from my mouth
Than it should do offence to Michael Cassio.

79

Iago gives an account of how Cassio started the affray. Asserting that Iago's honesty has made him play down Cassio's offence, Othello immediately dismisses Cassio from office.

1 Personal feelings, public judgement (whole class)

Iago gives a falsely sympathetic account of Cassio's behaviour (lines 201–27). Othello is taken in by Iago's cunning, and confirms that his 'honesty and love' have made the report 'light to Cassio'. In dismissing Cassio as one of his officers, Othello distinguishes between his private feelings for his friend and his public judgement of his lieutenant.

a Suggest how both these aspects are implied in Othello's line 231: 'Look if my gentle love be not raised up!'

b Othello declares his intention to make an example of Cassio (line 232). Think back on the play so far. On what other occasion has a character had to balance personal feelings against public judgement?

> ## Write about it
> ### Iago's diary
>
> Consider how well Iago has orchestrated the brawl. Do you think he would feel pleased with the way he has managed to convincingly play his part as a loyal friend to Cassio, while also seeming to reluctantly tell the truth to his commanding officer, Othello?
>
> * Write Iago's private diary, describing the events of the day from the point that he, Desdemona and Emilia disembark (Act 2 Scene 1, line 83).
> * Think about the kind of language he might use. To help you, look at his soliloquies during this act so far, where he speaks in the same type of confessional language that he is likely to use in his diary. (See Act 1 Scene 3, lines 365–86; Act 2 Scene 1, lines 267–93; Act 2 Scene 3, lines 40–6; Act 2 Scene 3, lines 303–29 and 347–53.) Don't forget that Iago also talks directly to the audience by means of asides, as in Act 2 Scene 1, lines 163–71 and 192–4.
> * In his diary, have Iago think back over his speech to Othello in lines 201–27 and comment on his own words.
> * At the end of the diary entry, indicate how successfully Iago believes he has set things up for his future plans.

entreats his pause begs him to stop

fall in fright become alarmed
I returned … that I thought it best to turn back because

indignity insult

mince this matter tone it down

Yet, I persuade myself, to speak the truth
Shall nothing wrong him. This it is, general: 205
Montano and myself being in speech,
There comes a fellow crying out for help,
And Cassio following him with determined sword
To execute upon him. Sir, this gentleman
Steps in to Cassio and entreats his pause;   210
Myself the crying fellow did pursue,
Lest by his clamour – as it so fell out –
The town might fall in fright. He, swift of foot,
Outran my purpose and I returned the rather
For that I heard the clink and fall of swords   215
And Cassio high in oath, which till tonight
I ne'er might say before. When I came back –
For this was brief – I found them close together
At blow and thrust, even as again they were
When you yourself did part them.   220
More of this matter can I not report;
But men are men; the best sometimes forget.
Though Cassio did some little wrong to him,
As men in rage strike those that wish them best,
Yet surely Cassio, I believe, received   225
From him that fled some strange indignity
Which patience could not pass.

OTHELLO   I know, Iago,
Thy honesty and love doth mince this matter,
Making it light to Cassio. Cassio, I love thee,
But never more be officer of mine.   230

                 Enter Desdemona attended.

Look if my gentle love be not raised up!
I'll make thee an example.

DESDEMONA   What's the matter, dear?

OTHELLO   All's well now, sweeting; come away to bed.
Sir, for your hurts myself will be your surgeon.

                   [Montano is led off]

After Othello has gone back to bed, Cassio bemoans the loss of his reputation to Iago. Iago tells him to make an appeal. Cassio curses what drink does to men.

Language in the play
From verse to prose (in pairs)

After Othello and Desdemona's exit (line 238), the script changes from verse to prose for the dialogue between Cassio and Iago.

* Read the information about verse and prose in 'The language of *Othello*' on page 230, then spend five minutes discussing possible reasons for this change of style here. How might you reflect this transition on stage (for example, by a change of lighting or the movement of characters)?

1 What is 'reputation'? (in pairs)

Read lines 242–9 to each other several times. Cassio uses the word 'reputation' six times in three lines, and defines it as 'the immortal part of myself', without which 'what remains is bestial'. In contrast, Iago defines reputation as 'an idle and most false imposition, oft got without merit and lost without deserving' (lines 247–8).

a Make notes about the different ways in which Iago and Cassio regard reputation as a concept.

b Write a paragraph reflecting on the importance of reputation and self-image for each of the following: you and your friends; celebrities you are familiar with from news stories and interviews; politicians in your country.

2 Alcohol awareness campaign (in small groups)

Imagine that Cassio has been employed by the Venetian Health Education Council to make an advertisement about the dangers of alcohol abuse. Design the campaign, making sure you include some of the following:

* a clear message about the dangers of alcohol abuse
* a focus on your target audience
* a well-known celebrity (Cassio)
* a suitable logo
* a slogan (taken from the script, if possible) to help your audience remember the message
* music and/or a jingle.

Improvise a three-minute television commercial featuring Cassio's account of his own experiences at the hands of the 'invisible spirit of wine'.

past all surgery nothing that medicine can cure

repute consider
cast in his mood dismissed in anger
in policy for political reasons
 Sue appeal

speak parrot talk nonsense
fustian rubbish, nonsense

nothing wherefore not what it was about

Iago, look with care about the town, 235
And silence those whom this vile brawl distracted.
Come, Desdemona, 'tis the soldier's life
To have their balmy slumbers waked with strife.

Exeunt [all but Iago and Cassio]

IAGO   What, are you hurt, lieutenant?

CASSIO Ay, past all surgery. 240

IAGO   Marry, God forbid!

CASSIO Reputation, reputation, reputation! O, I have lost my reputation! I have lost the immortal part of myself, and what remains is bestial. My reputation, Iago, my reputation!

IAGO   As I am an honest man, I thought you had received some bodily 245
wound: there is more of sense in that than in reputation.
Reputation is an idle and most false imposition, oft got without
merit and lost without deserving. You have lost no reputation at
all, unless you repute yourself such a loser. What, man! There
are ways to recover the general again. You are but now cast 250
in his mood, a punishment more in policy than in malice, even
so as one would beat his offenceless dog to affright an imperious
lion. Sue to him again, and he's yours.

CASSIO I will rather sue to be despised than to deceive so good a
commander with so light, so drunken, and so indiscreet an 255
officer. Drunk! And speak parrot! And squabble! Swagger!
Swear! And discourse fustian with one's own shadow! O thou
invisible spirit of wine, if thou hast no name to be known by, let
us call thee devil!

IAGO   What was he that you followed with your sword? What had he 260
done to you?

CASSIO I know not.

IAGO   Is't possible?

CASSIO I remember a mass of things, but nothing distinctly: a quarrel,
but nothing wherefore. O God, that men should put an enemy 265
in their mouths to steal away their brains! That we should with joy,
pleasance, revel and applause transform ourselves into beasts!

IAGO   Why, but you are now well enough. How came you thus
recovered?

CASSIO It hath pleased the devil drunkenness to give place to the devil 270
wrath; one unperfectness shows me another, to make me frankly
despise myself.

Iago suggests that Cassio should approach Desdemona about his reinstatement. He insists that her good nature and her influence over Othello will restore Cassio to office. Cassio accepts the advice.

Characters

Cassio (in small groups)

Cassio bemoans the fact that he no longer regards himself as 'a sensible man', but how does Cassio really see himself at this point in the play?

- Read lines 242–80. Find the ways in which Cassio describes himself (for example, in lines 267, 277 and 279). Then create a tableau or a collage based on the images Cassio uses.

1 Thought-track Iago (in pairs)

Iago deceitfully advises Cassio to ask Desdemona for help. Why do you think he suggests this course of action? What are his ulterior motives?

- With your partner, stand back to back. One person becomes Iago and reads the speech in lines 281–95, pausing at the end of each sentence. This is the cue for the second person to voice Iago's hidden thoughts. Present what is going on in Iago's mind, explaining what he really thinks and what his future plans are. Share your ideas with the rest of the class.

Write about it

Cassio's diary

Imagine Cassio keeps a personal journal. Write his diary entry for this evening. To help you decide what to include, consider the following questions while in role as Cassio:

- How has your life changed this evening? Give a brief description of the events that have taken place.
- How do you feel about yourself?
- Do you think Othello reacted fairly?
- What is your opinion of Iago and the advice he has given you?
- What do you hope to achieve by approaching Desdemona tomorrow?

Hydra a many-headed monster of Greek mythology

by and by very soon

inordinate superfluous, one too many

unblessed cursed

familiar creature friendly spirit

approved it tested it out

mark observation

parts qualities

splinter mend (apply a splint)

lay bet

betimes early

| IAGO | Come, you are too severe a moraler. As the time, the place, and the condition of this country stands, I could heartily wish this had not befallen; but since it is as it is, mend it for your own good. | 275 |

| CASSIO | I will ask him for my place again; he shall tell me I am a drunkard. Had I as many mouths as Hydra, such an answer would stop them all. To be now a sensible man, by and by a fool, and presently a beast! O strange! Every inordinate cup is unblessed, and the ingredience is a devil. | 280 |

| IAGO | Come, come, good wine is a good familiar creature, if it be well used; exclaim no more against it. And, good lieutenant, I think you think I love you. |

| CASSIO | I have well approved it, sir. I drunk! |

| IAGO | You or any man living may be drunk at a time, man. I'll tell you what you shall do. Our general's wife is now the general. I may say so in this respect, for that he hath devoted and given up himself to the contemplation, mark, and denotement of her parts and graces. Confess yourself freely to her, importune her help to put you in your place again. She is of so free, so kind, so apt, so blest a disposition, that she holds it a vice in her goodness not to do more than she is requested. This broken joint between you and her husband entreat her to splinter; and my fortunes against any lay worth naming, this crack of your love shall grow stronger than it was before. | 285 290 295 |

| CASSIO | You advise me well. |

| IAGO | I protest, in the sincerity of love and honest kindness. |

| CASSIO | I think it freely; and betimes in the morning I will beseech the virtuous Desdemona to undertake for me. I am desperate of my fortunes if they check me here. | 300 |

| IAGO | You are in the right. Good night, lieutenant, I must to the watch. |

| CASSIO | Good night, honest Iago. | *Exit* |

Left alone, Iago reveals his plan to lie to Othello about Desdemona and Cassio having an affair. When Desdemona pleads for Cassio's reinstatement, it will only make things worse. Roderigo tells Iago that he's fed up.

1 Iago's soliloquy – bare bones (in threes)

a Read through Iago's soliloquy in the script opposite (lines 303–29) in order to get the general sense. It demonstrates Iago's acute awareness that appearances can be deceptive. He uses **antitheses** (words with opposite meanings), culminating in the contrasting concepts of 'virtue' versus 'pitch' (line 327).

b In your group, take one line at a time and quickly agree what you consider to be the key word in each line (for example, in the first line this might be the word 'villain'). Write down each key word (one word per line). When you have done this for the whole speech, you will have a list of twenty-seven words. This is your 'bare-bones' script.

c Keeping the words in their original order, present this new script in any ways that seem appropriate (choral speech, movement, mime, sound effects, echoing individual words). Divide up the words between each group member however you like, but make sure everyone is fully involved. Afterwards, share your presentation with the rest of the class.

▼ **In this production, Iago is crouched – sinister and threatening. How would you have Iago deliver his soliloquy?**

Probal reasonable

inclining sympathetic

win persuade
baptism Christian faith
seals and symbols (for example, the sign of the cross)
list wishes
appetite sexual desire
function will

Divinity religious study

suggest tempt, seduce

repeals him tries to get him reinstated

pitch a black, tar-like substance

cudgelled beaten

IAGO   And what's he then that says I play the villain,
When this advice is free I give, and honest,
Probal to thinking, and indeed the course   305
To win the Moor again? For 'tis most easy
Th'inclining Desdemona to subdue
In any honest suit. She's framed as fruitful
As the free elements; and then for her
To win the Moor, were't to renounce his baptism,   310
All seals and symbols of redeemèd sin,
His soul is so enfettered to her love,
That she may make, unmake, do what she list,
Even as her appetite shall play the god
With his weak function. How am I then a villain   315
To counsel Cassio to this parallel course
Directly to his good? Divinity of hell!
When devils will the blackest sins put on,
They do suggest at first with heavenly shows
As I do now. For whiles this honest fool   320
Plies Desdemona to repair his fortunes,
And she for him pleads strongly to the Moor,
I'll pour this pestilence into his ear:
That she repeals him for her body's lust;
And by how much she strives to do him good,   325
She shall undo her credit with the Moor.
So will I turn her virtue into pitch,
And out of her own goodness make the net
That shall enmesh them all.

Enter Roderigo.

How now, Roderigo?

RODERIGO I do follow here in the chase, not like a hound that hunts,   330
but one that fills up the cry. My money is almost spent; I have
been tonight exceedingly well cudgelled; and I think the issue will
be, I shall have so much experience for my pains; and so, with
no money at all, and a little more wit, return again to Venice.

Iago bids Roderigo to be patient, and tells him they have already succeeded in disgracing Cassio. Left alone, Iago plans to make Emilia urge Desdemona to help Cassio, then to ensure that Othello sees his wife and Cassio together.

Stagecraft

Director's notes (in pairs)

For this activity you are going to work on both parts of Iago's soliloquy, from the previous page (lines 303–29) and from the script opposite (lines 347–53). One of you takes the role of director; the other is the actor playing Iago in a new production of the play. You need to prepare this key speech in detail before rehearsals. Annotate the speech, indicating:

- how Iago should speak (think about changes of tone of voice and of pace)
- what's Iago's movements should be and the way in which he will move around the stage
- what facial expressions and gestures he should employ
- where there might be pauses and silences
- what Iago might be thinking/feeling
- where the speech is set (if that is important)
- the props (if any) that Iago should have.

Overall, consider what relationship you want Iago to have with the audience. For example, does he draw the audience in to his plans? You may wish to work with an enlarged copy of the speech, which you can annotate similarly to the example below.

dilatory dragging, slow

cashiered Cassio got Cassio dismissed

By th'mass my God! (an expression of surprise)

move plead

the while meanwhile
jump at the very moment

device plot

Turns slowly to face audience directly	Speaks quite slowly	Half smiles, then puts on an innocent look	Slight pause on this word

IAGO

And what's he then that says I play the villain,
When this advice is free I give, and honest,
Probal to thinking, and indeed the course
To win the Moor again? For 'tis most easy
Th'inclining Desdemona to subdue
In any honest suit. She's framed as fruitful
As the free elements; and then for her
To win the Moor, were't to renounce his baptism,
All seals and symbols of redeemèd sin,

As he speaks, he walks to front of stage

Speed up a little

Make this word stand out (so many people have called him 'honest')

Light and quick

Allow word a little emphasis

Spoken with disgust

End of question, so pause

88

IAGO How poor are they that have no patience!   335
What wound did ever heal but by degrees?
Thou know'st we work by wit and not by witchcraft,
And wit depends on dilatory time.
Does't not go well? Cassio hath beaten thee,
And thou by that small hurt hath cashiered Cassio.   340
Though other things grow fair against the sun,
Yet fruits that blossom first will first be ripe.
Content thyself awhile. By th'mass, 'tis morning:
Pleasure and action make the hours seem short.
Retire thee, go where thou art billeted.   345
Away, I say, thou shalt know more hereafter –
Nay, get thee gone.

Exit Roderigo

Two things are to be done.
My wife must move for Cassio to her mistress –
I'll set her on.
Myself the while to draw the Moor apart,   350
And bring him jump when he may Cassio find
Soliciting his wife. Ay, that's the way:
Dull not device by coldness and delay.

Exit

Looking back at Act 2
Activities for groups or individuals

1 Headlines – what has happened so far?

Imagine you are a newspaper sub-editor. First of all, consider whether your newspaper is a tabloid or a broadsheet. Once you have decided, your job is to write brief, memorable headlines for each of the six scenes in the first two acts of the play. Make your headlines as accurate as possible. Try to use some of Shakespeare's own words.

2 Epithets and statues

An **epithet** is an adjective or describing phrase, added before a name or noun, that defines the person or thing – for example, 'honest Iago'. In Act 2, there are several epithets, which are applied to a number of different characters.

a In pairs, identify who said each of the following, then discuss what the description tells us about the speaker and the person described:

- 'the warlike Moor'
- 'brave Othello'
- 'valiant Cassio'
- 'divine Desdemon'
- 'bold Iago'
- 'the lusty Moor'
- 'virtuous Desdemona'
- 'honest Iago'
- 'good Michael'
- 'worthy Montano'.

b In your pairs, one person becomes a sculptor, the second person a block of marble. The sculptor must 'carve' three separate statues, choosing from the descriptions above. Swap roles and repeat the activity. Afterwards, share your statues with the rest of the class. Can they identify the statue from the list of titles above?

3 Judgements and justice

Differing notions of justice permeate the play. In both Act 1 and Act 2, a crucial judgement is made and 'justice' is publicly dispensed.

a With a partner, locate these judgements and the participants in each case. Identify the motive, the 'evidence' presented and the consequences of the ruling. What key similarities and/or differences can you find? Make notes as you work.

b On your own, write a short essay (approximately five paragraphs) examining how justice is represented in the first two acts of *Othello*. Use the notes that you and your partner generated in the activity above to support this piece of writing. Make sure that you make close references to the script, and include embedded quotations.

4 Staging the play

The pictures opposite show two different stage sets, both for outdoor performances of *Othello*. They may be rather different from how you imagined the set or from productions you have seen.

a Choose one of the sets and suggest how it might incorporate key locations that you have come across in the play so far:

- a street at night, including Brabantio's house
- outside the Sagittary
- the Council Chamber in Venice
- the storm at sea, and the quayside in Cyprus
- the herald's proclamation in Cyprus
- a barracks room in the castle in Cyprus.

b Design your own stage set, in which different locations can be suggested swiftly and without the need for major physical changes of scenery.

91

Cassio has hired Musicians to play for Othello and Desdemona. A Clown jokes with a Musician. Cassio sends the Clown to Emilia, to ask her to come out and speak with him.

1 The Clown and the Musicians (in threes)

Elizabethan and Jacobean acting companies always employed a comic actor, or clown. His main role was to play funny or witty parts, possibly embellishing the script with improvised jokes. Playwrights would create a specific role in order to accommodate the clown, even in tragic plays. One effect (for example, with the role of the Porter in *Macbeth*) was to momentarily relieve tension in the drama.

a Read the script opposite aloud, then talk together about what you think of the humour here, which relies heavily on puns and wordplay. For example, the Clown plays with the double meaning of the word 'Naples' – a joke on the nasal sound of a Neapolitan accent and 'Neapolitan disease', a venereal disease. He also generates puns around the word 'instrument', where the first reference in line 6 is to a kind of bagpipe, the second reference (line 10) to flatulence. Some people find the jokes to be rather crude and laboured, but others argue that the dramatic function of the Clown's punning is to foreshadow the misunderstandings that are shortly to happen in the play. Consider both points of view in your discussion.

b If you were directing a production of *Othello*, what popular stage or television comedian would you cast in the role of the Clown? Explain your choice.

c It was an Elizabethan custom to wake newlyweds with music outside their bedchamber. Discuss whether you would open the scene with musicians really playing on stage. In a modern production, what music would you choose, and why? Can you think of a particular song or piece of music that might have significant meaning for the characters at this point in the play?

2 Make a director's decision (in pairs)

Lines 1–27 are often cut from productions. Discuss with your partner whether you would include them in your own modern production of the play. Give at least two reasons for and against their inclusion before reaching your decision. Share your views with the rest of the class, then make some notes in your Director's Journal.

content your pains pay you for your trouble

speak i'th'nose thus talk with a nasal sound (as if through the nose)
How, sir, how? what do you mean?

for love's sake out of any affection you have for him

may not cannot

quillets puns and wordplays

stirring (line 24) awake

stirring (line 26) sexually active
seem arrange

Act 3 Scene 1

Cyprus   Outside Desdemona's bedchamber

Enter CASSIO, MUSICIANS *and* CLOWN.

CASSIO   Masters, play here; I will content your pains.
         Something that's brief, and bid 'Good morrow, general.'
                              [*They play.*]

CLOWN   Why, masters, have your instruments been in Naples, that
        they speak i'th'nose thus?

1 MUSICIAN   How, sir, how?   5

CLOWN   Are these, I pray you, wind instruments?

1 MUSICIAN   Ay, marry are they, sir.

CLOWN   O, thereby hangs a tail.

1 MUSICIAN   Whereby hangs a tale, sir?

CLOWN   Marry, sir, by many a wind instrument that I know. But,   10
        masters, here's money for you; and the general so likes your music
        that he desires you, for love's sake, to make no more noise with
        it.

1 MUSICIAN   Well sir, we will not.

CLOWN   If you have any music that may not be heard, to't again; but, 15
        as they say, to hear music the general does not greatly care.

1 MUSICIAN   We have none such, sir.

CLOWN   Then put up your pipes in your bag, for I'll away. Go,
        vanish into air, away!

                                        Exeunt Musicians

CASSIO   Dost thou hear, mine honest friend?   20

CLOWN   No, I hear not your honest friend; I hear you.

CASSIO   Prithee keep up thy quillets – there's a poor piece of gold for
         thee. If the gentlewoman that attends the general's wife be
         stirring, tell her there's one Cassio entreats her a little favour of
         speech. Wilt thou do this?   25

CLOWN   She is stirring, sir; if she will stir hither, I shall seem to notify
        unto her.

CASSIO   Do, good my friend.

                                          Exit Clown

Iago promises Cassio that he will take Othello out of the way for a while, so Cassio and Emilia can talk freely. Emilia tells Cassio that Othello feels obliged to make an example of him, but intends to reinstate him at a convenient moment.

1 The timescale of the play (in pairs)

Iago's opening comment, 'You have not been abed then?' suggests that this is the morning after the drunken party. The dramatic function might be to:

- give the impression that Cassio is too upset to sleep
- make the action seem to happen very quickly
- give the play continuity
- give a sense of urgency to the events
- keep the party fresh in the audience's mind
- heighten tension
- illustrate how astute or cunning Iago is.

Critics have argued about the timescale of the whole play, which is quite difficult to follow in any naturalistic way. As you read through the rest of the play, pay attention to the passage of time and consider what sense you get of the speed of the action. Construct a timeline of events as they unfold, either individually in your Director's Journal or collectively as a class display.

Characters

Emilia: role and relationships

In the dual role of Desdemona's companion and Iago's wife, Emilia becomes an increasingly important character in the play. In this part of the scene, she takes on the dramatic function of enabling Cassio to gain access to Desdemona, thereby becoming an unwitting pawn in Iago's elaborate plot.

a Read all that Emilia says in the script opposite, then write a paragraph outlining your impressions of Emilia. You might want to refer back to her first appearance (Act 2 Scene 1, lines 83–204) and compare how she came across then with your opinion of her now.

b Over the next two scenes, we will learn a great deal more about Emilia's relationship with Iago. As you read or watch Act 3, make notes on the way Emilia's character develops.

2 More dramatic irony

Find at least two examples of dramatic irony (see p. 38) in the script opposite. For each, explain in what way the comment is ironic and what the dramatic effect might be.

abed to bed

suit request

presently at once
a mean a way

Florentine someone from Florence (Cassio's place of birth)

For your displeasure that you have lost favour (with Othello)

stoutly loyally

great affinity important relations
refuse dismiss

safest occasion ... front first opportunity
in again back in favour

bosom mind, feelings
much bound very grateful

Enter IAGO.

                    In happy time, Iago.

IAGO	You have not been abed then?	
CASSIO	Why, no; the day had broke before we parted.	30

I have made bold, Iago,
To send in to your wife. My suit to her
Is that she will to virtuous Desdemona
Procure me some access.

IAGO   I'll send her to you presently;
And I'll devise a mean to draw the Moor   35
Out of the way, that your converse and business
May be more free.

CASSIO   I humbly thank you for't.

                                           Exit [*Iago*]

I never knew a Florentine more kind and honest.

Enter EMILIA.

EMILIA	Good morrow, good lieutenant; I am sorry	

For your displeasure; but all will sure be well.   40
The general and his wife are talking of it,
And she speaks for you stoutly. The Moor replies
That he you hurt is of great fame in Cyprus
And great affinity, and that in wholesome wisdom
He might not but refuse you; but he protests he loves you,   45
And needs no other suitor but his likings
To take the safest occasion by the front
To bring you in again.

CASSIO   Yet I beseech you,
If you think fit, or that it may be done,
Give me advantage of some brief discourse   50
With Desdemon alone.

EMILIA   Pray you, come in;
I will bestow you where you shall have time
To speak your bosom freely.

CASSIO   I am much bound to you.

                                         Exeunt

Othello goes off to inspect the fortifications. In Scene 3, Desdemona assures Cassio that she will help him. Cassio expresses his gratitude.

Write about it
Othello's official report

In line 1 of Scene 2, we discover that Othello has written an official report ('letters') to the Duke of Venice. In role as Othello, write this report. Firstly, think about the content, which might include:

- **Military mission** What has been the outcome of the mission to engage with the Turkish fleet and protect Cyprus from attack? Have all survived the storms at sea?
- **Current situation** What are you doing to make sure Cyprus is safe?
- **Incident involving Montano** How are you going to explain this? What changes in military personnel have there been?

What tone should you adopt as Othello (in your capacity as army general)? Find appropriate phrases from the script to include in your writing. Will you make any mention of your wedding celebration? If so, will the tone change when you turn to personal matters?

do my duties pay my respects
works ramparts, fortifications
Repair return

1 The dramatic function of Scene 2 (in pairs)

Scene 2 is very short. What dramatic purpose do you think this scene serves? Look back at the previous scene, and glance at the beginning of the next, then copy and complete the table below.

	Scene 1	Scene 2	Scene 3
Characters			
Where does it take place?			
What happens?			
How is the plot taken forward?			

What can you deduce about the function of Scene 2? Consider the following in your discussions:

- Othello's role as a military leader
- Iago's relationship with Othello
- Desdemona's whereabouts
- the time scheme
- Cassio's whereabouts
- Cyprus as a colonial outpost.

He shall … distance he will distance himself from you only while it is politically necessary

Act 3 Scene 2
Cyprus   Outside the castle

Enter OTHELLO, IAGO *and* GENTLEMEN.

OTHELLO	These letters give, Iago, to the pilot,
	And by him do my duties to the senate.
	That done, I will be walking on the works;
	Repair there to me.
IAGO	Well, my good lord, I'll do't. [*Exit*]
OTHELLO	This fortification, gentlemen, shall we see't?
GENTLEMEN	We'll wait upon your lordship.

5

Exeunt

Act 3 Scene 3
Cyprus   A room in the castle

Enter DESDEMONA, CASSIO *and* EMILIA.

DESDEMONA	Be thou assured, good Cassio, I will do
	All my abilities in thy behalf.
EMILIA	Good madam, do; I warrant it grieves my husband
	As if the case were his.
DESDEMONA	O, that's an honest fellow. Do not doubt, Cassio,
	But I will have my lord and you again
	As friendly as you were.
CASSIO	Bounteous madam,
	Whatever shall become of Michael Cassio,
	He's never anything but your true servant.
DESDEMONA	I know't; I thank you. You do love my lord,
	You have known him long, and be you well assured
	He shall in strangeness stand no farther off
	Than in a politic distance.

5

10

Cassio fears that Othello may not relent, but Desdemona again pledges her support. Othello sees them in conversation, and Iago draws attention to Cassio's hurried departure, implying furtiveness and guilt.

Themes

The position of women in the play (in pairs)

Desdemona promises Cassio: 'I give thee warrant of thy place.' She will help him back to his military position on the grounds of personal friendship.

- Briefly discuss Desdemona's role here, as friend, wife, woman and civilian. Then read on to the next page of script, and look at Activity 1 on page 100, which develops this issue further.

Stagecraft

Exits, entrances and movement (in small groups)

The manner and timing of characters' entrances and exits at this moment of the play are crucial to the dramatic development. In Shakespeare's day, the stage had a deep acting area with two entrance/exit doors at the back. The size of this area would make it possible for Othello and Iago to enter and pass by Cassio at a distance, allowing the remaining dialogue (notably, Iago's 'Ha! I like not that') to work theatrically. Look at the picture on page 186, which shows an Elizabethan stage similar in shape to the Globe Theatre, where *Othello* was originally performed.

- Try 'blocking' the moves of all the characters involved between line 25 and line 51 ('blocking' is working out different positions where people stand). Match the characters' movements and precise entrances and exits with lines of script. For example, decide how many lines it takes for Cassio to make his exit, and where Othello and Iago might be during those lines.

1 'Ha! I like not that' (in pairs)

a Read through lines 35–40. Annotate a copy of the script to show how Iago shapes what Othello thinks he sees.

b In role as Othello and Desdemona, read through lines 41–51. Experiment with ways in which Desdemona might speak her lines. For example, is she serious or playful?

c Discuss how chance yet again plays into Iago's hands. Consider what dramatic effect this combination of manipulation and chance creates, then add some notes to your Director's Journal.

---

nice meagre

breed itself … circumstance produce so few opportunities

supplied taken by someone else

doubt fear

warrant promise

watch him keep him awake (a way of taming hawks)

board dinner table, meals

shrift confessional, place for penance

solicitor advocate, helper

your discretion what you think best

CASSIO	Ay, but, lady,
	That policy may either last so long
	Or feed upon such nice and waterish diet,
	Or breed itself so out of circumstance,
	That I being absent and my place supplied,
	My general will forget my love and service.
DESDEMONA	Do not doubt that. Before Emilia here,
	I give thee warrant of thy place. Assure thee
	If I do vow a friendship, I'll perform it
	To the last article. My lord shall never rest,
	I'll watch him tame and talk him out of patience;
	His bed shall seem a school, his board a shrift;
	I'll intermingle every thing he does
	With Cassio's suit. Therefore be merry, Cassio;
	Thy solicitor shall rather die
	Than give thy cause away.

Enter OTHELLO *and* IAGO.

EMILIA	Madam, here comes my lord.
CASSIO	Madam, I'll take my leave.
DESDEMONA	Why, stay and hear me speak.
CASSIO	Madam, not now: I am very ill at ease,
	Unfit for mine own purposes.
DESDEMONA	Well, do your discretion.

Exit Cassio

IAGO	Ha! I like not that.
OTHELLO	What dost thou say?
IAGO	Nothing, my lord; or if – I know not what.
OTHELLO	Was not that Cassio parted from my wife?
IAGO	Cassio, my lord? No, sure I cannot think it
	That he would steal away so guilty-like,
	Seeing you coming.
OTHELLO	I do believe 'twas he.
DESDEMONA	How now, my lord?
	I have been talking with a suitor here,
	A man that languishes in your displeasure.
OTHELLO	Who is't you mean?

15

20

25

30

35

40

Desdemona playfully lobbies Othello about Cassio's reinstatement. She reminds him that Cassio accompanied Othello during their courtship. Othello agrees that Cassio may come to see him at any time.

1 Desdemona pleads for a friend (in pairs)

Several readers of the play have commented that Desdemona shows little understanding of the responsibilities of her husband's position. She confuses personal feelings with official duties, and believes that Cassio should be pardoned for a military offence simply because he has been a good friend to them.

a Discuss how far you believe Desdemona is justified in pleading on Cassio's behalf. Share your ideas with another pair of students.

b Make a list of other occasions in the play so far when it could be said that the boundary between public and private concerns has been blurred. Does this make any difference to your thoughts about Desdemona's intervention here?

Characters

Othello's response

Read through the exchange between Desdemona and Othello (lines 45–76), and decide what advice you would give the actor playing Othello at this point. What do you think Othello's tone would be by the time he says: 'I will deny thee nothing'? Consider the following suggestions in turn. Othello's mood is:

- weary
- condescending
- impatient
- loving and indulgent
- anxious
- angry
- surprised that Desdemona is so assertive.

Write a paragraph outlining what you would want an actor to convey here, including precisely how he should utter line 76.

2 A private conversation? (in fours)

When you read the script on the page, it is easy to forget that characters who have fallen silent are still on stage.

- Remind yourselves who else is on stage, then step into roles as the characters present and create a tableau of the line 'I shall not dine at home'. In turn, each person should bring their character to life and express his or her thoughts at this moment in the play.

His present reconciliation take make peace with him now

in cunning knowingly

sooth in truth

trespass misdeed
in our common reason by normal standards
check rebuke

mammering on stuttering

bring him in bring him back in favour
By'r Lady by the Virgin Mary

DESDEMONA	Why, your lieutenant, Cassio. Good my lord, 45
	If I have any grace or power to move you,
	His present reconciliation take.
	For if he be not one that truly loves you,
	That errs in ignorance, and not in cunning,
	I have no judgement in an honest face. 50
	I prithee call him back.
OTHELLO	Went he hence now?
DESDEMONA	Ay, sooth; so humbled
	That he hath left part of his grief with me
	To suffer with him. Good love, call him back.
OTHELLO	Not now, sweet Desdemon; some other time. 55
DESDEMONA	But shall't be shortly?
OTHELLO	The sooner, sweet, for you.
DESDEMONA	Shall't be tonight at supper?
OTHELLO	No, not tonight.
DESDEMONA	Tomorrow dinner then?
OTHELLO	I shall not dine at home.
	I meet the captains at the citadel.
DESDEMONA	Why, then, tomorrow night, or Tuesday morn, 60
	On Tuesday noon, or night; on Wednesday morn.
	I prithee name the time, but let it not
	Exceed three days. In faith, he's penitent;
	And yet his trespass, in our common reason –
	Save that, they say, the wars must make example 65
	Out of their best – is not almost a fault
	T'incur a private check. When shall he come?
	Tell me, Othello. I wonder in my soul
	What you would ask me that I should deny,
	Or stand so mammering on. What! Michael Cassio, 70
	That came a-wooing with you, and so many a time
	When I have spoke of you dispraisingly
	Hath tane your part, to have so much to do
	To bring him in? By'r Lady, I could do much –
OTHELLO	Prithee no more. Let him come when he will; 75
	I will deny thee nothing.

Othello dismisses Desdemona, promising to grant her requests. Iago continues to drop deceptive hints about Cassio. Othello tries to find out what's on Iago's mind.

1 Sowing the seeds of doubt (in small groups)

Right from Cassio's exit and Iago's accompanying 'I like not that' at line 35, Iago manages to plant ideas in Othello's mind without saying very much. His use of understatement is highly effective and suggestive.

- Share out the following quotations between the groups in your class. Each group should work out a dramatic presentation of its quote. Bring out the insidious way in which Iago works – probing, asking questions, vaguely hinting …

      'Ha! I like not that.'
      'My lord, for aught I know.'
      'Honest, my lord?'
      'No further harm.'
      'Nothing, my lord'
      'Think, my lord?'
      '… or if'
      'Cassio, my lord?'
      'Indeed?'
      '… acquainted with her?'

2 'Chaos is come again' – imagery, or a memory?

For Othello, falling out of love with Desdemona will be 'the end of the world'. Some Elizabethans believed that a state of Chaos existed before the creation, and that when the world ended Chaos would return. It was something to be feared, in the same way that even in the twenty-first century some people fear that a catastrophe (such as a comet striking Earth) will destroy the world. But consider Othello's comments at a personal level. He might mean that the effects of falling out of love will be personally catastrophic, or that personal chaos will literally return ('come again'), implying that he has experienced such a state of personal disorder once before.

- Which interpretation do you think is more likely? Or are they both equally likely? Try reading Othello's line aloud in different ways to convey the meaning you prefer.

boon personal favour

'Tis as it's as if

peculiar personal

profit benefit

touch your love put your love to the test

poise and difficult weight serious importance

fearful to be granted not easy to be decided

Whereon at this point

straight soon

fancies desires

Perdition damnation

But … of my thought I just wondered

went between took messages between

DESDEMONA	Why, this is not a boon;
	'Tis as I should entreat you wear your gloves,
	Or feed on nourishing dishes, or keep you warm,
	Or sue to you to do a peculiar profit
	To your own person. Nay, when I have a suit 80
	Wherein I mean to touch your love indeed,
	It shall be full of poise and difficult weight,
	And fearful to be granted.
OTHELLO	I will deny thee nothing,
	Whereon, I do beseech thee, grant me this,
	To leave me but a little to myself. 85
DESDEMONA	Shall I deny you? No; farewell, my lord.
OTHELLO	Farewell, my Desdemona, I'll come to thee straight.
DESDEMONA	Emilia, come. Be as your fancies teach you;
	Whate'er you be, I am obedient.

Exeunt Desdemona and Emilia

OTHELLO	Excellent wretch! Perdition catch my soul 90
	But I do love thee; and when I love thee not,
	Chaos is come again.
IAGO	My noble lord –
OTHELLO	What dost thou say, Iago?
IAGO	Did Michael Cassio,
	When you wooed my lady, know of your love?
OTHELLO	He did from first to last. Why dost thou ask? 95
IAGO	But for a satisfaction of my thought;
	No further harm.
OTHELLO	Why of thy thought, Iago?
IAGO	I did not think he had been acquainted with her.
OTHELLO	O yes, and went between us very oft.
IAGO	Indeed? 100
OTHELLO	Indeed? Ay, indeed. Discern'st thou aught in that?
	Is he not honest?
IAGO	Honest, my lord?
OTHELLO	Honest? Ay, honest.
IAGO	My lord, for aught I know.
OTHELLO	What dost thou think? 105
IAGO	Think, my lord?
OTHELLO	Think, my lord! By heaven, he echoes me,
	As if there were some monster in his thought
	Too hideous to be shown. Thou dost mean something.

Othello presses Iago to reveal his thoughts, assuring him that he knows him to be an honest and faithful man. Iago says he believes Cassio to be honest, but asks to be excused from telling his inner thoughts.

Language in the play
Qualified praise (in threes)

At line 126, Iago appears to be asserting his confidence in Cassio's honesty. Yet if you look carefully at the exact words he uses, he is cleverly and subtly suggesting just the opposite.

- Start with the basic statement 'he is honest' and see how Iago doubly modifies it with phrases that signal doubt. Take the following three statements and experiment with ways of presenting them to bring out Iago's qualified praise:

  'he is honest.'
  'I think that he is honest.'
  'I dare be sworn I think that he is honest.'

Themes
Appearance and reality (in pairs)

In lines 119–25 – shortly before Iago's breathtakingly hypocritical 'Men should be what they seem' – Othello talks of the 'just' man and the 'false' man. He says that both can speak in the same style or manner, but from different causes. For a 'false disloyal knave', hesitation in speech is a customary habit. For a 'just' man it arises because he is carefully weighing his words. It is ironic that Othello thinks Iago's 'stops' (hesitations) are a mark of honesty.

- Write a paragraph analysing lines 119–25 and 131–4, then write a further two paragraphs exploring the relationship between words and deeds in the play so far.

Stagecraft
Figures of authority

Othello's speech opposite is peppered with verbal signs that he is already filled with self-doubt (for example, in his repetition of 'I think' and his frequent use of questions or pleas for information).

- How might you direct the actors in this scene to suggest that Othello is no longer the authoritative figure he was in Acts 1 and 2? In what ways might you subtly suggest that Iago is taking control? Add your ideas to your Director's Journal.

my counsel in my confidence
In my whole course of wooing while I was courting (Desdemona)

conceit idea
Show tell

weigh'st consider
stops hesitations

tricks of custom familiar deceptions
just trustworthy
close dilations involuntary delays (note that there is much disagreement about the meaning of this phrase)

speak … thinkings tell me what you really think
ruminate think

leets local courts
law-days days on which courts are in session

	I heard thee say even now thou lik'st not that, 110
	When Cassio left my wife. What didst not like?
	And when I told thee he was of my counsel
	In my whole course of wooing, thou cried'st 'Indeed?'
	And didst contract and purse thy brow together,
	As if thou then hadst shut up in thy brain 115
	Some horrible conceit. If thou dost love me,
	Show me thy thought.
IAGO	My lord, you know I love you.
OTHELLO	I think thou dost;
	And for I know thou'rt full of love and honesty,
	And weigh'st thy words before thou giv'st them breath, 120
	Therefore these stops of thine fright me the more;
	For such things in a false disloyal knave
	Are tricks of custom; but in a man that's just,
	They're close dilations, working from the heart,
	That passion cannot rule.
IAGO	For Michael Cassio, 125
	I dare be sworn I think that he is honest.
OTHELLO	I think so too.
IAGO	Men should be what they seem;
	Or those that be not, would they might seem none!
OTHELLO	Certain, men should be what they seem.
IAGO	Why then, I think Cassio's an honest man. 130
OTHELLO	Nay, yet there's more in this.
	I prithee speak to me as to thy thinkings,
	As thou dost ruminate, and give thy worst of thoughts
	The worst of words.
IAGO	Good my lord, pardon me;
	Though I am bound to every act of duty, 135
	I am not bound to that all slaves are free to.
	Utter my thoughts! Why, say they are vile and false?
	As where's that palace, whereinto foul things
	Sometimes intrude not? Who has a breast so pure,
	But some uncleanly apprehensions 140
	Keep leets and law-days, and in session sit
	With meditations lawful?

Iago continues to seem reluctant to reveal what he claims to know about Cassio and Desdemona. He strongly defends the importance of a man's or woman's reputation, and warns Othello to beware of jealousy.

Language in the play
Metaphors (in small groups)

Earlier, Iago dismissed Cassio's lament about loss of 'reputation'. But now he describes 'Good name', or reputation, in a man or woman as 'the immediate jewel of their souls' (lines 156–7). He uses another visual image to describe jealousy: 'the green-eyed monster which doth mock / The meat it feeds on.'

a Choose one of these metaphors and create a tableau as a physical representation of the words (remember, you are not showing a picture of what is happening on stage, but creating an interpretation of the image). Make sure everyone in the group is involved.

b For the other metaphor, create a drawing or collage that seems to you to best illuminate the sense and connotations of the words. Share both visual interpretations with the rest of the class.

c Talk together about how Iago develops each of these images through practical examples in the lines that follow (158–62 and 168–72).

1 Game tactics (in threes)

Iago tactically approaches his task of heightening Othello's anxiety. It is as intriguing following his verbal 'moves' as it can be monitoring a game of football, chess or snooker, where each individual move is part of a much wider game strategy.

a Read aloud lines 143–78 to familiarise yourselves with the script. Discuss the points at which Iago cleverly shapes Othello's responses, and what kinds of tactics he employs.

b One of you then becomes a commentator on the game, and the other two take the parts of Iago and Othello. Present the dialogue as if it is a game being watched by a radio or television presenter, who comments throughout on the tactics Iago uses against Othello and Othello's responses. Iago and Othello may need to briefly freeze their dialogue at pre-arranged moments so that the commentary can be heard. Remember that the 'players' might gain or lose ground during the game.

c As an extension to this activity, try beginning your commentary from line 90 of this scene.

mak'st his ear … thoughts don't tell him what you're thinking

perchance perhaps
it is my nature's plague I can't help it
jealousy suspicion
Shapes imagines
conceits imagines
scattering … observance random and uncertain perceptions
quiet peace of mind

immediate most precious

filches steals

doth mock … it feeds on torments its victim
cuckold wronged husband
tells counts
dotes loves

106

OTHELLO	Thou dost conspire against thy friend, Iago,
	If thou but think'st him wronged, and mak'st his ear
	A stranger to thy thoughts.
IAGO	I do beseech you,	145
	Though I perchance am vicious in my guess –
	As I confess it is my nature's plague
	To spy into abuses, and oft my jealousy
	Shapes faults that are not – that your wisdom then,
	From one that so imperfectly conceits,	150
	Would take no notice, nor build yourself a trouble
	Out of his scattering and unsure observance.
	It were not for your quiet, nor your good,
	Nor for my manhood, honesty, and wisdom,
	To let you know my thoughts.
OTHELLO	What dost thou mean?	155
IAGO	Good name in man and woman, dear my lord,
	Is the immediate jewel of their souls.
	Who steals my purse, steals trash; 'tis something, nothing,
	'Twas mine, 'tis his, and has been slave to thousands:
	But he that filches from me my good name	160
	Robs me of that which not enriches him
	And makes me poor indeed.
OTHELLO	By heaven, I'll know thy thoughts.
IAGO	You cannot, if my heart were in your hand,
	Nor shall not, while 'tis in my custody.	165
OTHELLO	Ha!
IAGO	O beware, my lord, of jealousy:
	It is the green-eyed monster which doth mock
	The meat it feeds on. That cuckold lives in bliss
	Who certain of his fate loves not his wronger;	170
	But O, what damnèd minutes tells he o'er
	Who dotes, yet doubts, suspects, yet fondly loves?
OTHELLO	O misery!

Othello assures Iago he's not a naturally jealous man. He says he is confident of his wife's virtue. Iago warns him to watch Desdemona with Cassio, as she is capable of deception.

1 Key words and phrases (in pairs)

a Read lines 178–206. Between you, agree on what seems to be a key word or phrase in each line. Working only with those words or phrases you have chosen, experiment with ways of presenting the exchange between Iago and Othello to express Othello's apparent confidence but underlying uncertainty, and Iago's insinuations and warning. You could 'intercut' (interweave) the two sets of key words, for example, if you feel that contributes to an understanding of the dynamics of the dialogue. Make use of the dramatic approach that seems to be most appropriate. Compare your presentation with those of other pairs, and discuss similarities or differences.

b With a digital camera, take two or three photographs as you work with the script, then upload them to a computer. Compare your group's interpretations with those of other groups. You could create a class display of 'production photos', which you can add to as you continue to read or watch the play.

▼ How well do you think this photograph conveys the relationship between Iago and Othello at this point in the play?

fineless endless

To follow ... fresh suspicions to be overtaken by new suspicions as often as the moon waxes and wanes

to be once ... resolved the minute I'm in any doubt, I'll settle the matter

goat (goats were supposed to be particularly lecherous)

exsufflicate exaggerated

surmises suspicions

Matching thy inference equal to your interpretation

weak merits lack of physical attraction

revolt infidelity

bound duty-bound

Wear your eyes thus (what gesture might Iago make?)

self-bounty natural generosity and kindness

pranks sexual exploits

Their best conscience their idea of morality

IAGO	Poor and content is rich, and rich enough;
	But riches fineless is as poor as winter	175
	To him that ever fears he shall be poor.
	Good God, the souls of all my tribe defend
	From jealousy.
OTHELLO	Why, why is this?
	Think'st thou I'd make a life of jealousy,
	To follow still the changes of the moon	180
	With fresh suspicions? No, to be once in doubt
	Is once to be resolved. Exchange me for a goat
	When I shall turn the business of my soul
	To such exsufflicate and blown surmises
	Matching thy inference. 'Tis not to make me jealous	185
	To say my wife is fair, feeds well, loves company,
	Is free of speech, sings, plays, and dances well:
	Where virtue is, these are more virtuous.
	Nor from mine own weak merits will I draw
	The smallest fear or doubt of her revolt,	190
	For she had eyes and chose me. No, Iago,
	I'll see before I doubt; when I doubt, prove;
	And on the proof, there is no more but this:
	Away at once with love or jealousy!
IAGO	I am glad of this; for now I shall have reason	195
	To show the love and duty that I bear you
	With franker spirit. Therefore, as I am bound,
	Receive it from me. I speak not yet of proof.
	Look to your wife, observe her well with Cassio;
	Wear your eyes thus: not jealous, nor secure.	200
	I would not have your free and noble nature,
	Out of self-bounty, be abused. Look to't.
	I know our country disposition well:
	In Venice they do let God see the pranks
	They dare not show their husbands. Their best conscience	205
	Is not to leave't undone, but keep't unknown.

Iago reminds Othello that Desdemona has already deceived her father. He professes his love for Othello, but continues to drop hints about Desdemona's lack of fidelity.

Characters

Iago the manipulator (in pairs)

Iago continues to undermine Othello, using cunning strategies to heighten Othello's doubts. Each of Iago's speeches opposite employs a different technique of insidious persuasion.

a   Consider each of these speeches in turn. Trace the way Iago puts words into Othello's mouth and thoughts into his head to create suspicion of Desdemona.

b   Practise saying the lines, experimenting with physical distances between the characters. Start at far sides of the room and read through the script, raising your voices sufficiently to be heard; move closer and try again, finally moving towards each other until almost whispering into each others' ears. What works best? At what points might you move closer together and at what points would you move or turn away?

1 Who's deceiving whom?

Iago has already commented on Venetian women's ability to deceive (lines 203–6). Now, his 'She did deceive her father, marrying you' closely echoes Brabantio's parting words in Act 1 Scene 3, lines 288–9.

• Devise a diagrammatic way of representing which characters are being (or have been) deceived by Iago at this point, and who believes they are being deceived by others. You could use the example below as a starting point. For each 'strand' of your diagram, find a relevant quotation and include that in your design.

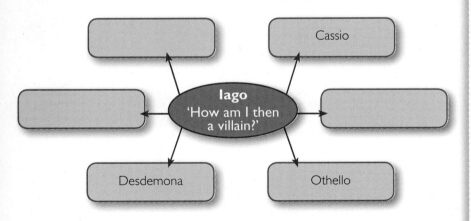

go to then! there you are!

seel stitch up
close as oak like the close grain of an oak tree

bound indebted

Not a jot not at all

moved distressed
strain push further
issues conclusions
larger reach go beyond

success result
aimed not at did not intend

honest chaste, virtuous

erring from itself straying from its true self

OTHELLO	Dost thou say so?	
IAGO	She did deceive her father, marrying you;	
	And when she seemed to shake and fear your looks	
	She loved them most.	
OTHELLO	And so she did.	
IAGO	Why, go to then!	210
	She that so young could give out such a seeming	
	To seel her father's eyes up close as oak	
	He thought 'twas witchcraft – but I am much to blame,	
	I humbly do beseech you of your pardon	
	For too much loving you.	
OTHELLO	I am bound to thee for ever.	215
IAGO	I see this hath a little dashed your spirits.	
OTHELLO	Not a jot, not a jot.	
IAGO	I'faith, I fear it has.	
	I hope you will consider what is spoke	
	Comes from my love. But I do see you're moved.	
	I am to pray you not to strain my speech	220
	To grosser issues nor to larger reach	
	Than to suspicion.	
OTHELLO	I will not.	
IAGO	Should you do so, my lord,	
	My speech should fall into such vile success	
	As my thoughts aimed not at. Cassio's my worthy friend –	225
	My lord, I see you're moved.	
OTHELLO	No, not much moved.	
	I do not think but Desdemona's honest.	
IAGO	Long live she so, and long live you to think so!	
OTHELLO	And yet how nature erring from itself –	

Iago implies that Desdemona is unnatural for preferring a black man over someone of her own colour. Othello orders Iago to set Emilia to watch Desdemona. Iago advises Othello to see how Desdemona pleads for Cassio.

Stagecraft
Stage directions: 'Going' and 'Returning'

Iago skilfully plays his victim. He even pretends to leave the stage, only to come straight back as if having a spontaneous second thought.

- Give advice to the actor playing Iago – how should he go and return? Add these ideas to your Director's Journal.

▶ Compare and contrast this image with the one on page 108. What does each image suggest about the relationship between the two characters? What has changed in the way Iago is 'playing' Othello in the picture here?

bold blunt
affect like
clime country

disproportion impropriety
in position positively
Distinctly specifically
recoiling returning
fall to match come to compare
country forms own countrymen
happily perhaps

unfolds reveals

scan consider
place professional position

means methods
strain his entertainment urges his reinstatement
importunity pleading
busy interfering

government self-control

1 Natural – then and now? (in small groups)

Iago's 'in all things nature tends' (line 233) echoes Othello's 'And yet how nature erring from itself' (line 229). But is Desdemona's marriage to Othello unnatural?

- Talk together about whether you feel that in your culture, people's views on 'mixed-race' marriage have changed since Shakespeare's time. (See 'Race and culture in *Othello*' on pp. 233–7 for additional information about seventeenth-century views about black people.)

IAGO	Ay, there's the point: as, to be bold with you,	230
	Not to affect many proposèd matches	
	Of her own clime, complexion, and degree,	
	Whereto we see in all things nature tends –	
	Foh! one may smell, in such, a will most rank,	
	Foul disproportion, thoughts unnatural.	235
	But pardon me: I do not in position	
	Distinctly speak of her; though I may fear	
	Her will, recoiling to her better judgement,	
	May fall to match you with her country forms,	
	And happily repent.	
OTHELLO	Farewell, farewell.	240
	If more thou dost perceive, let me know more;	
	Set on thy wife to observe. Leave me, Iago.	
IAGO	[*Going.*] My lord, I take my leave.	
OTHELLO	Why did I marry? This honest creature doubtless	
	Sees and knows more, much more, than he unfolds.	245
IAGO	[*Returning.*] My lord, I would I might entreat your honour	
	To scan this thing no farther. Leave it to time.	
	Although 'tis fit that Cassio have his place –	
	For sure he fills it up with great ability –	
	Yet if you please to hold him off awhile,	250
	You shall by that perceive him and his means.	
	Note if your lady strain his entertainment	
	With any strong or vehement importunity –	
	Much will be seen in that. In the mean time,	
	Let me be thought too busy in my fears –	255
	As worthy cause I have to fear I am –	
	And hold her free, I do beseech your honour.	
OTHELLO	Fear not my government.	
IAGO	I once more take my leave.	*Exit*

Othello reflects that his colour, speech and age may have lost him Desdemona. He sees women's unfaithfulness as the curse of marriage. But the sight of Desdemona seems to make him reject his suspicions.

Stagecraft

Othello's soliloquy: Iago's influence (in pairs)

Iago's success in troubling Othello's mind is evident. He even affects the language that Othello now begins to use.

a Read Othello's soliloquy opposite and identify the ways in which it is reminiscent of Iago's language and attitudes. First look at any references to creatures or animals – what kind of animals are they, and what are they used in reference to? Next, re-read one of Iago's previous speeches (e.g. Act 1 Scene 1, lines 87–93 and 110–13 or Act 3 Scene 3, lines 168–9) to remind yourself of the language Iago has used elsewhere. How does Othello's choice of image reflect Iago's growing influence over him?

b What advice would you give to an actor playing Othello at this point in the play? Would you suggest any shift in pace and tone when Desdemona comes on stage? How should this soliloquy be delivered: directly to the audience, or as if Othello is muttering to himself? Add these notes to your Director's Journal.

Language in the play

Hawking imagery

Using trained hawks for hunting small prey was a courtly pursuit in Elizabethan and Jacobean times. Othello uses a number of hawking images in his soliloquy about Desdemona. He wonders if she will prove to be a 'haggard' (a wild hawk), in which case he will set her free ('whistle her off') and untie the 'jesses' (straps). He will 'let her down the wind / To prey at fortune' – in other words, let her go to look after herself.

• Create a design that could be used as a symbolic stage backdrop, making use of this hawk or captive bird imagery.

haggard wild, untrained hawk
jesses straps tied around a trained hawk's legs
Haply for perhaps because

chamberers gallants, young men

vapour stinking air

Prerogatived privileged
destiny unshunnable inescapable fate
forkèd plague cuckold's horns (the mark of deceived husbands)
do quicken are born

114

OTHELLO This fellow's of exceeding honesty   260
And knows all qualities, with a learnèd spirit,
Of human dealings. If I do prove her haggard,
Though that her jesses were my dear heart-strings,
I'd whistle her off and let her down the wind
To prey at fortune. Haply for I am black,   265
And have not those soft parts of conversation
That chamberers have, or for I am declined
Into the vale of years – yet that's not much –
She's gone, I am abused, and my relief
Must be to loathe her. O curse of marriage,   270
That we can call these delicate creatures ours
And not their appetites! I had rather be a toad
And live upon the vapour of a dungeon
Than keep a corner in the thing I love
For others' uses. Yet 'tis the plague of great ones,   275
Prerogatived are they less than the base;
'Tis destiny unshunnable, like death:
Even then this forkèd plague is fated to us
When we do quicken. Look where she comes.

Enter Desdemona and Emilia.

If she be false, O then heaven mocks itself;   280
I'll not believe it.

Desdemona greets Othello, who claims he has a headache. She tries to bind his head with her handkerchief, but he pushes it aside. Emilia picks it up, remembering that Iago has urged her to steal it.

1 'I am to blame' (in pairs)

To whom does Othello address line 284? How does he say it? Try it out in a number of different ways, then decide which one is the best – and why. Discuss what reasons Othello might have to claim that he is to blame. What does he think he is to blame for?

2 Why does Iago want the handkerchief?

As Emilia holds the handkerchief ('napkin'), she reflects that Iago 'hath a hundred times / Wooed me to steal it'. Why?

• Predict what Iago might want to do with Desdemona's handkerchief.

▼ How does Emilia tell the audience about the 'napkin'? For example, consider how she describes her husband (see line 294). Is she triumphant at obtaining the handkerchief? Or should the actor suggest that Emilia has her doubts about her husband's motives?

generous noble

watching lack of sleep, being on duty

napkin handkerchief

remembrance keepsake
wayward unpredictable
Wooed persuaded
conjured her made her swear
reserves keeps
work tane out embroidery copied

fantasy whim

DESDEMONA   How now, my dear Othello?
Your dinner and the generous islanders,
By you invited, do attend your presence.

OTHELLO   I am to blame.

DESDEMONA   Why do you speak so faintly?
Are you not well?   285

OTHELLO   I have a pain upon my forehead here.

DESDEMONA   Faith, that's with watching; 'twill away again.
Let me but bind it hard, within this hour
It will be well.

OTHELLO   Your napkin is too little.
[*He puts the handkerchief from him, and she drops it.*]
Let it alone. Come, I'll go in with you.   290

DESDEMONA   I am very sorry that you are not well.

                              Exeunt Othello and Desdemona

EMILIA   I am glad I have found this napkin:
This was her first remembrance from the Moor.
My wayward husband hath a hundred times
Wooed me to steal it; but she so loves the token,   295
For he conjured her she should ever keep it,
That she reserves it evermore about her
To kiss and talk to. I'll have the work tane out
And give't Iago.
What he will do with it, heaven knows, not I: 300
I nothing but to please his fantasy.

Emilia hands the handkerchief over to her husband. Iago reveals to the audience what he intends to do with it.

1 Iago and Emilia: what relationship? (in threes)

Lines 302–21 present an exchange between husband and wife. It is possible to direct it in a way that brings out very different interpretations of the relationship between Iago and Emilia. You could even make an important statement about the institution of marriage as it is presented in the play.

a common thing used by anyone

a One person directs the other two, who take parts as Iago and Emilia. You will have to make decisions about Iago's attitude to his wife, Emilia's own mood and the way she approaches her husband. For example, Emilia may be:

- intimidated by Iago
- cheerful
- confident
- desperate for her husband's attention
- frustrated
- playfully flirtatious
- resentful and moody.

to th'advantage luckily

You may find it useful to know that in Elizabethan slang, 'thing' meant the female sexual organ. Does Emilia knowingly use it in this sense (line 303) or is Iago introducing the obscene meaning (line 304)? Decide at precisely what point she would reveal the handkerchief to Iago and how she would relinquish it according to your interpretation of the mood of the exchange. How does she leave the stage at line 321?

import importance

b Afterwards, watch at least two different film or stage versions of this scene and discuss how other directors have interpreted it. For example, in Oliver Parker's 1995 movie, this is a deeply disturbing scene in which Iago virtually sexually assaults his wife.

Be not acknown on't say you know nothing about it

c Write two paragraphs interpreting this dialogue in two contrasting ways chosen from the suggestions below (brief explanations of a range of different critical approaches to the play are given on p. 222).

- a feminist interpretation (which sympathetically presents an obviously oppressed Emilia)
- a fairly 'traditional' reading of the play, which focuses on the cleverness of Iago and regards Emilia as of little interest
- an approach that focuses on the interesting psychological interplay between Iago and Emilia, in which each character is playing games with the other.

holy writ the Bible

conceits imaginings
to distaste to be unpleasant
act action
mines of sulphur hell

Enter Iago.

IAGO	How now? What do you here alone?
EMILIA	Do not you chide; I have a thing for you.
IAGO	You have a thing for me? It is a common thing –
EMILIA	Ha!	305
IAGO	To have a foolish wife.
EMILIA	O, is that all? What will you give me now

For that same handkerchief?

IAGO   What handkerchief?

EMILIA   What handkerchief!

Why, that the Moor first gave to Desdemona,   310
That which so often you did bid me steal.

IAGO   Hast stolen it from her?

EMILIA   No, faith; she let it drop by negligence,
And to th'advantage I being here took't up.
Look, here it is.

IAGO   A good wench! Give it me.   315

EMILIA   What will you do with't, that you have been so earnest
To have me filch it?

IAGO   [*Snatching it.*]   Why, what's that to you?

EMILIA   If it be not for some purpose of import,
Give't me again. Poor lady, she'll run mad
When she shall lack it.

IAGO   Be not acknown on't: 320
I have use for it. Go, leave me.

Exit Emilia

I will in Cassio's lodging lose this napkin
And let him find it. Trifles light as air
Are to the jealous confirmations strong
As proofs of holy writ. This may do something.   325
The Moor already changes with my poison:
Dangerous conceits are in their natures poisons,
Which at the first are scarce found to distaste
But, with a little act upon the blood,
Burn like the mines of sulphur. I did say so.   330

Othello is convinced of Desdemona's infidelity. He wishes he was ignorant of it and declares he has lost interest in his life as a professional soldier. He demands that Iago provide him with hard evidence.

Characters

Othello's 'general camp' speech (in large groups)

Othello laments his loss of contentment, reputation and occupation.

a One member of the group reads lines 346–58 aloud. The others listen carefully and echo any words to do with military activity.

b Divide the speech (from line 349) between group members. Each person takes one or two lines or meaningful phrases. Learn your respective chunks of text, and work out a choral version, including actions, to present your group's delivery of the speech.

c Use your experience of the activities above to discuss what the speech suggests to you about Othello at this point in the play. Is there any evidence of the 'old' Othello here (i.e. Othello as he was presented in Act 1 and the first part of Act 2)?

1 'ocular proof' (in pairs)

a Decide what Othello might be referring to when he says 'ocular proof' in line 361 ('ocular' is to do with eyes). Can you detect any inconsistencies in the way Othello is thinking? Spend three or four minutes comparing your ideas.

b On page 122, there is a picture showing one director's interpretation of how Othello performed this speech. Discuss what is happening here in the relationship between Iago and Othello. How do you think this piece of dialogue should be directed?

2 'Is't come to this?' (in pairs)

a In your own words, explain what you think the situation has 'come to' (line 364) from your own perspective.

b One of you takes the part of Iago and the other Othello. Stand back to back. Take it in turns to answer the question 'Is't come to this?', briefly explaining what your character believes or hopes the situation has 'come to'. Make sure you stay in role.

c As an extension of this activity, regroup as a class and 'hot-seat' one of your classmates as Iago. Ask questions about the way his plot is developing. What has gone well, and what (if anything) has not gone as well as he hoped? What outcome is he looking for?

poppy … mandragora sleep-inducing drugs from plants

medicine drug

thou owed'st was yours

Avaunt go away

rack instrument of torture

sense awareness

general camp whole army

Pioners men of lowest rank

trump trumpet

quality essential nature

circumstance ceremony

engines cannons

clamours thunder

occupation reason for living

ocular visual

waked aroused

Enter Othello.

Look where he comes! Not poppy nor mandragora,
Nor all the drowsy syrups of the world,
Shall ever medicine thee to that sweet sleep
Which thou owed'st yesterday.

OTHELLO   Ha, ha, false to me!

IAGO   Why, how now, general! No more of that.   335

OTHELLO   Avaunt, be gone! Thou hast set me on the rack.
I swear 'tis better to be much abused
Than but to know't a little.

IAGO   How now, my lord!

OTHELLO   What sense had I of her stolen hours of lust?
I saw't not, thought it not, it harmed not me.   340
I slept the next night well, fed well, was free and merry;
I found not Cassio's kisses on her lips.
He that is robbed, not wanting what is stolen,
Let him not know't and he's not robbed at all.

IAGO   I am sorry to hear this.   345

OTHELLO   I had been happy if the general camp,
Pioners and all, had tasted her sweet body
So I had nothing known. O, now for ever
Farewell the tranquil mind! Farewell content!
Farewell the plumèd troops, and the big wars   350
That makes ambition virtue – O farewell!
Farewell the neighing steed and the shrill trump,
The spirit-stirring drum, th'ear-piercing fife,
The royal banner, and all quality,
Pride, pomp, and circumstance of glorious war!   355
And, O you mortal engines, whose rude throats
Th'immortal Jove's dread clamours counterfeit,
Farewell! Othello's occupation's gone.

IAGO   Is't possible, my lord?

OTHELLO   Villain, be sure thou prove my love a whore;   360
Be sure of it. Give me the ocular proof,
Or by the worth of mine eternal soul,
Thou hadst been better have been born a dog
Than answer my waked wrath!

IAGO   Is't come to this?

Othello curses Iago if his suspicions are without foundation. Iago protests that he was only acting as a friend and asks what proof Othello requires of his wife's infidelity.

Characters

In two minds (in pairs)

To experience Othello's tortured, contradictory emotions, share lines 384–91 between you, speaking them as an argument between two people. Try saying the lines standing face to face, or back to back, or standing on different levels. Decide which works best and share your interpretation with the rest of the class.

Write about it

'honesty's a fool'

Consider how far Iago's phrase in line 383 could be regarded as central to the play as a whole. Write two paragraphs outlining your views, supported by evidence from the script. You might like to structure your writing in the following way:

- For the first paragraph, outline all the characters who appear to be honest in the play, and consider what has happened to each so far.
- For the second paragraph, write about Iago. Which characters have described him as honest in the play? What do we (as readers or as viewers) know about Iago and how honest he really is? How is this ironic? Why might Iago conclude that honest people are fools?

probation proof

God bu'y you God be with you
office job, appointment

direct outspoken
profit lesson
sith since
breeds such offence causes such distress

that it works for what it works so hard to earn

just truthful

Dian (goddess of virginity)
begrimed soiled

satisfied certain

topped with a man on top of her

OTHELLO	Make me to see't; or, at the least, so prove it	365
	That the probation bear no hinge nor loop	
	To hang a doubt on – or woe upon thy life!	
IAGO	My noble lord –	
OTHELLO	If thou dost slander her and torture me,	
	Never pray more; abandon all remorse;	370
	On horror's head horrors accumulate;	
	Do deeds to make heaven weep, all earth amazed:	
	For nothing canst thou to damnation add	
	Greater than that.	
IAGO	O grace! O heaven forgive me!	
	Are you a man? Have you a soul? Or sense?	375
	God bu'y you; take mine office. O wretched fool,	
	That lov'st to make thine honesty a vice!	
	O monstrous world! Take note, take note, O world!	
	To be direct and honest is not safe.	
	I thank you for this profit, and from hence	380
	I'll love no friend, sith love breeds such offence.	
OTHELLO	Nay, stay: thou shouldst be honest.	
IAGO	I should be wise; for honesty's a fool	
	And loses that it works for.	
OTHELLO	By the world,	
	I think my wife be honest, and think she is not;	385
	I think that thou art just, and think thou art not.	
	I'll have some proof. Her name, that was as fresh	
	As Dian's visage, is now begrimed and black	
	As mine own face. If there be cords or knives,	
	Poison or fire or suffocating streams,	390
	I'll not endure it. Would I were satisfied!	
IAGO	I see, sir, you are eaten up with passion.	
	I do repent me that I put it to you.	
	You would be satisfied?	
OTHELLO	Would? Nay, I will.	
IAGO	And may. But how? How satisfied, my lord?	395
	Would you, the supervisor, grossly gape on?	
	Behold her topped?	
OTHELLO	Death and damnation! O!	

Iago warns that it will be impossible to catch Desdemona and Cassio in the act of adultery. He reports that he has heard Cassio talk of Desdemona in his sleep. Othello threatens murder.

1 'I'll tear her all to pieces' (in pairs)

At lines 280–1, Othello says: 'If she be false, O then heaven mocks itself; / I'll not believe it.' Only 150 lines later, he vows: 'I'll tear her all to pieces!' (line 432). What has happened in the intervening five pages of script?

- Trace the stages of Iago's manipulation and record them and Othello's responses in the form of a flow diagram. Your diagram might start something like this:

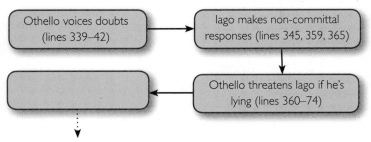

- Calculate how much time has elapsed in the time-scheme of the play. Add this dimension to your diagram.
- Discuss the dramatic effect of this timescale and write your conclusions on the diagram.

Language in the play

Bestial imagery (by yourself)

What effect does Iago's talk of animals on heat (lines 404–5) have on you as a reader or viewer? Read Iago's speech aloud to yourself, then write some suggestions as to how you might draw attention to the various examples of animal imagery in the play (for example, in the set design, use of digital projector, costumes and style of speech).

Stagecraft

Act it out (in pairs)

Iago graphically describes what happened during a night he spent in the barracks with Cassio (lines 411–32). Put actions to the words so that Iago creates a lifelike reconstruction of events. Try playing it in two or three different ways, using some of the following suggestions:

- make it funny – play for laughs
- make it creepy and/or menacing
- Iago is embarrassed by the lurid detail
- Iago is disgusted.

prospect situation
bolster share a pillow

prime lecherous
in pride on heat

imputation … circumstances strong circumstantial evidence

living valid
office task

Pricked spurred
lay with lay next to

loose indiscreet

gripe grasp

foregone conclusion previous consummation
shrewd doubt good guess
thicken strengthen
do demonstrate thinly give weaker evidence

IAGO	It were a tedious difficulty, I think,
	To bring them to that prospect. Damn them then,
	If ever mortal eyes do see them bolster

400

	More than their own. What then? How then?
	What shall I say? Where's satisfaction?
	It is impossible you should see this,
	Were they as prime as goats, as hot as monkeys,
	As salt as wolves in pride, and fools as gross

405

	As Ignorance made drunk. But yet, I say,
	If imputation and strong circumstances,
	Which lead directly to the door of truth,
	Will give you satisfaction, you might have't.

OTHELLO   Give me a living reason she's disloyal.   410

IAGO   I do not like the office;
           But sith I am entered in this cause so far –
           Pricked to't by foolish honesty and love –
           I will go on. I lay with Cassio lately,
           And being troubled with a raging tooth   415
           I could not sleep.
           There are a kind of men so loose of soul
           That in their sleeps will mutter their affairs.
           One of this kind is Cassio.
           In sleep I heard him say, 'Sweet Desdemona,   420
           Let us be wary, let us hide our loves.'
           And then, sir, he would gripe and wring my hand,
           Cry, 'O sweet creature!' and then kiss me hard,
           As if he plucked up kisses by the roots
           That grew upon my lips; then laid his leg   425
           Over my thigh, and sighed, and kissed, and then
           Cried, 'Cursèd fate that gave thee to the Moor.'

OTHELLO   O monstrous, monstrous!

IAGO   Nay, this was but his dream.

OTHELLO   But this denoted a foregone conclusion.

IAGO   'Tis a shrewd doubt, though it be but a dream;   430
           And this may help to thicken other proofs
           That do demonstrate thinly.

OTHELLO   I'll tear her all to pieces!

Iago claims that Cassio has Desdemona's handkerchief. Othello is overcome with jealous grief and vows revenge. To Iago's call for patience, Othello replies that his murderous thoughts will never change.

1 Evidence (in pairs)

Just a few lines ago, Othello asked repeatedly for proof of Desdemona's infidelity – 'a living reason' (line 410). Now he greets Iago's comment about the handkerchief with the words: 'Now do I see 'tis true.' Yet Othello has asked for 'ocular proof' (something he could see for himself).

- Up to now, what exactly has Iago offered by way of 'proof'?

> # Language in the play
> ## Imagery of revenge and hatred (in threes)
>
> **a** Express the following images through a series of two or three linked tableaux:
>
>   - 'Arise, black vengeance, from thy hollow cell!'
>   - 'Yield up, O love, thy crown and hearted throne / To tyrannous hate!'
>
> **b** Share your tableaux with another group, then select the one that both groups agree to be the most effective. Show these to the rest of the class, explaining what you think are the most successful features.

2 The tidal wave of Othello's emotions
(in large groups)

This activity (used by actors in rehearsal) will enable you to experience the relentless energy embodied in Othello's extended **simile** of the 'Pontic Sea' in lines 454–61. Work in quite a large space.

- Divide up the lines into small, meaningful chunks (lines or phrases) and distribute them amongst your group members. Memorise your lines, repeating them out loud as you walk around the available space.
- Get into a long line, not necessarily facing the same way, and link arms securely. The two students on either end must tug and pull the line around the room in opposite directions. As you are tugged around the room, say your lines in the correct order. Try performing the lines you have learnt in different ways – for example, shouting, or hissing them, or as if panting with exhaustion.

Afterwards, discuss what insights this activity has given you into Othello's state of mind at this point in the play. How does the style of his language (vocabulary, length of sentences, punctuation) reflect the intensity of his thoughts and feelings?

yet still

speaks against counts against

hearted in my heart
fraught burden, cargo
aspics venomous snakes

be content calm down

Pontic Sea Black Sea
compulsive course irresistible force
Propontic Sea of Marmora
Hellespont Dardanelles

capable ample
marble everlasting, unfeeling

engage pledge

126

IAGO	Nay, yet be wise; yet we see nothing done,
	She may be honest yet. Tell me but this:
	Have you not sometimes seen a handkerchief
	Spotted with strawberries in your wife's hand?
OTHELLO	I gave her such a one; 'twas my first gift.
IAGO	I know not that; but such a handkerchief –
	I am sure it was your wife's – did I today
	See Cassio wipe his beard with.
OTHELLO	If it be that –
IAGO	If it be that, or any that was hers,
	It speaks against her with the other proofs.
OTHELLO	O that the slave had forty thousand lives!
	One is too poor, too weak, for my revenge.
	Now do I see 'tis true. Look here, Iago,
	All my fond love thus do I blow to heaven;
	'Tis gone.
	Arise, black vengeance, from thy hollow cell!
	Yield up, O love, thy crown and hearted throne
	To tyrannous hate! Swell, bosom, with thy fraught,
	For 'tis of aspics' tongues.

He kneels.

IAGO	Yet be content.
OTHELLO	O, blood, blood, blood!
IAGO	Patience, I say; your mind perhaps may change.
OTHELLO	Never, Iago. Like to the Pontic Sea,
	Whose icy current and compulsive course
	Ne'er feels retiring ebb but keeps due on
	To the Propontic and the Hellespont,
	Even so my bloody thoughts with violent pace
	Shall ne'er look back, ne'er ebb to humble love,
	Till that a capable and wide revenge
	Swallow them up. Now by yond marble heaven,
	In the due reverence of a sacred vow
	I here engage my words.

435

440

445

450

455

460

Iago swears to serve Othello, who instructs him to kill Cassio. Othello vows to kill Desdemona himself. He appoints Iago to be his lieutenant. Scene 4 opens with Desdemona sending a messenger to Cassio.

1 'But let her live' (in pairs)

Why do you think Iago tells Othello to let Desdemona live (line 475)? Consider the following possibilities:

- He has no quarrel with Desdemona, and/or is attracted to her.
- He seeks only Cassio's death.
- He's displaying old-fashioned courtesy towards women.
- He needs her alive to torment Othello further – and to torment her.
- He actually means the opposite; he's planting the idea in Othello's mind on purpose.
- It's all happening too quickly; it's going beyond what Iago had planned.
- He wants to appear merciful in order to aid his deception.

Rank the statements from most likely to least likely, then give reasons for your choices. Pool your ideas with the rest of the class. Are there other possibilities?

2 What does Iago mean?

Scene 3 ends on Iago's statement, 'I am your own for ever.' It could simply mean 'Thanks for the promotion, I'll serve you well.' But what other, more ominous meanings could his words carry at the end of this scene, when Iago has successfully stirred Othello to hatred, jealousy and determination to murder?

Stagecraft
Scene changes: dramatic effect

An important feature of Shakespeare's plays is how scenes are often contrasted with one another. We have just witnessed a lengthy scene of sustained emotional charge, promising bloody violence and concluding with language that references scenes of damnation.

- If you were directing the play, what dramatic effect would you hope to achieve at the beginning of Scene 4? Make notes about the possibilities: how quickly the scene change takes place; whether there is a change in lighting (for example, a brighter, warmer effect) or scenery; how Desdemona's mood is signalled by her entrance; and how she and the Clown speak. What might be the dramatic effect of the Clown's inability to give a straight answer to her questions?
- In your Director's Journal, write up these notes into a plan for how to stage Scene 3, line 480 to Scene 4, line 18.

ever-burning lights the stars
clip enclose, embrace

execution activities

remorse compassion
What bloody … ever however murderous it gets

greet welcome
vain empty
acceptance bounteous generous reward
put thee to't put you to the test

furnish me equip myself

lies lodges

128

IAGO   Do not rise yet.
                    He kneels.
            Witness you ever-burning lights above,
            You elements that clip us round about,   465
            Witness that here Iago doth give up
            The execution of his wit, hands, heart,
            To wronged Othello's service. Let him command,
            And to obey shall be in me remorse,
            What bloody business ever.
                    [*They rise.*]
OTHELLO   I greet thy love,   470
            Not with vain thanks, but with acceptance bounteous;
            And will upon the instant put thee to't.
            Within these three days let me hear thee say
            That Cassio's not alive.
IAGO   My friend is dead;
            'Tis done at your request. But let her live.   475
OTHELLO   Damn her, lewd minx! O, damn her, damn her!
            Come, go with me apart. I will withdraw
            To furnish me with some swift means of death
            For the fair devil. Now art thou my lieutenant.
IAGO   I am your own for ever.   480
                                            Exeunt

Act 3 Scene 4
Cyprus   A room in the castle

Enter DESDEMONA, EMILIA *and* CLOWN.

DESDEMONA Do you know, sirrah, where Lieutenant Cassio lies?
CLOWN   I dare not say he lies anywhere.
DESDEMONA Why, man?
CLOWN   He's a soldier, and for one to say a soldier lies is
           stabbing.   5

The Clown leaves to tell Cassio to visit Desdemona. She expresses concern about the loss of her handkerchief to Emilia. Othello greets Desdemona and comments that her hand feels hot.

Characters

Emilia in the hot-seat (in large groups)

When Emilia lies that she knows nothing about the loss of Desdemona's handkerchief ('I know not, madam', line 20), what might be going through her mind?

- A volunteer steps into role as Emilia. The group questions her, exploring her possible motives. Try to work out where her loyalties lie. How does Emilia see her various positions as wife, employee and confidante?

1 A dramatic entrance (in fours)

At line 27, we see another dramatically charged entrance. Right on cue – just as Desdemona tells Emilia that Othello is incapable of suffering from jealousy – he enters the scene.

a In your group, three people take a role each and freeze the moment as Emilia says: 'Look where he comes.' The fourth person acts as director. Think carefully about positioning and the space between the three characters; also pay particular attention to facial expressions and the direction in which each character is looking. Once you are happy with your tableau, bring the stage picture alive and act out the next fifteen lines. End with a freeze on Othello's line, "Tis a good hand, / A frank one'. How are each of the characters now positioned?

b Share your performance with two or three groups. At the final tableau, bring each character alive in turn and ask them to share their immediate thoughts (in role).

2 Sweaty palms (in small groups)

Othello takes Desdemona's hand and remarks that it is 'hot, and moist' – supposedly a sign of a lecherous nature. He goes on to tell Desdemona that instead of giving her 'hand' in marriage as a love match ('hearts of old gave hands') she has merely given her hand – not her heart as well (lines 41–3).

- Read lines 28–43, then improvise a scene in which the main character wrongly (and privately) suspects his or her boyfriend or girlfriend of infidelity, and all sorts of quite innocent conversations and behaviour are misinterpreted. After watching one another's improvisations, discuss how easily this kind of situation arises, and under what circumstances.

devise make up, invent

in mine own throat tell a deliberate lie

edified instructed

catechise (a method of religious instruction)

moved persuaded

compass scope

crusadoes gold coins

humours moods

dissemble hide one's true feelings

sequester removal

castigation discipline

DESDEMONA   Go to. Where lodges he?

CLOWN   To tell you where he lodges is to tell you where I lie.

DESDEMONA   Can anything be made of this?

CLOWN   I know not where he lodges, and for me to devise a lodging, and say he lies here, or he lies there, were to lie in mine own throat.   10

DESDEMONA   Can you enquire him out, and be edified by report?

CLOWN   I will catechise the world for him: that is, make questions, and by them answer.

DESDEMONA   Seek him; bid him come hither; tell him I have moved my lord on his behalf and hope all will be well.   15

CLOWN   To do this is within the compass of man's wit, and therefore I will attempt the doing of it.   *Exit*

DESDEMONA   Where should I lose that handkerchief, Emilia?

EMILIA   I know not, madam.   20

DESDEMONA   Believe me, I had rather lose my purse
Full of crusadoes; and but my noble Moor
Is true of mind and made of no such baseness
As jealous creatures are, it were enough
To put him to ill thinking.

EMILIA   Is he not jealous?   25

DESDEMONA   Who, he? I think the sun where he was born
Drew all such humours from him.

Enter OTHELLO.

EMILIA   Look where he comes.

DESDEMONA   I will not leave him now; let Cassio
Be called to him. – How is't with you, my lord?

OTHELLO   Well, my good lady. [*Aside*] O hardness to dissemble!   30
How do you, Desdemona?

DESDEMONA   Well, my good lord.

OTHELLO   Give me your hand. This hand is moist, my lady.

DESDEMONA   It yet hath felt no age, nor known no sorrow.

OTHELLO   This argues fruitfulness and liberal heart.
Hot, hot, and moist. This hand of yours requires   35
A sequester from liberty, fasting and prayer,
Much castigation, exercise devout;
For here's a young and sweating devil here
That commonly rebels. 'Tis a good hand,
A frank one.

Othello asks for the handkerchief. When Desdemona denies she has lost it, Othello informs her of its magical powers and its great sentimental value. He claims it was magically made.

1 The myth of the handkerchief (in pairs)

Othello's description of the handkerchief's history (lines 51–71) is like a myth or folk tale.

- Read it dramatically, then experiment with retelling it as a fairy story for young children. (See p. 220 for a consideration of the dramatic significance of this handkerchief in the play as a whole.)

speak understand
chuck (term of endearment)

salt and sorry miserable
rheum cold

Write about it

What if?

What if Desdemona had told Othello the truth at this point – that she had indeed accidentally lost the handkerchief?

- Compose the next ten to twenty lines of dialogue, in which Desdemona tells Othello about losing the handkerchief. What exactly does she say? How does Othello react? What role does Emilia play – does she confess to giving the handkerchief to her husband or not?
- Remember to lay your dialogue out like a proper play script, with the name of the character speaking on the left and the stage directions in square brackets. Don't forget that you do not need speech marks in a script.
- Write in modern English, but try to make the characters' comments sound in keeping with what you know of them and the way they relate to one another.

charmer witch

amiable beloved

spirits desires
fancies lovers
wive take a wife

web weave
sibyl prophetess
numbered ... compasses was 200 years old
hallowed sacred
mummy substance from mummified bodies
Conserved of concocted from

132

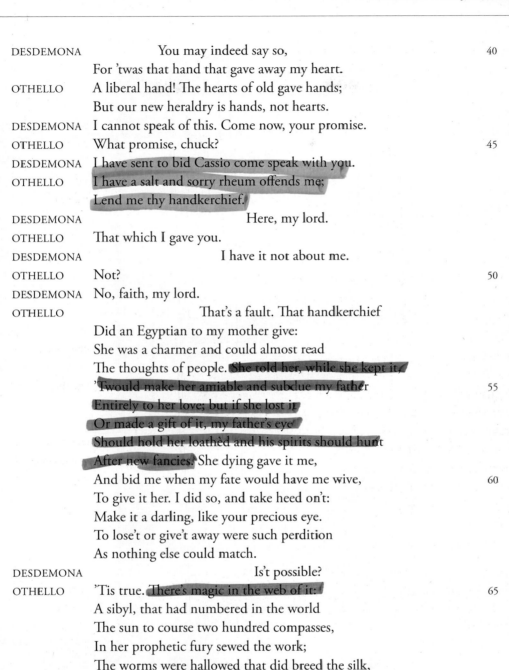

DESDEMONA	You may indeed say so, 40
	For 'twas that hand that gave away my heart.
OTHELLO	A liberal hand! The hearts of old gave hands;
	But our new heraldry is hands, not hearts.
DESDEMONA	I cannot speak of this. Come now, your promise.
OTHELLO	What promise, chuck? 45
DESDEMONA	I have sent to bid Cassio come speak with you.
OTHELLO	I have a salt and sorry rheum offends me;
	Lend me thy handkerchief.
DESDEMONA	Here, my lord.
OTHELLO	That which I gave you.
DESDEMONA	I have it not about me.
OTHELLO	Not? 50
DESDEMONA	No, faith, my lord.
OTHELLO	That's a fault. That handkerchief
	Did an Egyptian to my mother give:
	She was a charmer and could almost read
	The thoughts of people. She told her, while she kept it,
	'Twould make her amiable and subdue my father 55
	Entirely to her love; but if she lost it
	Or made a gift of it, my father's eye
	Should hold her loathèd and his spirits should hunt
	After new fancies. She dying gave it me,
	And bid me when my fate would have me wive, 60
	To give it her. I did so, and take heed on't:
	Make it a darling, like your precious eye.
	To lose't or give't away were such perdition
	As nothing else could match.
DESDEMONA	Is't possible?
OTHELLO	'Tis true. There's magic in the web of it: 65
	A sibyl, that had numbered in the world
	The sun to course two hundred compasses,
	In her prophetic fury sewed the work;
	The worms were hallowed that did breed the silk,
	And it was dyed in mummy, which the skilful 70
	Conserved of maidens' hearts.

Othello orders Desdemona to bring him the handkerchief. She tries to divert his attention by reminding him of Cassio's unresolved plight, but he leaves, swearing. Emilia comments unflatteringly on men.

1 Repetition (in threes)

Othello first asks Desdemona for the missing handkerchief at line 48, and he tells her to fetch it at line 81. In the following eleven lines he repeats the words 'The handkerchief' three times.

a How should Othello speak these lines? For example, each time he asks for it does he shout louder and louder, or does he get quieter and more menacing?

b Create a short mime around the action suggested by the command, 'Fetch me the handkerchief', in which 'the handkerchief' is the only phrase anyone can use (as many times as you like) in a variety of tones, volumes and moods.

2 Let's talk about Cassio! (in pairs)

a Desdemona draws the audience's attention to the fact that Othello is speaking 'startingly and rash'. Othello is clearly highly agitated about the lost handkerchief (as signalled by his frequent short or incomplete sentences), yet Desdemona persists in pursuing a conversation about Cassio. Why do you think she does this? What advice would you give to the actor playing Desdemona? Is she:

- completely naive
- bemused by Othello's anger
- forceful and assertive
- irritated by Othello's behaviour
- deliberately provocative
- afraid?

b Try reading line 71 (from 'I'faith, is't true?') to line 93 in three or four different ways.

▼ Emilia (right) expounds her philosophy concerning men in lines 97–100. She uses a food/appetite metaphor reminiscent of that used by Iago to talk about women in Act 2 Scene 1, lines 215–22. What do you think this suggests about Emilia and Iago's relationship?

look to't well take good care of it

Wherefore? why?

startlingly and rash disjointedly and violently

is't out of th'way? is it missing?

suit original purpose

My mind misgives I fear the worst

sufficient competent

founded based

wonder magic

'Tis not a year ... man it doesn't take very long to work out what a man is like

but stomachs merely appetites

the happiness good luck

importune beseech

134

DESDEMONA	I'faith, is't true?	
OTHELLO	Most veritable; therefore look to't well.	
DESDEMONA	Then would to God that I had never seen't!	
OTHELLO	Ha? Wherefore?	
DESDEMONA	Why do you speak so startingly and rash?	75
OTHELLO	Is't lost? Is't gone? Speak; is't out of th'way?	
DESDEMONA	Heaven bless us!	
OTHELLO	Say you?	
DESDEMONA	It is not lost, but what and if it were?	
OTHELLO	How?	80
DESDEMONA	I say it is not lost.	
OTHELLO	Fetch't, let me see't.	
DESDEMONA	Why so I can, sir; but I will not now.	
	This is a trick to put me from my suit.	
	Pray you let Cassio be received again.	
OTHELLO	Fetch me the handkerchief. My mind misgives.	85
DESDEMONA	Come, come;	
	You'll never meet a more sufficient man.	
OTHELLO	The handkerchief!	
DESDEMONA	I pray, talk me of Cassio.	
OTHELLO	The handkerchief!	
DESDEMONA	A man that all his time	
	Hath founded his good fortunes on your love,	90
	Shared dangers with you –	
OTHELLO	The handkerchief!	
DESDEMONA	I'faith, you are to blame.	
OTHELLO	Zounds!	*Exit*
EMILIA	Is not this man jealous?	
DESDEMONA	I ne'er saw this before.	
	Sure there's some wonder in this handkerchief;	95
	I am most unhappy in the loss of it.	
EMILIA	'Tis not a year or two shows us a man.	
	They are all but stomachs, and we all but food;	
	They eat us hungerly, and when they are full,	
	They belch us.	

Enter IAGO *and* CASSIO.

	Look you, Cassio and my husband.	100
IAGO	There is no other way: 'tis she must do't.	
	And lo, the happiness! Go, and importune her.	

Cassio again asks Desdemona to plead with Othello on his behalf. She tells him he will have to be patient, since Othello seems to be behaving strangely. Iago leaves to find Othello.

Write about it
'My lord is not my lord'

In line 118, Desdemona states that 'My lord is nor my lord'. She is confused by the changes in Othello's manner towards her, and uses this phrase in the colloquial sense, meaning 'he's not himself'. However, in another sense it could be argued that Othello's identity has literally changed and that he is a different man than the one we encountered at the beginning of the play. His identity has been undermined by Iago, who is busy constructing a new one for him.

- Write one or two paragraphs describing the way Iago has worked on Othello through this act and has brought about these startling changes. You could write a second paragraph assessing how important the context has been in contributing towards Othello's feeling of instability (for example, think about Othello as an isolated black man living in white society; also think about his position as commander of an occupying force on a colonial outpost, and the loss of his trusted lieutenant). Prioritise the factors you believe to be important.

Exist be myself

office loyal service

would not be delayed
don't want to waste any time

nor … nor neither … nor

purposed merit what I intend to deserve

in futurity in times to come

ransom buy my way

But merely

shall I clothe … content
I shall have to be satisfied with that

shut myself up in
confine myself to

To fortune's alms
accepting whatever chance may put my way

advocation advocacy

in tune appropriate

favour appearance

every spirit sanctified
all the angels

blank centre of target

1 Unspoken thoughts (in threes)

Look over Iago's short interchange with Emilia and Desdemona (lines 126–34). Both Emilia and Iago know more than they reveal, yet on the surface they appear innocent. Iago falsely expresses surprise at Othello's anger. He even finds four different ways of commenting that anger is an emotion unfamiliar to Othello.

- First, play with the lines, experimenting with ways of acting them out and exploring the undercurrent of (partially) shared knowledge between Emilia and her husband.
- Next, attempt to intercut the script with the unspoken thoughts and preoccupations of the three characters. For example, if in your initial explorations with acting out the script, you had actors exchanging significant looks, explain in each character's words what is going through their minds at that point.
- When you are happy with your intercut script, share it with other groups and discuss any similarities or differences.

of moment momentous

DESDEMONA	How now, good Cassio! What's the news with you?
CASSIO	Madam, my former suit. I do beseech you
	That, by your virtuous means, I may again 105
	Exist and be a member of his love,
	Whom I, with all the office of my heart,
	Entirely honour. I would not be delayed.
	If my offence be of such mortal kind
	That nor my service past nor present sorrows, 110
	Nor purposed merit in futurity,
	Can ransom me into his love again,
	But to know so must be my benefit:
	So shall I clothe me in a forced content,
	And shut myself up in some other course 115
	To fortune's alms.
DESDEMONA	Alas, thrice-gentle Cassio,
	My advocation is not now in tune:
	My lord is not my lord; nor should I know him,
	Were he in favour as in humour altered.
	So help me every spirit sanctified, 120
	As I have spoken for you all my best,
	And stood within the blank of his displeasure
	For my free speech! You must awhile be patient.
	What I can do, I will; and more I will
	Than for myself I dare. Let that suffice you. 125
IAGO	Is my lord angry?
EMILIA	He went hence but now
	And certainly in strange unquietness.
IAGO	Can he be angry? I have seen the cannon
	When it hath blown his ranks into the air,
	And like the devil from his very arm 130
	Puffed his own brother – and is he angry?
	Something of moment then. I will go meet him.
	There's matter in't indeed if he be angry.
DESDEMONA	I prithee do so.

Exit Iago

Desdemona reassures herself that Othello must be upset by some affair of state. Emilia hopes he is not growing jealous. Desdemona prays he has no such thought in mind and leaves to seek Othello. Bianca greets Cassio.

Write about it

Desdemona: the public face

In the scenes with Desdemona, it is easy to forget that Othello's primary role in Cyprus is to administer Venetian rule. In Desdemona's words about 'some unhatched practice' (secret plot), she draws attention to their position as quasi-colonial rulers once again. Keep this political dimension in mind as subsequent events unfold.

• Up to now, what has been Desdemona's main public role in the play? Write a paragraph about Desdemona's actions and reputation in her position as a high-ranking army officer's wife and as a senator's daughter.

Characters

Directing Desdemona (in pairs)

Desdemona assures Cassio and Emilia that 'men are not gods'. She excuses Othello's rudeness towards her on the grounds that he has a very important job to do and that personal matters must take second place to this. Talk together about what advice you would give to the actor playing Desdemona. For example, should she come across as:

• meek and mild
• fresh and innocent
• strong and independent
• world weary and cynical
• nervous and shy?

Give reasons for your decision. For an additional challenge, look back through the play so far and find examples from the text to support your reasoning.

1 Jealousy: 'a monster / Begot upon itself, born on itself'

Again, Emilia's language is an unconscious echo of Iago's. Look back to Act 3 Scene 3, lines 168–9 and read through Iago's graphic jealousy metaphor. How are the two images similar? Sketch a design based on Emilia's metaphor.

endues brings, leads (or infects)

observancy loving attention
bridal wedding night

Arraigning accusing
suborned the witness made the witness give false evidence
indicted accused

toy fancy

'Save you God save you (a greeting like 'good morning!')

138

                    Something sure of state,
Either from Venice, or some unhatched practice   135
Made demonstrable here in Cyprus to him,
Hath puddled his clear spirit; and in such cases
Men's natures wrangle with inferior things,
Though great ones are their object. 'Tis even so;
For let our finger ache, and it endues   140
Our other healthful members even to a sense
Of pain. Nay, we must think men are not gods,
Nor of them look for such observancy
As fits the bridal. Beshrew me much, Emilia,
I was – unhandsome warrior as I am –   145
Arraigning his unkindness with my soul;
But now I find I had suborned the witness
And he's indicted falsely.

EMILIA   Pray heaven it be state matters, as you think,
And no conception nor no jealous toy   150
Concerning you.

DESDEMONA Alas the day, I never gave him cause.

EMILIA   But jealous souls will not be answered so.
They are not ever jealous for the cause,
But jealous for they're jealous. 'Tis a monster   155
Begot upon itself, born on itself.

DESDEMONA Heaven keep that monster from Othello's mind.

EMILIA   Lady, amen!

DESDEMONA I will go seek him. Cassio, walk here about.
If I do find him fit, I'll move your suit   160
And seek to effect it to my uttermost.

CASSIO   I humbly thank your ladyship.

Exeunt Desdemona and Emilia

Enter BIANCA.

BIANCA   'Save you, friend Cassio.

CASSIO   What make you from home?
How is it with you, my most fair Bianca?
I'faith, sweet love, I was coming to your house.   165

Bianca accuses Cassio of neglecting her. He pleads that worries have kept him away and gives Bianca the handkerchief, saying he found it in his bedroom. He asks Bianca to leave so that he may meet Othello.

Characters

Who is Bianca? (in pairs)

a What are your first impressions of Bianca, and what relationship do you think she has with Cassio? Explore this question by taking parts. Create a series of tableaux to tell the story of this scene between Bianca and Cassio. Either freeze the moment at each of the following lines, or select your own to create a sequence of five still pictures:

- 'Save you, friend Cassio'
- 'This is some token from a newer friend'
- 'I found it in my chamber'
- 'Not that I love you not'
- ''Tis but a little way I can bring you'

b After you have performed your tableaux, talk about Bianca and how she appears to relate to Cassio. Do we learn anything new about Cassio in this scene?

Write about it

Bianca: dramatic purpose

Write at least two paragraphs exploring the dramatic purpose of this short episode with Bianca. Think about:

- the plot (does this episode further the main plot in any way?)
- themes or central ideas in the play (for example, the position of women, relationships, jealousy)
- dramatic tension (this episode comes straight after the high drama of Othello and Iago's pact to commit a double murder)
- characterisation (does this episode add to our knowledge of Cassio?)
- the passage of time (Bianca's words at line 167 suggest that a whole week has passed by since the Venetian fleet arrived at Cyprus, yet Othello wanted Cassio dead within three days at the end of Scene 3).

Once you have finished, exchange your writing with another student and compare your ideas.

---

dial clock

with leaden ... pressed tortured by heavy thoughts
continuate uninterrupted
Take me this work out copy this embroidery for me
whence came this? where did you get this?
To the felt ... cause now I know why you have been absent from me

And think it no addition I don't think it will do me any good
womaned with a woman

bring me accompany me

be circumstanced put up with

BIANCA	And I was going to your lodging, Cassio.
	What! Keep a week away? Seven days and nights?
	Eight score eight hours? And lovers' absent hours
	More tedious than the dial eight score times!
	O weary reckoning!
CASSIO	Pardon me, Bianca.	170
	I have this while with leaden thoughts been pressed;
	But I shall in a more continuate time
	Strike off this score of absence. Sweet Bianca,
	Take me this work out.
BIANCA	O Cassio, whence came this?
	This is some token from a newer friend.	175
	To the felt absence now I feel a cause.
	Is't come to this? Well, well.
CASSIO	Go to, woman!
	Throw your vile guesses in the devil's teeth
	From whence you have them. You are jealous now
	That this is from some mistress, some remembrance.	180
	No, by my faith, Bianca.
BIANCA	Why, whose is it?
CASSIO	I know not neither; I found it in my chamber.
	I like the work well. Ere it be demanded –
	As like enough it will – I'd have it copied.
	Take it and do't, and leave me for this time.	185
BIANCA	Leave you? Wherefore?
CASSIO	I do attend here on the general;
	And think it no addition, nor my wish,
	To have him see me womaned.
BIANCA	Why, I pray you?
CASSIO	Not that I love you not.
BIANCA	But that you do not love me.	190
	I pray you, bring me on the way a little,
	And say if I shall see you soon at night.
CASSIO	'Tis but a little way that I can bring you,
	For I attend here; but I'll see you soon.
BIANCA	'Tis very good; I must be circumstanced.	195

Exeunt

Looking back at Act 3
Activities for groups or individuals

1 Iago's tempting

At the beginning of Scene 1, Othello is in control of himself; by the end of Scene 4, he seems to be verging on insanity. This activity concentrates on the insidious way in which Iago works upon Othello's mind.

a Get together in large groups. Each group member learns one or two of the following lines:

1 'Ha! I like not that.'
2 'Cassio, my lord? … so guilty-like'
3 'Did Michael Cassio … know of your love?'
4 'Honest, my lord?'
5 'I dare be sworn I think that he is honest.'
6 'I think Cassio's an honest man.'
7 'I perchance am vicious in my guess'
8 'it is my nature's plague / To spy into abuses'
9 'O beware, my lord, of jealousy'
10 'cuckold'
11 'Who dotes, yet doubts, suspects, yet fondly loves?'
12 'the souls of all my tribe defend / From jealousy.'
13 'Look to your wife'
14 'observe her well with Cassio'
15 'She did deceive her father, marrying you'
16 'Foul disproportion'
17 'thoughts unnatural'
18 'Note if your lady strain his entertainment'
19 'Behold her topped'
20 'as prime as goats, as hot as monkeys'.

Move around the room, using all the available space. Speak your lines in different ways. For example, you might speak as if you are all spies passing on secrets, small children telling tales, neighbours gossiping.

b Form a large circle with one student in the centre, blindfolded (this helps to focus on the words). Those in the circle hiss their lines at the central person, sometimes very close to them, sometimes at a distance from them. Experiment with different ways of presenting your lines, perhaps devising a way of showing the progressive nature of the taunts.

c Individually, write an analysis of how skilfully you think Iago has played Othello during Act 3.

2 Sculptures of trust and jealousy

Issues of trust and jealousy are prominent throughout the act.

a In groups of three, one person takes on the job of sculptor again and the other two become the raw material. Create two sculptures, the first called 'Trust' and the second called 'Jealousy'.

b Talk together about how each of the themes of trust and jealousy are developed in Act 3. Choose two or three main characters and re-create your sculptures to reflect an appropriate type of trust or jealousy for that person. For example, how would a sculpture entitled 'Bianca's Jealousy' differ from one called 'Othello's Jealousy'? Remember, you are creating sculptures, not statues of real people. You could take photographs of these sculptures and create a classroom display. Add an appropriate quotation from the script as a caption for each sculpture.

3 Key moments in Act 3

Act 3 is the pivotal section of the play, where Iago's malevolent influence poisons Othello's mind irrevocably. The four photographs of Iago and Othello opposite show key moments in Act 3.

• Decide which moment each photo represents, and find an appropriate quotation. Write a short paragraph for each, explaining what is happening and why this is such a significant moment.

Iago encourages Othello's jealousy with increasingly graphic references to Desdemona's supposed infidelity. He teases Othello with mention of the handkerchief.

1 Role play (in pairs)

Iago's opening words in the scene suggest that he and Othello are part-way through a conversation, and that Iago continues to chip away at Othello's grasp on reality.

- Speculate about what Iago might have been saying before the opening line in the script opposite. Role-play the dialogue you create, then read through to line 34, where Iago further stimulates Othello's imaginings of Desdemona and Cassio's sexual relationship.

2 Iago's lies (in fives)

a Iago tells Othello four separate lies in the first thirty lines of this scene, some prompting Othello to merely echo his words in response. Identify each of the lies.

b Look closely at the punctuation and you will see that a number of Iago's comments are either in the form of a question or of an unfinished sentence, marked by a dash (–). Talk together about the way Iago uses language here, and about the effect it has on Othello.

c For each of the lies you identified above, write down the specific words Iago uses. One person takes the role of Othello and the other four become Iago. Each Iago selects one of the lies from the script and memorises it. The person playing Othello memorises the line 'Think so, Iago?' (line 2). The four Iagos surround Othello and taunt him with their lies, repeating the words as many times as they like. Othello may only respond with his memorised line. Try saying the lines in different ways and at different speeds. How many kinds of dramatic effect can you create?

Language in the play
Animal imagery

In describing his obsession with the lost handkerchief (lines 19–22), Othello uses a simile based on the belief that a croaking raven prophesied death to the inmates of a house, particularly in times of plague.

- Create a visual design that incorporates the image of the bird of ill omen and the handkerchief. Don't worry if your design is only rough – ideas are the most important element in this activity, not your artistic skills.

---

tempt heaven tempt God to curse them
So so long as
venial slip trivial misdeed

essence spiritual phenomenon
They have it … not the very women who are called honourable often don't deserve it

infected plague-ridden
Boding prophesying doom

importunate suit persistent chatting-up, wooing
voluntary dotage willing infatuation
Convincèd or supplied overpowered or seduced
But they must blab have to brag about it

Act 4 Scene 1

Cyprus   A room in the castle

Enter OTHELLO *and* IAGO.

IAGO	Will you think so?
OTHELLO	Think so, Iago?
IAGO	What,
	To kiss in private?
OTHELLO	An unauthorised kiss!
IAGO	Or to be naked with her friend in bed
	An hour or more, not meaning any harm?
OTHELLO	Naked in bed, Iago, and not mean harm?

5

It is hypocrisy against the devil.
They that mean virtuously and yet do so,
The devil their virtue tempts, and they tempt heaven.

IAGO   So they do nothing, 'tis a venial slip;
But if I give my wife a handkerchief –

10

OTHELLO   What then?

IAGO   Why, then 'tis hers, my lord; and being hers,
She may, I think, bestow't on any man.

OTHELLO   She is protectress of her honour too.
May she give that?

15

IAGO   Her honour is an essence that's not seen:
They have it very oft that have it not.
But for the handkerchief –

OTHELLO   By heaven, I would most gladly have forgot it.
Thou said'st – O it comes o'er my memory,

20

As doth the raven o'er the infected house,
Boding to all! – he had my handkerchief.

IAGO   Ay, what of that?

OTHELLO   That's not so good now.

IAGO   What
If I had said I had seen him do you wrong?
Or heard him say – as knaves be such abroad,

25

Who having by their own importunate suit
Or voluntary dotage of some mistress
Convincèd or supplied them, cannot choose
But they must blab –

Iago implies that Cassio has boasted about having sex with Desdemona. Othello is so upset that it appears to bring on an epileptic fit. Cassio enters but is persuaded by Iago to leave again.

1 Othello's breakdown (in pairs)

What effect does Othello's seizure have on you as a reader or spectator? Discuss the following suggestions in turn with your partner, and decide which statements you most agree with. Make sure you can explain why.

* You wonder what kind of man is in charge of law and order in Cyprus.
* Your sympathy for Othello increases.
* It presents the audience with a stereotypical view of a black man who easily loses physical and mental control.
* Iago knows exactly where his victim's weak points are.
* It shows how much Othello loves Desdemona.
* It demonstrates how insanely possessive Othello is towards women.
* Even though Othello is a tough and powerful military leader, it exposes how deeply insecure he is.

As an extension to this activity, use the statements you have selected as a prompt for writing an analysis of this highly charged dramatic moment in the play.

Language in the play
Dramatic grammar (whole class)

a To discover something about the state of Othello's mind, read lines 35–41 aloud while walking around the room. Change direction sharply at every punctuation mark. Increase the pace – go as fast as you dare! You'll find it's dizzying, underlining how Othello's tortured imaginings are accompanied by a breakdown in his language.

b Write a paragraph about the way Shakespeare structures language to reflect a character's state of mind in a dramatic way. Consider such things as sentence structure, sentence length, types of sentence (such as questions, exclamations, statements), and punctuation.

c Look back at Activity 2 on page 144, then write another paragraph about Iago's use of language.

belie slander
fulsome revolting

shadowing overwhelming
instruction reason

reproach shame

forbear leave him
lethargy loss of consciousness
have his quiet course follow its nature
savage madness (notice Iago's racial stereotyping)
withdraw yourself step outside
on great occasion about a serious matter

OTHELLO	Hath he said anything?
IAGO	He hath, my lord; but be you well assured 30
	No more than he'll unswear.
OTHELLO	What hath he said?
IAGO	Faith, that he did – I know not what he did.
OTHELLO	What, what?
IAGO	Lie –
OTHELLO	With her?
IAGO	With her, on her, what you will.

OTHELLO Lie with her? Lie on her? We say lie on her when they belie 35
her. Lie with her! Zounds, that's fulsome! Handkerchief –
confessions – handkerchief! To confess and be hanged for his
labour. First to be hanged and then to confess. I tremble at it.
Nature would not invest herself in such shadowing passion without
some instruction. It is not words that shakes me thus. Pish! Noses, 40
ears, and lips. Is't possible? – Confess? Handkerchief? O devil!

[*He*] *falls in a trance.*

IAGO Work on,
My medicine, work! Thus credulous fools are caught;
And many worthy and chaste dames even thus,
All guiltless, meet reproach. What ho, my lord! 45
My lord, I say! Othello!

Enter CASSIO.

How now, Cassio!

CASSIO	What's the matter?
IAGO	My lord is fallen into an epilepsy.
	This is his second fit; he had one yesterday.
CASSIO	Rub him about the temples.
IAGO	No, forbear. 50

The lethargy must have his quiet course.
If not, he foams at mouth and by and by
Breaks out to savage madness. Look, he stirs.
Do you withdraw yourself a little while;
He will recover straight. When he is gone, 55
I would on great occasion speak with you.

[*Exit Cassio*]

Othello regains consciousness. Iago again assures him of the unfaithfulness of women, then instructs him to eavesdrop on a conversation in which Cassio will tell of his sexual intercourse with Desdemona.

Write about it

'be a man' (in pairs)

a Iago makes four jibes at Othello's 'manhood' in the script opposite. Find the four comments and, in your pairs, agree what aspect of 'being a man' each comment refers to.

b Discuss why Iago chooses to employ such terms of criticism. In doing so, it might help to think about the roles that Othello is trying to fulfil (soldier/war hero, husband, commander…). What is there about Othello, and the society that has formed him, that might make these terms of criticism particularly appropriate?

c Together, write a couple of paragraphs about the ways in which Othello has tried to 'be a man' up to this point in the play.

1 Iago takes control

In lines 72–87, Iago swiftly sets out a course of action for Othello to follow. Earlier, he used insidious persuasive techniques, but now he is direct and unambiguous as he takes command of the situation.

- Take turns to speak the lines to bring out the urgency and seeming good sense of the plan Iago outlines. Emphasise words and phrases that will especially heighten Othello's fury.

hornèd man cuckold (a man thought to have an unfaithful wife was said to grow horns)

civil civilised

yoked 'hitched', married

draw with you share with you

unproper not solely theirs

peculiar their own

arch-mock supreme mockery

lip kiss

wanton lecherous person

secure free from suspicion

a patient list the bounds of patience

shifted him got rid of him on a pretext

laid good scuse came up with a good excuse

ecstasy fit, trance

anon soon

encave conceal

fleers mocks and jokes

cope copulate with

Marry by Mary! (a mild oath)

all in spleen eaten up with passion

cunning crafty

	How is it, general? Have you not hurt your head?	
OTHELLO	Dost thou mock me?	
IAGO	I mock you? No, by heaven!	
	Would you would bear your fortune like a man!	
OTHELLO	A hornèd man's a monster and a beast.	60
IAGO	There's many a beast then in a populous city,	
	And many a civil monster.	
OTHELLO	Did he confess it?	
IAGO	Good sir, be a man:	
	Think every bearded fellow that's but yoked	
	May draw with you. There's millions now alive	65
	That nightly lie in those unproper beds	
	Which they dare swear peculiar. Your case is better.	
	O, 'tis the spite of hell, the fiend's arch-mock,	
	To lip a wanton in a secure couch	
	And to suppose her chaste! No, let me know;	70
	And knowing what I am, I know what she shall be.	
OTHELLO	O, thou art wise; 'tis certain.	
IAGO	Stand you awhile apart,	
	Confine yourself but in a patient list.	
	Whilst you were here, o'erwhelmèd with your grief –	
	A passion most unsuiting such a man –	75
	Cassio came hither. I shifted him away	
	And laid good scuse upon your ecstasy;	
	Bade him anon return and here speak with me,	
	The which he promised. Do but encave yourself,	
	And mark the fleers, the gibes, and notable scorns	80
	That dwell in every region of his face;	
	For I will make him tell the tale anew,	
	Where, how, how oft, how long ago, and when	
	He hath and is again to cope your wife.	
	I say but mark his gesture. Marry, patience,	85
	Or I shall say you're all in all in spleen	
	And nothing of a man.	
OTHELLO	Dost thou hear, Iago?	
	I will be found most cunning in my patience,	
	But – dost thou hear – most bloody.	

Othello hides and Iago reveals he will question Cassio about Bianca. Othello overhears part of their conversation about Cassio's love life. He wrongly thinks they speak of Desdemona.

Stagecraft

Mime the 'eavesdropping' episode (in threes)

Lines 101–61 are often called the 'eavesdropping' episode, because in them Othello overhears (and misinterprets) Cassio's responses to Iago's questions and statements.

a Gain a first impression of this part of the scene by taking parts and running through the lines, adding some movement and gesture where appropriate.

b Prepare a 'silent movie' performance of these lines. Although your gestures are likely to be exaggerated, ensure they are clear to an audience. Make sure characterisation is communicated through the way people move, stand or position themselves. Create at least two captions (ideally, lines from the script) and either display them on large pieces of card or voice them at appropriate moments. Show your performance to the rest of your class.

▼ How would you set up the 'eavesdropping' episode so that the audience can see and hear Othello but he is still hidden from the other characters on stage?

keep time in all control yourself

strumpet's plague whore's curse

unbookish ignorant
construe interpret
light cheerful
addition title
Whose want the lack of which

speed prosper
poor caitiff poor thing

faintly a bit

importunes urges
said done
gives it out tells people

Roman like a victorious Roman warrior
customer slut
bear some charity give some credit

150

IAGO That's not amiss.
But yet keep time in all. Will you withdraw? 90
[Othello withdraws.]
Now will I question Cassio of Bianca,
A housewife that by selling her desires
Buys herself bread and clothes. It is a creature
That dotes on Cassio; as 'tis the strumpet's plague
To beguile many and be beguiled by one. 95
He, when he hears of her, cannot refrain
From the excess of laughter. Here he comes.

Enter Cassio.

As he shall smile, Othello shall go mad;
And his unbookish jealousy must construe
Poor Cassio's smiles, gestures, and light behaviours 100
Quite in the wrong. How do you now, lieutenant?

CASSIO The worser that you give me the addition
Whose want even kills me.

IAGO Ply Desdemona well and you are sure on't.
Now if this suit lay in Bianca's power, 105
How quickly should you speed!

CASSIO Alas, poor caitiff!

OTHELLO *[Aside]* Look how he laughs already!

IAGO I never knew a woman love man so.

CASSIO Alas, poor rogue! I think, i'faith, she loves me.

OTHELLO *[Aside]* Now he denies it faintly, and laughs it out. 110

IAGO Do you hear, Cassio?

OTHELLO *[Aside]* Now he importunes him
To tell it o'er. Go to, well said, well said!

IAGO She gives it out that you shall marry her.
Do you intend it?

CASSIO Ha, ha, ha! 115

OTHELLO *[Aside]* Do you triumph, Roman? Do you triumph?

CASSIO I marry her? What! A customer! I prithee, bear some
charity to my wit. Do not think it so unwholesome. Ha, ha, ha!

OTHELLO *[Aside]* So, so, so, so: they laugh that wins.

Othello continues to believe, wrongly, that Cassio speaks of Desdemona. He watches as Bianca meets Cassio and flings the handkerchief back in his face, supposing it had been given to him by some other woman.

▼ Is this how you imagine Bianca to look and dress? What alternative interpretations of Bianca can you suggest? Think of an actor or famous person you would cast in a film version of *Othello* and the costume you would have them wear.

Characters

Versions of Bianca (by yourself, then in pairs)

According to Iago, Bianca is a 'housewife' (pronounced 'huzif') or hussy, who sells her 'desires' to earn a living. He goes on to make his meaning clearer by calling her a 'strumpet' (a whore). Some editors of *Othello* assume that Bianca is a prostitute, and refer to her in that way in the list of characters at the beginning of the play.

a   Consider how accurate Iago is as a judge of women. Can you take his description at face value? Can you remember some of the things that Iago has said about other women so far in the play?

b   With a partner, compare your findings on Iago's attitude to women. Talk together about what difference it makes to a production of the play if Bianca is unequivocally presented as a prostitute. Think about how it reflects on Cassio, and what general image of women is offered through the play. Remember, Bianca is one of only three women in the cast.

cry rumour

scored wounded
the monkey's own giving out rumours started by the little monkey

bauble pretty thing

hales tugs

plucked drew

must leave her company must stop seeing her
such another fitchew none other than that polecat
a perfumed one a woman drenched in cheap perfume, like a prostitute
dam mother

take out the work copy the embroidery
piece of work story

hobby-horse whore

next prepared for (i.e. never)

IAGO	Faith, the cry goes that you shall marry her.	120
CASSIO	Prithee, say true.
IAGO	I am a very villain else.
OTHELLO	[*Aside*] Have you scored me? Well.
CASSIO	This is the monkey's own giving out. She is persuaded I will marry her out of her own love and flattery, not out of my promise.	125
OTHELLO	[*Aside*] Iago beckons me. Now he begins the story.
CASSIO	She was here even now. She haunts me in every place. I was the other day talking on the sea-bank with certain Venetians, and thither comes this bauble and, by this hand, falls me thus about my neck.	130
OTHELLO	[*Aside*] Crying 'O dear Cassio!' as it were. His gesture imports it.
CASSIO	So hangs and lolls and weeps upon me, so hales and pulls me. Ha, ha, ha!	135
OTHELLO	[*Aside*] Now he tells how she plucked him to my chamber. O, I see that nose of yours, but not that dog I shall throw it to!
CASSIO	Well, I must leave her company.
IAGO	Before me, look where she comes!	140
CASSIO	'Tis such another fitchew! Marry, a perfumed one.

Enter BIANCA.

	What do you mean by this haunting of me?
BIANCA	Let the devil and his dam haunt you! What did you mean by that same handkerchief you gave me even now? I was a fine fool to take it. I must take out the work? A likely piece of work that you should find it in your chamber and not know who left it there! This is some minx's token, and I must take out the work? There, give it your hobby-horse, wheresoever you had it. I'll take out no work on't.	145
CASSIO	How now, my sweet Bianca! How now, how now!	150
OTHELLO	[*Aside*] By heaven, that should be my handkerchief!
BIANCA	If you'll come to supper tonight, you may. If you will not, come when you are next prepared for. *Exit*

Cassio leaves to prevent further outbursts by Bianca. Othello determines to kill both Cassio and Desdemona, but is torn between violent hatred and love for his wife. Iago persuades him to put aside any remaining affection.

Write about it

'How shall I murder him …?'

Othello's immediate reaction is to plan a murder. As a reader or spectator, are you shocked by the brutality of the words? Write two paragraphs, one from a perspective that is sympathetic to Othello and his situation, and one that is highly critical of Othello. Include embedded quotations to back up your points.

- **Paragraph 1** Consider the way Iago has manipulated Othello. Could you argue that Othello has particular vulnerabilities? What has his life been like? Since Othello is a professional soldier, do you think he has been conditioned to react in violent ways? How has chance played a role in helping Iago's lies seem believable?
- **Paragraph 2** Think about how good a judge of character Othello appears to be. You might like to consider the secretive manner in which Othello courted Desdemona, and the disloyalty he showed Brabantio, one of his benefactors. Why is Othello so ready to believe his ensign, but not his ensign's wife, nor his own wife? In the end, just how believable *are* Iago's lies?

Stagecraft

In action (in threes)

a Explore different ways of reading lines 162–200, in which Iago cunningly deepens Othello's murderous impulses. Try, for example, whispering, ranting, reasoning. You will find that Othello's feelings fluctuate, but Iago ensures that his hatred eventually triumphs.

b With two group members as Othello and the third as Iago, share Othello's lines according to the mood and attitude they reflect. Experiment with movement and positioning:

- the two Othellos standing back-to-back
- all three moving constantly around the room
- all three staying in the same place
- having Iago always behind Othello, whispering in his ear
- Iago standing on a higher level than the two Othellos
- the 'violent' Othello gradually gaining volume, stature, moving towards Iago.

rail shout

else otherwise

sup have supper

fain like to

by this hand I swear it

nine years a-killing dying a slow death

command him tasks be in control

your way the way for you to go about this

invention imagination

so gentle a condition so refined, so mild-mannered

too gentle too easy to please

fond over foolish about

patent licence

if it touch not … nobody if it doesn't hurt you, it doesn't affect anyone else

messes minced meat

IAGO	After her, after her!
CASSIO	Faith, I must. She'll rail in the streets else.	155
IAGO	Will you sup there?
CASSIO	Faith, I intend so.
IAGO	Well, I may chance to see you; for I would very fain speak with you.
CASSIO	Prithee, come; will you?	160
IAGO	Go to; say no more.

Exit Cassio

OTHELLO	[*Coming forward.*] How shall I murder him, Iago?
IAGO	Did you perceive how he laughed at his vice?
OTHELLO	O, Iago!
IAGO	And did you see the handkerchief?	165
OTHELLO	Was that mine?
IAGO	Yours, by this hand. And to see how he prizes the foolish woman your wife: she gave it him, and he hath given it his whore.
OTHELLO	I would have him nine years a-killing. A fine woman, a fair woman, a sweet woman!	170
IAGO	Nay, you must forget that.
OTHELLO	Ay, let her rot and perish, and be damned tonight, for she shall not live. No, my heart is turned to stone: I strike it and it hurts my hand. O, the world hath not a sweeter creature! She might lie by an emperor's side and command him tasks.	175
IAGO	Nay, that's not your way.
OTHELLO	Hang her, I do but say what she is: so delicate with her needle, an admirable musician – O, she will sing the savageness out of a bear – of so high and plenteous wit and invention –
IAGO	She's the worse for all this.	180
OTHELLO	O, a thousand, thousand times – and then of so gentle a condition!
IAGO	Ay, too gentle.
OTHELLO	Nay, that's certain; but yet the pity of it, Iago! O Iago, the pity of it, Iago!	185
IAGO	If you are so fond over her iniquity, give her patent to offend; for if it touch not you, it comes near nobody.
OTHELLO	I will chop her into messes. Cuckold me!
IAGO	O, 'tis foul in her.
OTHELLO	With mine officer!	190
IAGO	That's fouler.

Othello determines to follow Iago's suggestion to strangle Desdemona in her bed. Iago promises to kill Cassio that night. Lodovico brings Othello a letter from Venice, and asks about Cassio.

Themes

Justice

According to Othello, to strangle his wife in bed represents 'justice' (line 197). In Act 3, a false notion of proof was introduced in the dialogue between Iago and Othello, and since Othello believes that he has been supplied with the 'ocular proof' he demanded, he can now dispense 'justice' for crimes committed. In this way, the concepts of proof and justice have become completely distorted in the course of the play.

a Look up the word 'justice' in a dictionary, then attempt to write your own definition of the term. Give an example of what might be called 'justice' in daily life.

b Write a definition of the word 'justice' as three different characters from the play might understand it. Choose from Othello, Iago, Desdemona, the Duke, Brabantio and Roderigo.

Stagecraft

'*Enter* LODOVICO'

Step into role as director and write an outline of how you would stage Lodovico's entrance. Work out who would accompany him and how they would be dressed. Detail the advice you would give an actor playing Lodovico regarding his tone, manner and general bearing. Add a justification for each of your decisions, and make some notes in your Director's Journal.

1 Two words (whole class)

Tiny sections of a play can be highly charged with significance. At line 212, Iago says only 'Lives, sir.' But how does he say it? And how does Lodovico (and everyone else) react?

• Four volunteers come to the front of the class and take the roles of Iago, Othello, Desdemona and Lodovico. Read the script from line 204 to line 214. In turn, volunteers from the rest of the class come forward as director and ask the actors to speak and show reactions in a variety of ways. Decide which is the most effective and why.

expostulate discuss
unprovide weaken

be his undertaker deal with him

I kiss … pleasures I welcome whatever they command

unkind breach unfortunate falling out

in the paper reading the letter
division difference of opinion

T'atone them to reconcile them

OTHELLO	Get me some poison, Iago, this night. I'll not expostulate with her, lest her body and beauty unprovide my mind again – this night, Iago.
IAGO	Do it not with poison; strangle her in her bed, even the bed she hath contaminated.
OTHELLO	Good, good! The justice of it pleases; very good!
IAGO	And for Cassio, let me be his undertaker. You shall hear more by midnight.
OTHELLO	Excellent good!

A trumpet [sounds within].

What trumpet is that same?

IAGO I warrant something from Venice.

Enter LODOVICO, DESDEMONA *and* ATTENDANTS.

'Tis Lodovico. This comes from the duke. See, your wife's with him.

LODOVICO	God save you, worthy general!
OTHELLO	With all my heart, sir.
LODOVICO	The duke and senators of Venice greet you.

[He gives Othello a letter.]

OTHELLO I kiss the instrument of their pleasures.

[He opens the letter and reads.]

DESDEMONA	And what's the news, good cousin Lodovico?
IAGO	I am very glad to see you, signior; Welcome to Cyprus.
LODOVICO	I thank you. How does Lieutenant Cassio?
IAGO	Lives, sir.
DESDEMONA	Cousin, there's fallen between him and my lord An unkind breach; but you shall make all well.
OTHELLO	Are you sure of that?
DESDEMONA	My lord?
OTHELLO	'This fail you not to do, as you will –'
LODOVICO	He did not call; he's busy in the paper. Is there division 'twixt my lord and Cassio?
DESDEMONA	A most unhappy one; I would do much T'atone them, for the love I bear to Cassio.
OTHELLO	Fire and brimstone!
DESDEMONA	My lord?

Line numbers: 195, 200, 205, 210, 215, 220

Lodovico reveals that the letter orders Othello to be recalled to Venice and Cassio be made governor of Cyprus. Desdemona says she is pleased. Othello strikes her in front of the Venetian delegation, and rages at her.

1 'He strikes her' (in pairs)

Some nineteenth-century directors thought that Othello striking Desdemona was too shocking to show on stage, so they left this out.

- Talk together about what difference it would make to a production if this act of violence was omitted. Would you retain it? Give reasons for your decision.

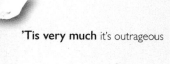

'Tis very much it's outrageous

prove turn into

crocodile (supposed to shed false tears)

Mistress (term used to address a prostitute in a brothel)

turn turn back, or move on to a new customer

obedient do whatever you ask of her (with sexual overtones)

mandate command

avaunt get out of my sight

place position, role as commander in Cyprus

Goats and monkeys (supposedly lecherous beasts)

Stagecraft

Show the moment (in groups of five or six)

Create a tableau of line 231: 'I have not deserved this.' Make sure that the characters are recognisable from their reactions, their spatial relationships and their frozen gestures. Show your tableau to the rest of the class and ask them to guess who the different characters are. Ask individual characters to step out of the freeze-frame and explain what is going through their mind at that moment.

Characters

Interpreting Desdemona (in pairs)

Some commentators suggest that in lines 202–31, Desdemona is deliberately provoking Othello in order to bring his increasingly disturbed behaviour out into the open.

- What do you think of that reading? Is there any evidence from the play so far that Desdemona is assertive enough to do this? Discuss this with a partner.

OTHELLO	Are you wise?
DESDEMONA	What, is he angry?
LODOVICO	Maybe the letter moved him; 225
	For as I think they do command him home,
	Deputing Cassio in his government.
DESDEMONA	By my troth, I am glad on't.
OTHELLO	Indeed!
DESDEMONA	My lord?
OTHELLO	I am glad to see you mad.
DESDEMONA	Why, sweet Othello?
OTHELLO	Devil! 230

[He strikes her.]

DESDEMONA	I have not deserved this.
LODOVICO	My lord, this would not be believed in Venice,
	Though I should swear I saw't. 'Tis very much.
	Make her amends; she weeps.
OTHELLO	O devil, devil!
	If that the earth could teem with woman's tears, 235
	Each drop she falls would prove a crocodile.
	Out of my sight!
DESDEMONA	I will not stay to offend you.
LODOVICO	Truly, an obedient lady.
	I do beseech your lordship, call her back.
OTHELLO	Mistress! 240
DESDEMONA	My lord?
OTHELLO	What would you with her, sir?
LODOVICO	Who? I, my lord?
OTHELLO	Ay, you did wish that I would make her turn.
	Sir, she can turn, and turn, and yet go on,
	And turn again. And she can weep, sir, weep. 245
	And she's obedient; as you say, obedient,
	Very obedient – proceed you in your tears –
	Concerning this, sir, – O, well-painted passion! –
	I am commanded home – get you away!
	I'll send for you anon. – Sir, I obey the mandate, 250
	And will return to Venice. – Hence, avaunt!

[Exit Desdemona]

Cassio shall have my place. And, sir, tonight
I do entreat that we may sup together.
You are welcome, sir, to Cyprus. Goats and monkeys! *Exit*

Lodovico expresses his horror to Iago at what he has just seen. Iago remarks that Othello is greatly changed. The next scene opens with Othello questioning Emilia about his wife's infidelity.

Language in the play
The man 'Whom passion could not shake' (in pairs)

Lodovico comments on how the Venetians had always considered Othello to be a man blessed with great self-control.

a Discuss whether or not you consider self-control to be an admirable quality in a man. Relate your discussion to Othello.

b Look carefully at Othello's syntax (sentence structure) in lines 243–54. What is different about his way of speaking here in comparison with his early speeches (for example, Act 1 Scene 3, lines 127–69)? Discuss what this comparison tells you about Othello's changing state of mind.

c Individually, write three paragraphs on the way Othello's language indicates the way he has changed since the beginning of the play. Use the ideas you discussed in the activity above. (Referring back to the 'Language' box on p. 146 may help you add some additional detail to your writing.)

Characters
Iago's persuasive skill

Some readers have interpreted the character of Othello as rather stupid and gullible for having been taken in by Iago. On the other hand, Iago has succeeded in convincing everyone – including Lodovico at this point. It is testimony to Iago's acting skill that he has been so convincing to so many people. At line 273, Lodovico tells Iago with heavy (unconscious) irony, 'I am sorry that I am deceived in him' – meaning that he believes Othello has been misleading them.

a Examine each of Iago's comments to Lodovico in the script opposite. Assess the skill with which he imparts an opinion without seeming to do so.

b Think about why Iago adopts a very plain, down-to-earth way of speaking. What effect is this designed to have?

---

all-in-all sufficient fully competent

shot of accident ... chance whatever fate threw at him

Are his wits safe? is he in his right mind?
light of brain losing his grip on sanity
censure judgement
If what ... he were if it's down to mental illness, at least he's got an excuse
Faith it's true
yet would ... the worst if only I could say that's the worst of it
use custom
work upon his blood anger him

courses actions
denote reveal

I am deceived in him I got the wrong impression of him

LODOVICO	Is this the noble Moor whom our full senate	255

LODOVICO Is this the noble Moor whom our full senate   255
          Call all-in-all sufficient? Is this the nature
          Whom passion could not shake? Whose solid virtue
          The shot of accident nor dart of chance
          Could neither graze nor pierce?
IAGO   He is much changed.
LODOVICO Are his wits safe? Is he not light of brain?   260
IAGO   He's that he is; I may not breathe my censure
          What he might be. If what he might he is not,
          I would to heaven he were.
LODOVICO   What! Strike his wife!
IAGO   Faith, that was not so well; yet would I knew
          That stroke would prove the worst.
LODOVICO   Is it his use?   265
          Or did the letters work upon his blood
          And new-create this fault?
IAGO   Alas, alas!
          It is not honesty in me to speak
          What I have seen and known. You shall observe him,
          And his own courses will denote him so,   270
          That I may save my speech. Do but go after,
          And mark how he continues.
LODOVICO I am sorry that I am deceived in him.

                                        Exeunt

Act 4 Scene 2
Cyprus   Another room in the castle

Enter OTHELLO *and* EMILIA.

OTHELLO You have seen nothing then?
EMILIA   Nor ever heard, nor ever did suspect.
OTHELLO Yes, you have seen Cassio and she together.
EMILIA   But then I saw no harm, and then I heard
         Each syllable that breath made up between them.   5

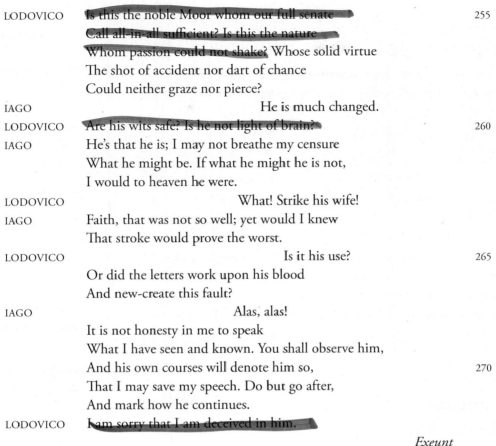

Emilia states categorically that Desdemona is innocent. Othello sends for his wife. He dismisses Emilia, treating her as a brothel-keeper.

Themes

Attitudes to women

Most people who come under Iago's influence begin to adopt offensively sexist language. Here, Othello refers to Emilia as a 'simple bawd' and Desdemona as a 'subtle whore'. He suggests that Emilia is a brothel-keeper and that Desdemona is a prostitute.

a Explain the three or four ways this image is used in lines 26–9.

b Note down other characters who have had their views and language debased by Iago, particularly when they are talking about women.

c Pool your ideas with other students on a flipchart or whiteboard, then discuss how important you consider this theme to be in the play so far.

d As an extension, you might like to consider Emilia's views about marriage, fidelity and men. Look back at Act 3 Scene 4.

Characters

Othello in the hot-seat (whole class)

Look at the questions Othello asks Emilia (lines 1–18) and the answers she gives. Why does Othello not believe Emilia? And why do you think he asks the questions in the first place?

- One student steps into role as Othello in the hot-seat. The rest of the class asks questions about what he thinks of Desdemona, Emilia and Iago. What proof does he have that his wife is unfaithful? Why is he so convinced? Try to include short quotations in the questions and answers.

1 Desdemona's question

Only a little while earlier, Desdemona was struck and then angrily dismissed by Othello. Now she has been sent for, she enters and asks a question.

- Decide how Desdemona would behave and sound as she asks 'My lord, what is your will?' (line 23). Experiment, then make a directorial decision and justify it to the rest of the class. Once you have shared your ideas, add notes to your Director's Journal.

durst dare

serpent's curse
(Biblical reference)

bawd brothel-keeper

closet lock and key … secrets
furtive keeper of vile secrets

Some of your function get on with your job (as brothel-keeper)
procreants those engaged in sex

Your mystery get on with your trade
dispatch get on with it

OTHELLO	What! Did they never whisper?
EMILIA	Never, my lord.
OTHELLO	Nor send you out o'th'way?
EMILIA	Never.
OTHELLO	To fetch her fan, her gloves, her mask, nor nothing?
EMILIA	Never, my lord.
OTHELLO	That's strange.
EMILIA	I durst, my lord, to wager she is honest,

10

Lay down my soul at stake. If you think other,
Remove your thought; it doth abuse your bosom.
If any wretch have put this in your head,
Let heaven requite it with the serpent's curse!   15
For if she be not honest, chaste, and true,
There's no man happy. The purest of their wives
Is foul as slander.

OTHELLO   Bid her come hither; go!

Exit Emilia

She says enough; yet she's a simple bawd
That cannot say as much. This is a subtle whore,   20
A closet lock and key of villainous secrets;
And yet she'll kneel and pray. I have seen her do't.

Enter DESDEMONA *and Emilia.*

DESDEMONA	My lord, what is your will?
OTHELLO	Pray, chuck, come hither.
DESDEMONA	What is your pleasure?
OTHELLO	Let me see your eyes.

Look in my face.

DESDEMONA   What horrible fancy's this?   25

OTHELLO [*To Emilia*] Some of your function, mistress:
Leave procreants alone and shut the door;
Cough or cry 'hem' if anybody come.
Your mystery, your mystery! Nay, dispatch!

Exit Emilia

DESDEMONA Upon my knees, what doth your speech import?   30
I understand a fury in your words,
But not the words.

OTHELLO   Why? What art thou?

Othello accuses Desdemona of gross dishonesty. She doesn't understand what he is talking about, but thinks his anger may be because he has been recalled to Venice by Brabantio's plotting.

1 Why does he not reply? (in pairs)

Spend five minutes discussing why you think Othello avoids answering Desdemona's direct questions: 'To whom …? With whom? How …?' (line 39). He merely responds with 'away, away, away!' How does this moment contribute to your understanding of Othello's character?

Language in the play

Othello's language: soliloquy? (in threes)

a Read through Othello's lines 46–68. Much of what he says is almost like a soliloquy. As one person reads, the other two echo any words or phrases connected with nature – for example, images of beauty or decay.

b Go through the speeches in more detail, sentence by sentence, and talk together about who you think he is addressing: the audience, himself, Desdemona or someone else? Explore ways in which each section of the speeches might be spoken on stage to give the audience insight into Othello's thoughts and feelings from moment to moment.

c Take turns to present a delivery to the class, explaining before or after your presentation how you hope to show Othello's mental state and emotions. Pinpoint what you consider to be the key words or phrases in contributing to the meaning.

Themes

Images of nature (in threes)

Re-read lines 47–8, 60–1 and 65–6. Each pair of lines contains a strong visual image, all concerned in some way with the world of nature, but from a disturbing perspective.

• Create a collage or other visual display using these images as your inspiration. When you have finished, give the collage a title and create an exhibition of the completed artworks. Provide a paragraph of explanatory notes that can be fastened alongside your display.

one of heaven an angel

heavy sorrowful

haply by chance

lost him lost his favour

try test

Steeped submerged

garnered up my heart stored up my love

fountain source

current stream

cistern water tank

knot and gender writhe around and breed

cherubin angel

esteems considers

shambles slaughterhouses

quicken even with blowing hatch as soon as the eggs are laid

ignorant unknowing

DESDEMONA	Your wife, my lord; your true and loyal wife.
OTHELLO	Come, swear it; damn thyself;
	Lest, being like one of heaven, the devils themselves 35
	Should fear to seize thee. Therefore be double-damned:
	Swear thou art honest.
DESDEMONA	Heaven doth truly know it.
OTHELLO	Heaven truly knows that thou art false as hell.
DESDEMONA	To whom, my lord? With whom? How am I false?
OTHELLO	Ah, Desdemon, away, away, away! 40
DESDEMONA	Alas, the heavy day! Why do you weep?
	Am I the motive of these tears, my lord?
	If haply you my father do suspect
	An instrument of this your calling back,
	Lay not your blame on me. If you have lost him, 45
	I have lost him too.
OTHELLO	Had it pleased heaven
	To try me with affliction, had they rained
	All kind of sores and shames on my bare head,
	Steeped me in poverty to the very lips,
	Given to captivity me and my utmost hopes, 50
	I should have found in some place of my soul
	A drop of patience. But, alas, to make me
	The fixèd figure for the time of scorn
	To point his slow unmoving finger at!
	Yet could I bear that too, well, very well; 55
	But there where I have garnered up my heart,
	Where either I must live or bear no life,
	The fountain from the which my current runs
	Or else dries up – to be discarded thence
	Or keep it as a cistern for foul toads 60
	To knot and gender in! Turn thy complexion there,
	Patience, thou young and rose-lipped cherubin;
	Ay, there look grim as hell!
DESDEMONA	I hope my noble lord esteems me honest.
OTHELLO	O ay: as summer flies are in the shambles, 65
	That quicken even with blowing. O, thou weed,
	Who art so lovely fair and smell'st so sweet
	That the sense aches at thee, would thou hadst ne'er been born!
DESDEMONA	Alas, what ignorant sin have I committed?

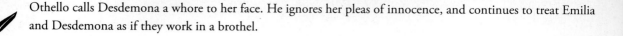

Othello calls Desdemona a whore to her face. He ignores her pleas of innocence, and continues to treat Emilia and Desdemona as if they work in a brothel.

Language in the play

Exaggeration (in pairs)

Othello uses extravagant imagery of the heavens in his answer to Desdemona's innocent question, 'what ignorant sin have I committed?' (line 69). He focuses on the word 'committed', and states that 'Heaven stops the nose at it' (the smell of Desdemona's sin), 'the moon winks' (the moon refuses to look) and 'The bawdy wind, that kisses all it meets, / Is hushed within the hollow mine of earth / And will not hear it' (lines 76–9). He is saying that her sin is so revolting and so far-reaching that heaven, moon and wind are unable to bear it. This is a gross exaggeration if taken literally (the literary term is **hyperbole**).

* What does such exaggeration suggest about Othello's state of mind and how he interprets his wife's behaviour? Discuss this with a partner.

Write about it

Emilia's version (in pairs)

In his last two encounters with Emilia, Othello has persisted in addressing her as if she is a 'madam' and Desdemona is one of her prostitutes. At line 92 he tells Emilia, 'We have done our course' (finished our business) and then proceeds to pay her.

What does Emilia make of all this? Write a letter in which she shares her version of all that has happened since their arrival in Cyprus, and how she thinks events might unfold in the future. What details does she reveal honestly? Are there any facts that she decides not to mention? Does she ask her friend for advice? Step into role and consider including the following:

* surviving the storm
* the wedding celebration between your 'mistress' and 'the Moor'
* Cassio losing his job and Desdemona's attempt to get him reinstated
* giving your husband Desdemona's lost 'napkin'
* Othello's sudden mood swings and inexplicable jealousy
* any suspicion you have about what your husband is up to.

Try to include some of Emilia's phrases or lines from the script.

What committed? what sins have you committed?

commoner common whore

forges furnaces

stops the nose holds its nose

winks closes its eye

hollow mine depths

vessel body

cry you mercy I beg your pardon

took mistook

Saint Peter (the saint who guards the gates of heaven)

done our course finished our business

keep our counsel keep quiet about what we've been doing

conceive imagine

half-asleep dazed

OTHELLO	Was this fair paper, this most goodly book,	70
	Made to write 'whore' upon? What committed!	
	Committed? O thou public commoner!	
	I should make very forges of my cheeks	
	That would to cinders burn up modesty	
	Did I but speak thy deeds. What committed!	75
	Heaven stops the nose at it, and the moon winks;	
	The bawdy wind, that kisses all it meets,	
	Is hushed within the hollow mine of earth	
	And will not hear it. What committed?	
	Impudent strumpet!	
DESDEMONA	By heaven, you do me wrong.	80
OTHELLO	Are not you a strumpet?	
DESDEMONA	No, as I am a Christian.	
	If to preserve this vessel for my lord	
	From any other foul unlawful touch	
	Be not to be a strumpet, I am none.	
OTHELLO	What, not a whore?	
DESDEMONA	No, as I shall be saved.	85
OTHELLO	Is't possible?	
DESDEMONA	O, heaven forgive us!	
OTHELLO	I cry you mercy then:	
	I took you for that cunning whore of Venice	
	That married with Othello. You, mistress,	
	That have the office opposite to Saint Peter,	90
	And keeps the gate of hell! You, you, ay, you!	

Enter Emilia.

	We have done our course; there's money for your pains.	
	I pray you turn the key, and keep our counsel. *Exit*	
EMILIA	Alas, what does this gentleman conceive?	
	How do you, madam? How do you, my good lady?	95
DESDEMONA	Faith, half-asleep.	
EMILIA	Good madam, what's the matter with my lord?	
DESDEMONA	With who?	
EMILIA	Why, with my lord, madam.	
DESDEMONA	Who is thy lord?	
EMILIA	He that is yours, sweet lady.	100

167

Desdemona expresses her distress and bewilderment at Othello's treatment of her. She cannot speak the word 'whore'. Emilia speculates it is all the trick of a villain seeking promotion.

1 Desdemona's soliloquy (in small groups)

Many modern readers of the play have found Desdemona's submissiveness in the face of severe provocation rather frustrating. However, others have argued that in previous centuries, her behaviour might have been regarded as exemplary for a married woman.

a Lines 106–8 are Desdemona's only soliloquy in the play. It is conventional that in a soliloquy a character always speaks truthfully. What 'truths' does Desdemona utter in these three lines?

b What advice would you give to the actor playing Desdemona in the way she should deliver these lines? First, think about who she is addressing the lines to. Then consider her tone of voice, pace and volume. Add these thoughts to your Director's Journal.

c Attitudes towards domestic violence have changed a lot since Shakespeare's time. Carry out some research into seventeenth-century beliefs about men's rights over women. Share your findings with other groups.

2 'some eternal villain' (whole class)

Emilia's guess that 'some eternal villain' is responsible for the 'slander' (lines 129–32) is extremely accurate. The dramatic irony is made even more acute by the fact that Iago is present. Has Emilia finally recognised the truth? Or is it just a case of unconscious irony?

a As a whole class, nominate one student to play Iago, who comes to the front of the class. While someone reads out Emilia's words, 'Iago' shows how he reacts. Freeze on 'I'll be hanged else'.

b Then bring forward two volunteers to play Emilia. One performs the role as if unconscious of the truth; the second performs it as if she is beginning to realise her husband is at the root of the trouble. Which works better? Can you explain why?

c Predict what Iago's next line will be and write it down. Then turn the page and find out what response Iago actually makes at this moment of high dramatic tension.

should go by water should be expressed in tears

meet fitting, appropriate
that he might … least misuse? to lead him to misinterpret my deeds like this?

a child to chiding not used to being verbally abused
bewhored her called her a whore
despite and heavy terms contempt and insults

in his drink drunken
callet slut

forsook given up

Beshrew curse
trick delusion

eternal damned
busy interfering
cogging, cozening cheating, deceiving

DESDEMONA	I have none. Do not talk to me, Emilia.
	I cannot weep, nor answers have I none
	But what should go by water. Prithee tonight
	Lay on my bed my wedding sheets, remember;
	And call thy husband hither.
EMILIA	Here's a change indeed! *Exit* 105
DESDEMONA	'Tis meet I should be used so, very meet!
	How have I been behaved that he might stick
	The smallest opinion on my least misuse?

Enter IAGO *and Emilia.*

IAGO	What is your pleasure, madam? How is't with you?
DESDEMONA	I cannot tell. Those that do teach young babes 110
	Do it with gentle means and easy tasks.
	He might have chid me so; for, in good faith,
	I am a child to chiding.
IAGO	What is the matter, lady?
EMILIA	Alas, Iago, my lord hath so bewhored her,
	Thrown such despite and heavy terms upon her 115
	As true hearts cannot bear.
DESDEMONA	Am I that name, Iago?
IAGO	What name, fair lady?
DESDEMONA	Such as she said my lord did say I was.
EMILIA	He called her whore. A beggar in his drink
	Could not have laid such terms upon his callet. 120
IAGO	Why did he so?
DESDEMONA	I do not know; I am sure I am none such.
IAGO	Do not weep, do not weep! Alas the day!
EMILIA	Hath she forsook so many noble matches,
	Her father, and her country, and her friends, 125
	To be called whore? Would it not make one weep?
DESDEMONA	It is my wretched fortune.
IAGO	Beshrew him for't!
	How comes this trick upon him?
DESDEMONA	Nay, heaven doth know.
EMILIA	I will be hanged if some eternal villain,
	Some busy and insinuating rogue, 130
	Some cogging, cozening slave, to get some office,
	Have not devised this slander; I'll be hanged else.

Emilia continues to suggest that a villain has poisoned Othello's mind. She reminds Iago that he has suspected her of infidelity with Othello. Desdemona professes her undying love for Othello, whatever happens.

1 'Here I kneel': intercut two scenes (in threes)

At line 150, Desdemona kneels to Iago to enlist his help. Not only is this heavy with irony, it also parallels the scene where Othello kneels before Iago to swear vengeance (Act 3 Scene 3, line 451).

a Read through these two incidents and the relevant sections of surrounding script. Copy and complete the table below. Some of Othello's key words and images are listed in the left-hand column. Pick out clear echoes from Desdemona's speech and add them to the right-hand column. What are the similarities and what are the differences? (For example, both mention heaven, but from different perspectives.)

Othello kneels (Act 3 Scene 3)	Desdemona kneels (Act 4 Scene 2)
'blood, blood, blood'	
'icy current … compulsive course'	
'bloody thoughts'	
'violent pace'	
'ne'er ebb to humble love'	'ever will … love him dearly'
'revenge'	
'marble heaven'	'the light of heaven'
'sacred vow'	

b In your groups, experiment to find a way of performing these speeches, intercutting the two episodes where husband and wife both kneel unwittingly before their tormentor. The actions are similar, but what differences exist between the two?

▶ What might Iago make of Emilia's telling description of the 'scurvy fellow' who might be behind Othello's uncharacteristic behaviour?

halter noose
keeps her company is meant to be her lover
form appearance
scurvy miserable
unfold reveal

within door quietly
squire fellow
the seamy side without inside out
suspect me (i.e. suspect me of committing adultery)

in discourse … deed either in thought or deed

Comfort forswear me! may all happiness forsake me!

abhor horrify
addition title
vanity finery
humour mood
does him offence irritates him
chide with rebuke, criticise

170

IAGO	Fie, there is no such man; it is impossible.
DESDEMONA	If any such there be, heaven pardon him.
EMILIA	A halter pardon him and hell gnaw his bones!

135

Why should he call her whore? Who keeps her company?
What place, what time, what form, what likelihood?
The Moor's abused by some most villainous knave,
Some base notorious knave, some scurvy fellow.
O heaven, that such companions thou'dst unfold,

140

And put in every honest hand a whip
To lash the rascals naked through the world,
Even from the east to th'west!

IAGO	Speak within door.
EMILIA	O fie upon them! Some such squire he was

That turned your wit the seamy side without

145

And made you to suspect me with the Moor.

IAGO	You are a fool, go to.
DESDEMONA	O good Iago,

What shall I do to win my lord again?
Good friend, go to him; for, by this light of heaven,
I know not how I lost him. Here I kneel:

150

If e'er my will did trespass 'gainst his love
Either in discourse of thought or actual deed;
Or that mine eyes, mine ears, or any sense
Delighted them in any other form;
Or that I do not yet, and ever did,

155

And ever will – though he do shake me off
To beggarly divorcement – love him dearly,
Comfort forswear me! Unkindness may do much,
And his unkindness may defeat my life,
But never taint my love. I cannot say 'whore':

160

It does abhor me now I speak the word;
To do the act that might the addition earn
Not the world's mass of vanity could make me.

IAGO	I pray you be content; 'tis but his humour.

The business of the state does him offence,

165

And he does chide with you.

DESDEMONA	If 'twere no other –
IAGO	It is but so, I warrant.

Emilia and Desdemona go off to dinner with the Venetian visitors. Roderigo is fed up with Iago, accusing him of tricking him out of jewellery that was meant to have been passed on to Desdemona. He threatens Iago.

1 What happened at dinner? (in groups of six or seven)

After the highly emotional episode of marital strife, Desdemona is called to a formal dinner to entertain her Venetian guests. The scene is not included in the play, but there are strong dramatic possibilities in such an artificially polite and formal occasion, with seething undercurrents of highly charged emotional discord.

- Improvise or write the imagined scene, giving due consideration to how Othello, Desdemona, Emilia and Lodovico might speak and behave towards one another in public.

Stagecraft

Playng the scene (in pairs)

The final part of Scene 2 brings in Roderigo, who bitterly complains that he is being exploited and cheated by Iago, and has no prospect of winning Desdemona. Iago displays his usual quick-wittedness, and his initially brief replies incite Roderigo's anger and a threat of a duel ('seek satisfaction'). On the next page of the script, Iago flatters Roderigo and devises a murderous plan to kill Cassio, thus enabling Roderigo to win Desdemona. This episode between Iago and Roderigo has been interpreted in different ways by commentators and directors. Some see it as continuing to raise the tension. Others believe it has strong comic possibilities to temporarily lower the tension.

a Take parts and read lines 171–235, then discuss how you would play the episode in two or three different ways. Try out different readings. Decide which works best, and why.

b Annotate an enlarged copy of the script, making precise suggestions about how you think it should be acted. Then write a paragraph outlining the reasons for your decisions. You might like to refer to:

- your knowledge of the two characters so far
- the situation at this point in the story, including Iago's complex balancing act with all the lies he is telling
- the need to lighten the mood at this point in the play (or not)
- the need to heighten the tension even further (or not).

stay the meat await the meal

daff'st me fob me off
device excuse
conveniency opportunity
endure it put up with it

performances actions
no kin together bear no relation to each other
I have wasted … means I am facing financial ruin
half easily
votarist nun
expectations encouragements
sudden respect immediate attention
scurvy despicable
fopped fooled

seek satisfaction of you challenge you to a duel
You have said now? have you finished?

[*Trumpets sound within.*]
Hark how these instruments summon to supper!
The messengers of Venice stay the meat.
Go in, and weep not; all things shall be well.   170

                Exeunt Desdemona and Emilia

        Enter RODERIGO.

       How now, Roderigo?

RODERIGO I do not find that thou deal'st justly with me.

IAGO   What in the contrary?

RODERIGO Every day thou daff'st me with some device, Iago, and
rather, as it seems to me now, keep'st from me all conveniency   175
than suppliest me with the least advantage of hope. I will indeed
no longer endure it. Nor am I yet persuaded to put up in peace
what already I have foolishly suffered.

IAGO   Will you hear me, Roderigo?

RODERIGO Faith, I have heard too much; for your words and   180
performances are no kin together.

IAGO   You charge me most unjustly.

RODERIGO With naught but truth. I have wasted myself out of my
means. The jewels you have had from me to deliver to Desdemona
would half have corrupted a votarist. You have told me she hath   185
received them, and returned me expectations and comforts of
sudden respect and acquaintance, but I find none.

IAGO   Well, go to; very well.

RODERIGO Very well, go to! I cannot go to, man, nor 'tis not very
well. By this hand, I say 'tis very scurvy and begin to find myself   190
fopped in it.

IAGO   Very well.

RODERIGO I tell you 'tis not very well. I will make myself known to
Desdemona. If she will return me my jewels, I will give over my
suit and repent my unlawful solicitation; if not, assure yourself I   195
will seek satisfaction of you.

IAGO   You have said now?

Iago promises Roderigo that Desdemona will be available for him soon. He plots that Roderigo shall kill Cassio that night as Cassio leaves Bianca's house.

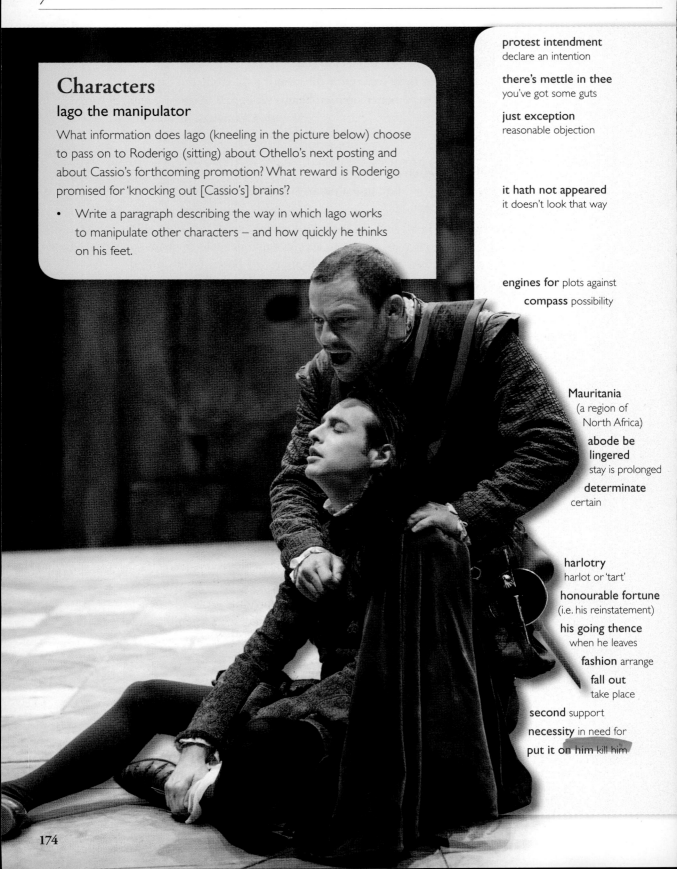

Characters

Iago the manipulator

What information does Iago (kneeling in the picture below) choose to pass on to Roderigo (sitting) about Othello's next posting and about Cassio's forthcoming promotion? What reward is Roderigo promised for 'knocking out [Cassio's] brains'?

- Write a paragraph describing the way in which Iago works to manipulate other characters – and how quickly he thinks on his feet.

protest intendment
declare an intention

there's mettle in thee
you've got some guts

just exception
reasonable objection

it hath not appeared
it doesn't look that way

engines for plots against
compass possibility

Mauritania
(a region of
North Africa)
**abode be
lingered**
stay is prolonged
determinate
certain

harlotry
harlot or 'tart'
honourable fortune
(i.e. his reinstatement)
his going thence
when he leaves
fashion arrange
fall out
take place
second support
necessity in need for
put it on him kill him

RODERIGO Ay, and said nothing but what I protest intendment of
doing.

IAGO Why, now I see there's mettle in thee, and even from this instant   200
do build on thee a better opinion than ever before. Give me thy
hand, Roderigo. Thou hast taken against me a most just
exception; but yet I protest I have dealt most directly in thy
affair.

RODERIGO It hath not appeared.   205

IAGO I grant indeed it hath not appeared; and your suspicion is not
without wit and judgement. But, Roderigo, if thou hast that in
thee indeed, which I have greater reason to believe now than ever – I
mean purpose, courage, and valour – this night show it. If thou the
next night following enjoy not Desdemona, take me from this   210
world with treachery, and devise engines for my life.

RODERIGO Well, what is it? Is it within reason and compass?

IAGO Sir, there is especial commission come from Venice to depute
Cassio in Othello's place.

RODERIGO Is that true? Why, then Othello and Desdemona return again   215
to Venice.

IAGO O no, he goes into Mauritania and takes away with him the
fair Desdemona, unless his abode be lingered here by some
accident; wherein none can be so determinate as the removing of
Cassio.   220

RODERIGO How do you mean 'removing' of him?

IAGO Why, by making him uncapable of Othello's place – knocking out
his brains.

RODERIGO And that you would have me to do?

IAGO Ay, if you dare do yourself a profit and a right. He sups tonight   225
with a harlotry, and thither will I go to him. He knows not yet of
his honourable fortune. If you will watch his going thence – which
I will fashion to fall out between twelve and one – you may take
him at your pleasure. I will be near to second your attempt, and
he shall fall between us. Come, stand not amazed at it, but go along   230
with me. I will show you such a necessity in his death that you shall
think yourself bound to put it on him. It is now high supper-time
and the night grows to waste. About it!

RODERIGO I will hear further reason for this.

IAGO And you shall be satisfied.   235

Exeunt

Othello bids goodnight to Lodovico after their dinner, and orders Desdemona to go to bed to await him. She talks with Emilia of her love for Othello, of death, and of Barbary, her mother's maid.

1 Inner dilemmas/outward politeness (in sixes)

In lines 1–9 of Scene 3, all three characters are troubled by what they have seen or heard recently, yet all maintain a veneer of calm politeness.

- Three people take on the roles of Lodovico, Desdemona and Othello. The remaining three represent each character's innermost thoughts. Perform the script, punctuating each line with what you think is really going on in the mind of the speaker.

Characters

Emilia and Desdemona (in pairs)

Scene 3 is often referred to as the 'willow' scene. It focuses on Emilia and Desdemona, and provides a quietly moving final moment, in contrast to the recent turmoil.

a Take parts and read from line 10 to the end of the scene (line 101). As you read, think about the relationship between the two women. Is it a close friendship, or that of mistress and servant. What evidence can you find in the script to back up your view? Look, for instance, at the terms of address used (if any). Who gives commands or asks questions? Who gives advice, and in what terms?

b Write two paragraphs describing the relationship between Emilia and Desdemona at this point in the play. How has it developed from the beginning of Act 2?

2 Foreboding

In this scene, there is a general sense of foreboding. Devise a diagram or collage to show how each of the following contributes to the ominous atmosphere, in the context of Iago's earlier suggestion that Othello should 'strangle her in her bed' and Othello's desire for 'blood, blood, blood':

- bedsheets
- the order to dismiss Emilia
- Barbary's story and the willow song
- Desdemona's complete obedience.

In each case, add a quotation from the play. Your diagram or collage should help others to understand the dramatic effect of this part of the play.

---

on th'instant at once
forthwith immediately

incontinent straight away

nightly wearing night-dress

So would not I that's not my wish
approve value
checks rebukes

All's one it's all the same to me

you talk you're talking rubbish

willow (willow trees were traditionally symbolic of forsaken lovers)
I have … But I find it hard to stop myself
hang my head … one side hold my head to one side

Act 4 Scene 3
Cyprus   A room in the castle

Enter OTHELLO, LODOVICO, DESDEMONA,
EMILIA *and* ATTENDANTS.

LODOVICO   I do beseech you, sir, trouble yourself no further.

OTHELLO   O, pardon me; 'twill do me good to walk.

LODOVICO   Madam, good night. I humbly thank your ladyship.

DESDEMONA   Your honour is most welcome.

OTHELLO   Will you walk, sir? O, Desdemona.   5

DESDEMONA   My lord?

OTHELLO   Get you to bed on th'instant. I will be returned forthwith.
Dismiss your attendant there. Look't be done.

DESDEMONA   I will, my lord.

Exeunt [Othello, Lodovico and Attendants]

EMILIA   How goes it now? He looks gentler than he did.   10

DESDEMONA   He says he will return incontinent;
He hath commanded me to go to bed
And bade me to dismiss you.

EMILIA   Dismiss me?

DESDEMONA   It was his bidding; therefore, good Emilia,
Give me my nightly wearing, and adieu.   15
We must not now displease him.

EMILIA   I would you had never seen him.

DESDEMONA   So would not I: my love doth so approve him
That even his stubbornness, his checks, his frowns –
Prithee, unpin me – have grace and favour in them.   20

EMILIA   I have laid those sheets you bade me on the bed.

DESDEMONA   All's one. Good faith, how foolish are our minds!
If I do die before thee, prithee shroud me
In one of those same sheets.

EMILIA   Come, come, you talk.

DESDEMONA   My mother had a maid called Barbary: 25
She was in love, and he she loved proved mad
And did forsake her. She had a song of willow;
An old thing 'twas but it expressed her fortune,
And she died singing it. That song tonight
Will not go from my mind. I have much to do   30
But to go hang my head all at one side

Desdemona sings a sad song from her childhood as she prepares for bed. She and Emilia discuss their differing attitudes to marriage and fidelity.

1 'a proper man' (in pairs)

Desdemona refers to Lodovico as being 'a proper man' (a good-looking man) and someone who 'speaks well'. Emilia agrees.

- Spend about five minutes discussing why Desdemona says this. What interpretations of this comment are possible? As director, how would you want Desdemona to say this in order to encourage an audience to share your interpretation? Add a short note to your Director's Journal.

Stagecraft
The Willow Song

The first edition of the play (published in 1622) omits the song altogether. Perhaps the boy actor who played Desdemona at that time couldn't sing!

- From your reading of the script, and/or viewing of either a live or filmed performance, what was your reaction to the song? What effect did it have on you? List what a performance would gain or lose if the song were omitted. Compare your feelings with those of other students.

▶ Explore ways of presenting the Willow Song to create a moving and dramatic effect between the two women at this point in the play.

dispatch hurry up

proper good-looking

touch of his nether lip a kiss

Lay by these put these (clothes) away
hie thee go away

moe more
couch sleep
bode foretell

in conscience honestly

And sing it like poor Barbary – prithee, dispatch.

EMILIA   Shall I go fetch your nightgown?

DESDEMONA   No, unpin me here.

This Lodovico is a proper man.

EMILIA   A very handsome man.

DESDEMONA   He speaks well.   35

EMILIA   I know a lady in Venice would have walked barefoot to Palestine
for a touch of his nether lip.

DESDEMONA   [*Sings*]
       The poor soul sat sighing by a sycamore tree,
           Sing all a green willow;
       Her hand on her bosom, her head on her knee,   40
           Sing willow, willow, willow;
       The fresh streams ran by her and murmured her moans;
           Sing willow, willow, willow.
       Her salt tears fell from her and softened the stones –
Lay by these.
           Sing willow, willow, willow –   45
Prithee, hie thee; he'll come anon.
           Sing all a green willow must be my garland.
           Let nobody blame him; his scorn I approve –
Nay that's not next. Hark, who is't that knocks?   50

EMILIA   It's the wind.

DESDEMONA   [*Sings*]
       I called my love false love, but what said he then?
           Sing willow, willow, willow;
       If I court moe women, you'll couch with moe men –
So get thee gone; good night. Mine eyes do itch –   55
Does that bode weeping?

EMILIA   'Tis neither here nor there.

DESDEMONA   I have heard it said so. O, these men, these men!
Dost thou in conscience think – tell me, Emilia –
That there be women do abuse their husbands
In such gross kind?

EMILIA   There be some such, no question.   60

DESDEMONA   Wouldst thou do such a deed for all the world?

EMILIA   Why, would not you?

DESDEMONA   No, by this heavenly light.

EMILIA   Nor I neither by this heavenly light;
I might do't as well i'th'dark.

Emilia says she would commit adultery if it gained her husband the world. Desdemona can't believe this. Emilia asserts that husbands are to blame, and argues for equality and mutual respect in marriage.

▲ Role-play Emilia and Desdemona. Justify their views, making reference to their respective social positions, their experience of men and married life.

Characters

Emilia and Desdemona's contrasting views (in pairs)

a Compare the two women's views of men and marriage. With a partner, discuss what the women say to each other in lines 57–101. Would you agree that one is a romanticised view, whilst the other is much more practical? What difference does each woman's social position make to their separate views?

b To develop your discussion, look at the production photographs of Emilia and Desdemona here and on pages 170, 178 and 183. What does each photograph suggest about their relationship (look at positioning, expressions and direction of gaze, costume, lighting)? Add some notes to your Director's Journal to explain how you think these two women characters should be played.

undo't put it right

joint-ring cheap ring

measures of lawn lengths of fabric

exhibition amount of money

Ud's God's

venture purgatory risk being condemned to the torture of purgatory

to th'advantage in addition

store populate

slack their duties fail to perform (sexually)

pour … laps give out what's rightfully ours to other women

Throwing restraint upon us restricting our freedom

scant reduce

our former having what we used to have

in despite out of spite

galls the guts (to get revenge)

sport for amusement

Is't frailty that thus errs? is it weakness that makes men stray?

use us well treat us kindly

ills wrongs

pick learn

by bad mend learn from our bad ways

DESDEMONA	Wouldst thou do such a deed for all the world?	65
EMILIA	The world's a huge thing; it is a great price For a small vice.	
DESDEMONA	In troth, I think thou wouldst not.	
EMILIA	In troth, I think I should, and undo't when I had done it. Marry, I would not do such a thing for a joint-ring, nor for measures of lawn, nor for gowns, petticoats, nor caps, nor any petty exhibition. But for all the whole world! Ud's pity, who would not make her husband a cuckold, to make him a monarch? I should venture purgatory for't.	70
DESDEMONA	Beshrew me, if I would do such a wrong for the whole world.	75
EMILIA	Why, the wrong is but a wrong i'th'world; and having the world for your labour, 'tis a wrong in your own world, and you might quickly make it right.	
DESDEMONA	I do not think there is any such woman.	
EMILIA	Yes, a dozen; and as many to th'advantage as would store the world they played for. But I do think it is their husbands' faults If wives do fall. Say that they slack their duties And pour our treasures into foreign laps, Or else break out in peevish jealousies, Throwing restraint upon us; or say they strike us, Or scant our former having in despite – Why, we have galls, and though we have some grace, Yet have we some revenge. Let husbands know Their wives have sense like them: they see, and smell, And have their palates both for sweet and sour As husbands have. What is it that they do When they change us for others? Is it sport? I think it is. And doth affection breed it? I think it doth. Is't frailty that thus errs? It is so too. And have not we affections, Desires for sport, and frailty, as men have? Then let them use us well; else let them know The ills we do, their ills instruct us so.	80 85 90 95
DESDEMONA	Good night, good night. God me such uses send, Not to pick bad from bad, but by bad mend!	100

Exeunt

Looking back at Act 4
Activities for groups or individuals

1 The focus of Act 4

Act 4 takes on a much narrower, more domestic focus than the previous three acts, and it is worth considering how Act 4 furthers the action of the play.

- As a first step, draw a table similar to the one below and compile a summary of each act so far, suggesting (as far as you know) where each scene is set.

	Summary of events	Where set

Act 1	Iago and Roderigo tell Brabantio that his daughter has secretly married Othello.
	    Brabantio takes his complaint to the Duke of Venice. Othello (and Desdemona) defend themselves in front of the Senate; the Duke allows the marriage.
	    News that Cyprus is under threat from a Turkish attack means that Othello must set sail immediately and command the troops.
		Venice:
		a in the streets
		b in the Senate

Act 2		Cyprus: **a** the quayside **b** …
Act 3		
Act 4		

- Suggest some ideas about staging, set designs, sound and lighting that could help to emphasise this movement from public to private affairs. What would you highlight as key dramatic moments in Act 4?

2 Abuse of Desdemona

The following lines are all spoken by Othello directly to Desdemona's face:

- 'thou art false as hell'
- 'look grim as hell!'
- 'O, thou weed'

- 'Was this fair paper … Made to write "whore" upon?'
- 'O thou public commoner!'
- 'Impudent strumpet!'
- 'Are not you a strumpet?'
- 'What, not a whore?'
- 'I took you for that cunning whore of Venice'
- 'We have done our course'.

a In large groups, each person learns one of the lines above. Move around the room, and every time you encounter another student, shout, hiss or sneer your line in their face.

b Stand in a long line, all facing one way. Go swiftly down the row, spinning round one by one so that you are facing the next person, and snap your lines harshly. Then try standing in a tight circle with one student kneeling in the middle – volunteers only! Hurl your lines of abuse at them.

c Use the physical experience of the activities above to help you write a short essay analysing Othello's motives for such language, and Desdemona's feelings in response to it.

3 Private thoughts

At the end of Act 4, each of the main characters is poised on the brink of a significant event.

- Choose three from the following characters: Roderigo, Desdemona, Iago, Othello, Emilia. In role, write down one sentence for each that you feel best encapsulates their hope or wish at this moment. Then share these sentences with the rest of the class, by reading out in role.

- Discuss any variations, and talk about why some of you may have interpreted characters and their motivation in different ways at this point in the play.

Iago positions Roderigo for the murder. He hopes both Cassio and Roderigo will die. Roderigo fails to kill Cassio, who wounds him instead. Iago leaps out of hiding, strikes Cassio and runs off.

Language in the play
Count the commands

How many commands can you find in the opening five lines of Iago's conversation? What does the repeated use of the imperative ('Stand!' 'Be bold!') emphasise about the relationship between Iago and Roderigo?

1 Intrigue again

Act 5 opens in a very similar way to Act 1, with Iago and Roderigo plotting villainy in the streets late at night. What other similarities are there with that opening scene – and what key differences?

- Create a poster or display to explore the parallels between the opening of this scene and of Act 1 Scene 1. Include some short quotations (words, phrases or lines) that you believe to be significant. Display your poster in the classroom.

Characters
Iago: motiveless malignity? (in pairs)

The nineteenth-century poet and writer Samuel Taylor Coleridge was intrigued by the character of Iago, whose activities he described as arising out of 'motiveless malignity' (wickedness that cannot be explained). Iago himself has already given several reasons for his vendetta against Othello and Cassio, but these seem rather flimsy and inconsistent.

- **a** Read through Iago's aside in lines 11–22. What reason does he give here for his behaviour?
- **b** What other reasons has Iago already given for his hatred of Othello and Cassio?
- **c** Discuss what you think is meant by Iago's comment 'He hath a daily beauty in his life / That makes me ugly' (lines 19–20).
- **d** Write a paragraph outlining your thoughts about Iago's motivation (or lack of it) to do harm to others.

bulk projecting wall
bare unsheathed
put it home thrust it deep
at thy elbow near at hand
it makes us … mars us it will either make our fortunes or ruin us
resolution determination
miscarry make a mistake

quat spot or boil
almost to the sense almost until it bursts
makes my gain I win
Live Roderigo if Roderigo lives
calls me … restitution it's pay-back time
bobbed conned, tricked

unfold expose
soft hush

his gait the way he walks

make proof of test

Act 5 Scene 1
Cyprus A street at night

Enter IAGO *and* RODERIGO.

IAGO   Here, stand behind this bulk, straight will he come.
         Wear thy good rapier bare, and put it home.
         Quick, quick, fear nothing; I'll be at thy elbow.
         It makes us or it mars us; think on that,
         And fix most firm thy resolution.   5

RODERIGO Be near at hand; I may miscarry in't.

IAGO   Here, at thy hand; be bold, and take thy stand.
                         [*He retires.*]

RODERIGO I have no great devotion to the deed,
         And yet he hath given me satisfying reasons.
         'Tis but a man gone. Forth my sword! He dies!   10

IAGO   [*Aside*] I have rubbed this young quat almost to the sense,
         And he grows angry. Now, whether he kill Cassio,
         Or Cassio him, or each do kill the other,
         Every way makes my gain. Live Roderigo,
         He calls me to a restitution large   15
         Of gold and jewels that I bobbed from him
         As gifts to Desdemona.
         It must not be. If Cassio do remain,
         He hath a daily beauty in his life
         That makes me ugly; and besides, the Moor   20
         May unfold me to him – there stand I in much peril.
         No, he must die. But soft, I hear him coming.

Enter CASSIO.

RODERIGO I know his gait; 'tis he. Villain, thou diest!
                         [*He lunges at Cassio.*]

CASSIO   That thrust had been mine enemy indeed
         But that my coat is better than thou think'st.   25
         I will make proof of thine.
                         [*He wounds Roderigo.*]

RODERIGO   O, I am slain!
                         [*Iago wounds Cassio in the leg and exit*]

CASSIO   I am maimed forever. Help, ho! Murder, murder!

Enter OTHELLO.

Othello hears the scuffles and, satisfied Cassio is dead, goes off to kill Desdemona. Lodovico and Gratiano cautiously investigate the cries of the two wounded men. Iago arrives to help.

1 Who's doing what, and when? (in pairs)

There is a great deal of action in the first fifty-five lines of Scene 1. As you can imagine, on stage it is both fast-moving and exciting. Below is one person's idea for staging it at the Globe Theatre (now rebuilt on London's Bankside). The drawing shows different characters at different moments, and the events are numbered in the order in which they occur in the script.

* Identify each person in the drawing, then work out which moment in the script is being represented in each case. Find a suitable quotation for each one (five in all). Copy and complete the table below.

	Character	Moment	Quotation
1			
2			
3			
4			
5			

Minion darling (used contemptuously about Desdemona)

dear beloved

unblest cursed

hies is coming fast

Forth of my heart out of my heart

blotted wiped out

watch night patrol

passage passers-by

mischance accident

direful distressed

heavy dark

counterfeits fraudsters

think't assume it to be

in to the cry to the rescue

in his shirt (i.e. as if he has just got out of bed)

spoiled wounded

undone injured

OTHELLO	[*Aside*] The voice of Cassio: Iago keeps his word.	
RODERIGO	O villain that I am!	
OTHELLO	[*Aside*] It is even so.	
CASSIO	O help, ho! Light! A surgeon!	30
OTHELLO	[*Aside*] 'Tis he. O brave Iago, honest and just,	
	That hast such noble sense of thy friend's wrong!	
	Thou teachest me. Minion, your dear lies dead,	
	And your unblest fate hies. Strumpet, I come!	
	Forth of my heart those charms, thine eyes, are blotted;	35
	Thy bed, lust-stained, shall with lust's blood be spotted.	

Exit Othello

Enter LODOVICO *and* GRATIANO.

CASSIO	What, ho! No watch? No passage? Murder, murder!	
GRATIANO	'Tis some mischance; the cry is very direful.	
CASSIO	O, help!	
LODOVICO	Hark!	40
RODERIGO	O, wretched villain!	
LODOVICO	Two or three groan. It is a heavy night.	
	These may be counterfeits: let's think't unsafe	
	To come in to the cry without more help.	
RODERIGO	Nobody come? Then I shall bleed to death.	45
LODOVICO	Hark!	

Enter Iago, with a light.

GRATIANO	Here's one comes in his shirt, with light and weapons.	
IAGO	Who's there? Whose noise is this that cries on murder?	
LODOVICO	We do not know.	
IAGO	Did you not hear a cry?	
CASSIO	Here, here; for heaven's sake, help me!	
IAGO	What's the matter?	50
GRATIANO	This is Othello's ancient, as I take it.	
LODOVICO	The same indeed, a very valiant fellow.	
IAGO	What are you here that cry so grievously?	
CASSIO	Iago? O, I am spoiled, undone by villains!	
	Give me some help.	55

In pretending to investigate what has happened, Iago secretly stabs the injured Roderigo. Cassio is discovered to have a severe leg wound. Bianca arrives to see what has happened, and Iago insults her.

Stagecraft

Darkness – and Iago's play-acting (in pairs)

In Shakespeare's time, the play would have been acted at the Globe in broad daylight, so Shakespeare provides his actors with language and action to suggest that this scene takes place at night. Audiences would have been familiar with such dramatic presentations, and accepted them willingly, ready to suspend their disbelief.

- What examples can you find in the script opposite of words or phrases that act as signals to the actors and the audience that it is very dark and difficult to make out what is happening?

Shakespeare continues to present Iago as a cunning manipulator, ready to seize any opportunity under cover of darkness to further his own interests. He plays the innocent, honest soldier yet again, calling in Lodovico and Gratiano to help, and even binding Cassio's wound with his shirt to show friendship. But he also takes advantage of the darkness to stab Roderigo, whose last words are: 'O damned Iago! O inhuman dog!'

- Read through Iago's lines in the script opposite, pausing after every sentence. In the pause, the other person describes what impression Iago is attempting to create through his words.

Language in the play

Sentence structure (in small groups)

a The script is full of short, simple sentences. To catch the mood and the speed of the action, try these ways of reading lines 56–84:

- Read around the group, with each person exclaiming a single sentence before handing on.
- Repeat the exercise, but this time exclaim only one word – the one you think most important – in each sentence.
- Repeat both exercises, but as quickly as possible.

Identify which of these are questions, statements or exclamations.

b Talk together about the speed at which you think the lines should be spoken, and why Shakespeare chose to use so many short sentences here.

make away escape

As you shall … praise us make your mind up once you know who we are

I cry you mercy I beg your pardon

notable notorious
may you suspect can you guess
mangled injured

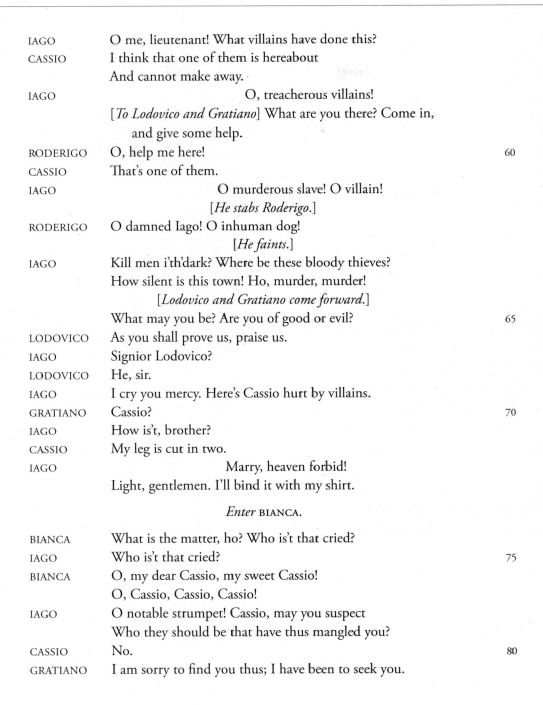

IAGO	O me, lieutenant! What villains have done this?	
CASSIO	I think that one of them is hereabout	
	And cannot make away.	
IAGO	O, treacherous villains!	
	[*To Lodovico and Gratiano*] What are you there? Come in,	
	and give some help.	
RODERIGO	O, help me here!	60
CASSIO	That's one of them.	
IAGO	O murderous slave! O villain!	
	[*He stabs Roderigo.*]	
RODERIGO	O damned Iago! O inhuman dog!	
	[*He faints.*]	
IAGO	Kill men i'th'dark? Where be these bloody thieves?	
	How silent is this town! Ho, murder, murder!	
	[*Lodovico and Gratiano come forward.*]	
	What may you be? Are you of good or evil?	65
LODOVICO	As you shall prove us, praise us.	
IAGO	Signior Lodovico?	
LODOVICO	He, sir.	
IAGO	I cry you mercy. Here's Cassio hurt by villains.	
GRATIANO	Cassio?	70
IAGO	How is't, brother?	
CASSIO	My leg is cut in two.	
IAGO	Marry, heaven forbid!	
	Light, gentlemen. I'll bind it with my shirt.	

Enter BIANCA.

BIANCA	What is the matter, ho? Who is't that cried?	
IAGO	Who is't that cried?	75
BIANCA	O, my dear Cassio, my sweet Cassio!	
	O, Cassio, Cassio, Cassio!	
IAGO	O notable strumpet! Cassio, may you suspect	
	Who they should be that have thus mangled you?	
CASSIO	No.	80
GRATIANO	I am sorry to find you thus; I have been to seek you.	

Iago accuses Bianca of involvement in the affray. He pretends to be surprised at identifying Roderigo as Cassio's attacker. He shows great concern for Cassio, and has him carried off to receive treatment.

Write about it

Clever Iago? Or helped by chance?

Iago continues to play the role of the concerned friend. He bustles about, accusing Bianca, feigning distress at discovering Roderigo, and calling for a chair for Cassio. Iago seems to have avoided personal disaster very narrowly, through a combination of chance and his own skill. However, if Lodovico and Gratiano had immediately and properly investigated the screams from the street (line 37), the scene might have unfolded in a very different way.

a Write a paragraph explaining which aspects of this incident you think are down to Iago's skill. Then write a second paragraph outlining how you think chance works in Iago's favour at this point.

b Write about another incident in the play where chance has helped Iago and he has been lucky to get away with his scheme without anyone discovering what he's up to. What general observations can you make about the relationship between chance and intention in the play?

Themes

Attitudes to women (by yourself)

Iago immediately casts doubt on Bianca, calling her 'this trash' (language similar to that used by Cassio in Act 4). He even insinuates that Bianca might be an accessory to the murder attempt (lines 105–10). Iago can rely on other characters sharing his insulting view of women. Bianca becomes an easy target for Emilia, too, who calls her a 'strumpet' (whilst Cassio is thought of as a poor victim!).

• Read up to line 129, noting the way Iago and others treat Bianca, and how she responds. Then imagine you are Bianca, arrested on suspicion of being accessory to murder. In role, write a short statement defending yourself against Iago's charge of being 'a party in this injury'. Explain how you know Cassio, what your movements have been this evening, how you came to be in the street at that time, and what you heard or saw. Practise reading it in role, and then share it with the rest of the class, who can question Bianca once she has read her statement.

garter a band worn by men and women to keep stockings up

trash rubbish (referring to Bianca)
be a party in have something to do with

a chair (probably a sedan chair to carry off Cassio)

well said well done

Save you your labour stop interfering

190

IAGO	Lend me a garter: so. O for a chair
	To bear him easily hence!
BIANCA	Alas, he faints!
	O, Cassio, Cassio, Cassio!
IAGO	Gentlemen all, I do suspect this trash 85
	To be a party in this injury.
	Patience awhile, good Cassio. Come, come,
	Lend me a light. Know we this face or no?
	Alas, my friend and my dear countryman!
	Roderigo? No – yes, sure – O, heaven, Roderigo! 90
GRATIANO	What, of Venice?
IAGO	Even he, sir; did you know him?
GRATIANO	Know him? Ay.
IAGO	Signior Gratiano! I cry your gentle pardon.
	These bloody accidents must excuse my manners
	That so neglected you.
GRATIANO	I am glad to see you. 95
IAGO	How do you, Cassio? O, a chair, a chair!
GRATIANO	Roderigo?
IAGO	He, he, 'tis he.

[*Enter* ATTENDANTS *with a chair.*]

              O, that's well said, the chair!
Some good men bear him carefully from hence.
I'll fetch the general's surgeon. [*To Bianca*] For you, mistress,   100
Save you your labour. – He that lies slain here, Cassio,
Was my dear friend. What malice was between you?

CASSIO	None in the world, nor do I know the man.
IAGO	[*To Bianca*] What, look you pale? – O, bear him out o'th'air.

          [*Cassio is carried off; Roderigo's body is removed*]

Iago accuses Bianca of looking guilty. He explains to Emilia what has happened, and she verbally abuses Bianca. Iago sends Emilia to Othello with the news.

1 'I am no strumpet' (in pairs)

The embedded directions for the actor playing Bianca here are to specifically look 'pale' with 'gastness of eye' (lines 105–6). Yet she is strong enough to mount a robust defence, ironically telling Iago and Emilia that she leads as honest a life as her accusers.

a Traditionally, Bianca has not been depicted as a sympathetic character. Discuss the ways a director can influence the sympathies of an audience at moments like this.

b Emilia is quick to support her husband's view of Bianca as a prostitute. Why do you think she does this?

Stagecraft

Fast forward (in groups of eight to ten)

For this activity you need to work in a large, clear space as you will be rushing around. Make sure that it is safe for your needs.

a Think of old silent movies when the action gets ridiculously fast-moving, and is usually accompanied by breathlessly rapid music. Or consider what happens when you hold down the fast-forward control when watching a movie and the action becomes comically frenetic. Try staging Act 5 Scene 1 as if it is being played like that. You will find the need for speed adds to your understanding of the sequence of events.

- Share out parts; each person will need to familiarise themselves with the script so that they feel confident in reading it very quickly.
- Agree on a way to 'block' the basic moves.
- Act it out as fast as you can – keep going even if someone makes a mistake.
- If you do it properly, you should be completely out of breath at the end! To make it more fun, find some suitable musical accompaniment, for example old silent-movie chase music.

b While you are still catching your breath, sit in a circle and launch immediately into a reading of the next scene. This way you'll gain an appreciation of how Shakespeare effects a dramatic change in tone and pace between Scenes 1 and 2.

gastness terrified look

'Las alas

'scaped escaped

Go know of find out from

I therefore shake not I'm not afraid to say so
charge order

Foh! (an expression of contempt)
dressed have wounds treated

afore ahead
fordoes me quite ruins me completely

Stay you, good gentlemen. Look you pale, mistress? 105
Do you perceive the gastness of her eye?
[*To Bianca*] Nay, if you stare, we shall hear more anon.
Behold her well; I pray you, look upon her.
Do you see, gentlemen? Nay, guiltiness
Will speak, though tongues were out of use. 110

Enter EMILIA.

EMILIA   'Las, what's the matter? What's the matter, husband?
IAGO   Cassio hath here been set on in the dark
             By Roderigo and fellows that are 'scaped.
             He's almost slain and Roderigo dead.
EMILIA   Alas, good gentleman! Alas, good Cassio! 115
IAGO   This is the fruits of whoring. Prithee, Emilia,
             Go know of Cassio where he supped tonight.
             [*To Bianca*] What, do you shake at that?
BIANCA   He supped at my house, but I therefore shake not.
IAGO   O, did he so? I charge you go with me. 120
EMILIA   O, fie upon thee, strumpet!
BIANCA   I am no strumpet, but of life as honest
             As you that thus abuse me.
EMILIA   As I? Foh! Fie upon thee!
IAGO   Kind gentlemen, let's go see poor Cassio dressed.
             Come, mistress, you must tell's another tale. 125
             Emilia, run you to the citadel
             And tell my lord and lady what hath happed.
             Will you go on afore? [*Aside*] This is the night
             That either makes me, or fordoes me quite.

                                                    Exeunt

Othello reasons why Desdemona needs to die and that the dead cannot be restored to life. He kisses her and nearly abandons his intent to kill her, but resolves that she must die.

Language in the play
Othello's soliloquy (in pairs)

a Read through Othello's soliloquy (lines 1–22), swapping the reading at each full stop, colon or semi-colon. Discuss what you think Othello means in this speech.

b Rewrite this soliloquy in modern English, without using any euphemisms, metaphors or imagery.

c Talk about Othello's language in the original script. What are the key differences between your plain version and Shakespeare's? What effects do you think such language might have at this moment in the play? How might it position the audience to respond?

d A soliloquy can be seen as a form of internal dialogue, where a character develops an argument focused on a core dilemma. Consider ways of performing this speech as if it is a conversation. Experiment with ways of dividing up the speech, and how to say the words to create different effects. Decide how you might stand, move, use different volumes and so on.

e In your Director's Journal, write some notes advising the actor playing Othello on how to deliver the lines. Then share your ideas with the rest of the class, either presenting the speech as a 'two-hander' or with a single person speaking the lines.

It (i.e. adultery)

whiter … than snow skin that's whiter than snow

alabaster pale stone used for monuments

betray be unfaithful to

flaming minister burning torch

Should if

cunning'st most intricate

pattern model or exemplar to be copied

Promethean heat (in Greek mythology, Prometheus stole fire from the gods and used it to give life to mortals)

relume light again

sword traditional symbol of justice

1 Othello's 'cause' (in small groups)

Othello repeats the word 'cause' three times in the opening three lines of the scene. This word could carry several meanings:

- an action that prompts a reaction (Desdemona's infidelity)
- a morally justifiable end that one is pursuing, 'all in a good cause' (Othello wishing to protect 'more men' and restore moral order)
- a legal usage describing an accusation brought against someone in court (Othello sees himself as an agent of impartial justice – but at lines 16–17, as he kisses her, his emotions threaten to reject his role as a minister of 'justice').

Take the phrase 'It is the cause' and illustrate the three meanings above in a way that relates to Othello's situation and state of mind at this point in the play. Use whatever dramatic method of presentation seems appropriate to you (for example, mime, tableaux, improvisation).

It strikes … love (a biblical phrase: 'for whom the Lord loveth, he chasteneth')

Act 5 Scene 2
Cyprus   Desdemona's bedchamber

Enter OTHELLO, *with a light, and* DESDEMONA *in bed.*

OTHELLO It is the cause, it is the cause, my soul:
Let me not name it to you, you chaste stars.
It is the cause. Yet I'll not shed her blood,
Nor scar that whiter skin of hers than snow
And smooth as monumental alabaster —   5
Yet she must die, else she'll betray more men.
Put out the light, and then put out the light:
If I quench thee, thou flaming minister,
I can again thy former light restore,
Should I repent me; but once put out thy light,   10
Thou cunning'st pattern of excelling nature,
I know not where is that Promethean heat
That can thy light relume. When I have plucked thy rose,
I cannot give it vital growth again;
It needs must wither. I'll smell it on the tree.   15
He kisses her.
O balmy breath, that dost almost persuade
Justice to break her sword! One more, one more!
Be thus when thou art dead, and I will kill thee
And love thee after. One more, and this the last.
So sweet was ne'er so fatal. I must weep.   20
But they are cruel tears: this sorrow's heavenly —
It strikes where it doth love. She wakes.

Desdemona wakes. Othello orders her to confess her sins before her death. Desdemona, fearful, replies that her only sin is in loving him.

1 Desdemona's last moments (in pairs)

a Desdemona is apparently lying asleep in her bed when Othello enters. In some productions, she passively awaits her fate; in others, she puts up a spirited struggle, physically fighting back as Othello finally smothers her. Discuss what your instructions to the actor would be.

b The photograph below suggests a moment of quiet desperation. To gain a first impression of this final dialogue between husband and wife, take roles as Othello and Desdemona and read lines 23–85, adding movement and action at appropriate points (the script hints at facial expressions and other reactions).

bethink yourself remember
Unreconciled unforgiven, not absolved
Solicit pray for forgiveness
straight at once
I will walk by I'll step aside to give you some privacy (to pray)
unpreparèd (i.e. not prepared for heaven)
forfend forbid

fatal terrible

They are loves I bear to you (i.e. loving a human being more than God)
for loving out of love
nether lower
very frame whole body
portents bad signs for the future
point on point at

DESDEMONA	Who's there? Othello?
OTHELLO	Ay, Desdemona.
DESDEMONA	Will you come to bed, my lord?
OTHELLO	Have you prayed tonight, Desdemon?
DESDEMONA	Ay, my lord.

OTHELLO   If you bethink yourself of any crime
Unreconciled as yet to heaven and grace,
Solicit for it straight.

DESDEMONA   Alack, my lord, what may you mean by that?

OTHELLO   Well, do it, and be brief: I will walk by:
I would not kill thy unpreparèd spirit;
No – heaven forfend! – I would not kill thy soul.

DESDEMONA   Talk you of killing?

OTHELLO   Ay, I do.

DESDEMONA   Then heaven
Have mercy on me!

OTHELLO   Amen, with all my heart!

DESDEMONA   If you say so, I hope you will not kill me.

OTHELLO   Hum!

DESDEMONA   And yet I fear you, for you're fatal then
When your eyes roll so. Why I should fear I know not,
Since guiltiness I know not, but yet I feel I fear.

OTHELLO   Think on thy sins.

DESDEMONA   They are loves I bear to you.

OTHELLO   Ay, and for that thou diest.

DESDEMONA   That death's unnatural that kills for loving.
Alas, why gnaw you so your nether lip?
Some bloody passion shakes your very frame:
These are portents; but yet I hope, I hope
They do not point on me.

Line numbers: 25, 30, 35, 40, 45

Othello accuses Desdemona of giving her handkerchief to Cassio. She denies this, yet Othello is convinced he has enough proof. He tells her that Cassio has confessed to sexual relations with Desdemona, but is now dead.

Themes

'Justice'? (in pairs)

Desdemona's request to 'Send for the man and ask him' (line 50) is reminiscent of Act 1, when Othello calls for Desdemona to support his testimony when Brabantio accuses him of abduction. In that case, the Duke agreed to send for Desdemona, who was able to corroborate Othello's story. Here, Othello cannot hear what the key witness (Cassio) has to say, and he merely accuses Desdemona of 'perjury'. Othello's view of justice and of evidence has changed in the course of the play.

a There is much legal language in this bedroom episode, almost as if it were some kind of courtroom in session, with Othello taking on the roles of both judge and executioner. Read through the script (lines 47–76) and pick out any examples of legal-sounding language you can find. Identify what constitutes the case for the prosecution, what the case for the defence, and what is presented as evidence.

b Perform a version of this section of the scene as if it is taking place in a court of law. Play with the script as much as you like, but retain fragments of the original language. Try playing it in different styles and tones (for example, as a parody of a television courtroom drama). This experiment may help you decide on effective ways of performing the episode on stage.

Characters

Othello the executioner

Othello asks Desdemona the questions he should have asked her in Act 3 or 4. Yet he is on the verge of killing her, and appears not to be interested in any answer that does not match his view of events.

a How do you read Othello's mood? Do you agree with critics who argue that his tone is calm and rational?

b In what ways have directors interpreted this scene? View two movie versions of this scene and try reading Othello's part in different ways (is he calm, quiet, resigned, angry, frustrated?) Write some notes in your Director's Journal, suggesting what advice you would give to the actor playing Othello.

perjury untruthfulness, lying on oath

freely fully
article item in a list of accusations (a legal term)
conception suspicion
do groan withal am pained by, give birth to

general warranty ordinary permission

stone my heart turn my heart to stone

Send for him hither tell him to come here

used thee (i.e. sexually)

his mouth is stopped he has been silenced
tane order for it done the deed
interprets understands
Had ... lives if he had as many lives as he has hairs on his head
stomach appetite

OTHELLO	Peace, and be still!
DESDEMONA	I will so. What's the matter?
OTHELLO	That handkerchief which I so loved and gave thee,
	Thou gav'st to Cassio.
DESDEMONA	No, by my life and soul!
	Send for the man and ask him.
OTHELLO	Sweet soul, take heed.
	Take heed of perjury: thou art on thy death-bed.
DESDEMONA	Ay, but not yet to die.
OTHELLO	Yes, presently.
	Therefore confess thee freely of thy sin;
	For to deny each article with oath
	Cannot remove nor choke the strong conception
	That I do groan withal. Thou art to die.
DESDEMONA	Then Lord have mercy on me!
OTHELLO	I say, Amen.
DESDEMONA	And have you mercy too! I never did
	Offend you in my life; never loved Cassio
	But with such general warranty of heaven
	As I might love. I never gave him token.
OTHELLO	By heaven, I saw my handkerchief in's hand.
	O perjured woman! Thou dost stone my heart,
	And mak'st me call what I intend to do
	A murder, which I thought a sacrifice.
	I saw the handkerchief.
DESDEMONA	He found it then;
	I never gave it him. Send for him hither;
	Let him confess a truth.
OTHELLO	He hath confessed.
DESDEMONA	What, my lord?
OTHELLO	That he hath used thee.
DESDEMONA	How? Unlawfully?
OTHELLO	Ay.
DESDEMONA	He will not say so.
OTHELLO	No, his mouth is stopped:
	Honest Iago hath tane order for't.
DESDEMONA	O, my fear interprets! What, is he dead?
OTHELLO	Had all his hairs been lives, my great revenge
	Had stomach for them all.

Line numbers: 50, 55, 60, 65, 70, 75

In spite of her pleas, Othello suffocates Desdemona. He is disturbed by Emilia calling from outside the door.

1 Action – avoiding melodrama (in threes)

Take parts and act lines 78–106. Make decisions about the pace, timing of stage directions, positioning and delivery of words to suit the dramatic effect you wish to achieve. Think about the way Othello interprets Desdemona's ironically innocent words: 'Alas, he is betrayed, and I undone.' How do you avoid the scene becoming melodramatic, and therefore bordering on the ridiculous? Share your version with one other group, then discuss any differences of interpretation.

Stagecraft

'He smothers her' (whole class)

The photographs below demonstrate two very different interpretations of the stage direction: 'He smothers her.'

- Discuss how these dramatisations differ in terms of dramatic focus (on Desdemona or on Othello?), force and level of brutality. If you had to choose just one picture to illustrate this page of script, which one would it be, and why?

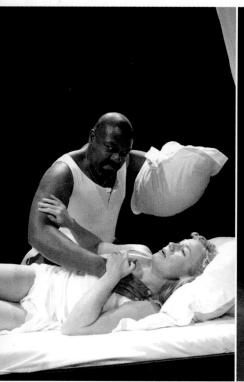

undone ruined

But only
Being done ... pause
now I've started, I can't stop

'Tis like it's likely
high loud

insupportable I can't bear it

globe whole world
yawn tear apart (in an earthquake)
alteration the change (brought about by Desdemona's death)
beseech beg

the curtains draw (on the Globe stage, the bed was probably in the recess behind curtains – see illustration on p. 186; here, Othello closes the curtains)

DESDEMONA	Alas, he is betrayed, and I undone.
OTHELLO	Out, strumpet! Weep'st thou for him to my face?
DESDEMONA	O banish me, my lord, but kill me not!
OTHELLO	Down, strumpet!
DESDEMONA	Kill me tomorrow; let me live tonight!
OTHELLO	Nay, if you strive –
DESDEMONA	But half an hour!
OTHELLO	Being done, there is no pause.
DESDEMONA	But while I say one prayer!
OTHELLO	It is too late.
DESDEMONA	O, Lord, Lord, Lord!

He smothers her.

EMILIA (*Within*) My lord, my lord! What, ho! My lord, my lord!
OTHELLO What noise is this? Not dead? Not yet quite dead?
I that am cruel am yet merciful;
I would not have thee linger in thy pain.
So, so.
EMILIA (*Within*) What, ho! My lord, my lord!
OTHELLO Who's there?
EMILIA [*Within*] O, good my lord, I would speak a word with you.
OTHELLO Yes – 'tis Emilia – by and by. – She's dead.
'Tis like she comes to speak of Cassio's death:
The noise was high. Ha! No more moving?
Still as the grave. Shall she come in? Were't good?
I think she stirs again. No. What's best to do?
If she come in, she'll sure speak to my wife –
My wife, my wife! What wife? I have no wife.
O insupportable! O heavy hour!
Methinks it should be now a huge eclipse
Of sun and moon, and that th'affrighted globe
Should yawn at alteration.
EMILIA [*Within*] I do beseech you
That I may speak with you. O, good my lord!
OTHELLO I had forgot thee. O, come in, Emilia.
Soft, by and by. Let me the curtains draw.
Where art thou?

[*He unlocks the door.*]

What's the matter with thee now?

80

85

90

95

100

105

Emilia reports that Roderigo is dead but Cassio lives. Desdemona revives briefly, only to protect her husband in her dying breath. Othello confesses to Emilia and attempts to explain.

Characters

Desdemona's death (in small groups)

Even in her dying breath, Desdemona supports her husband. She tells a lie on her death-bed, in an attempt to protect him from a murder charge. Do you admire her for her faithfulness, or do you find her action difficult to believe – even within the social and historical context of the play? Is it possible to regard Desdemona as a dramatic construct rather than as a 'real' person or character?

a Discuss your attitudes to the way Desdemona has been portrayed in Scene 2. Focus your discussion on:

- how twenty-first century readers might react to Desdemona
- how a reader's gender and culture might affect the way he or she sees Desdemona
- how Desdemona reflects early seventeenth-century attitudes to women and marriage (the research you did as part of Activity 1 on p. 28 may help with this)
- how Desdemona as a dramatic figure embodies or relates to the play's themes and concerns (see also pp. 224–5)
- whether it is possible to reconcile the earlier Desdemona of Act 1 with the one here in Act 5.

b Present your views to the rest of the class and explore any differences of opinion.

Themes

Contrasts and opposites (in pairs)

The script opposite contains a number of sharply contrasting images:

- angel/devil
- false/true
- water/fire
- hell/heavenly
- sweet/harsh.

Locate each pair and explore ways of presenting them through movement only (mime). After this physical activity, talk together about the significance of each pair of contrasts in their dramatic context (e.g. what they suggest about characters, themes or mood).

error of the moon
moon straying off course
(the influence of the moon
was said to cause madness)
was wont used to do

out of tune gone wrong

like a liar like the liar that she is

folly sin
belie tells lies about
false as water (proverbial saying)

Enter EMILIA.

EMILIA	O, my good lord, yonder's foul murders done.
OTHELLO	What? Now?
EMILIA	But now, my lord.
OTHELLO	It is the very error of the moon: 110
	She comes more nearer earth than she was wont
	And makes men mad.
EMILIA	Cassio, my lord, hath killed a young Venetian
	Called Roderigo.
OTHELLO	Roderigo killed?
	And Cassio killed?
EMILIA	No, Cassio is not killed. 115
OTHELLO	Not Cassio killed! Then murder's out of tune,
	And sweet revenge grows harsh.
DESDEMONA	O, falsely, falsely murdered!
EMILIA	O Lord! What cry is that?
OTHELLO	That? What?
EMILIA	Out and alas, that was my lady's voice! 120
	[*She draws the bed-curtains.*]
	Help, help, ho, help! O, lady, speak again!
	Sweet Desdemona, O sweet mistress, speak!
DESDEMONA	A guiltless death I die.
EMILIA	O, who hath done this deed?
DESDEMONA	Nobody; I myself. Farewell. 125
	Commend me to my kind lord. O farewell! *She dies*
OTHELLO	Why, how should she be murdered?
EMILIA	Alas, who knows?
OTHELLO	You heard her say herself it was not I.
EMILIA	She said so; I must needs report the truth.
OTHELLO	She's like a liar gone to burning hell: 130
	'Twas I that killed her.
EMILIA	O, the more angel she,
	And you the blacker devil!
OTHELLO	She turned to folly, and she was a whore.
EMILIA	Thou dost belie her, and thou art a devil.
OTHELLO	She was false as water.
EMILIA	Thou art rash as fire to say 135
	That she was false. O, she was heavenly true!

Othello reveals that Iago gave him the details of Desdemona's infidelity. Emilia increasingly questions Iago's part in Othello's story and curses them both. She is unmoved by Othello's threats and calls for help.

Write about it

'honest, honest Iago' (in threes)

Emilia's shocked response, and the ten repetitions of the word 'husband', culminate in Othello's exclamation: 'My friend, thy husband, honest, honest Iago.'

a Produce a series of tableaux based on your interpretation of line 153. Take digital photos of each.

b Using the three photographs from the activity above as stimulus, write three paragraphs about 'honest' Iago in his roles as:

- husband
- friend
- colleague.

1 'Ha!'

Speed-write (five minutes only) what you think Othello means by his exclamation 'Ha!' at line 157. Compare your notes with others and discuss what led to your interpretation.

top her mount her (i.e. have sex with her)
else if you don't believe it
But except
extremity final punishment (legal term)

entire pure
chrysolite a semi-precious stone

told me on told me about

iterance repetition
made mocks with mocked

pernicious evil
half a grain a day very slowly
to th'heart completely
too fond of infatuated with
filthy bargain (i.e. she paid a high price for her choice of husband)
no more worthy heaven damnable
Peace … best you'd better keep quiet
gull fool
dolt idiot
I care not … sword don't threaten me with your sword

204

OTHELLO	Cassio did top her: ask thy husband else.
	O, I were damned beneath all depth in hell
	But that I did proceed upon just grounds
	To this extremity. Thy husband knew it all.	140
EMILIA	My husband?
OTHELLO	Thy husband.
EMILIA	That she was false to wedlock?
OTHELLO	Ay, with Cassio. Nay, had she been true,
	If heaven would make me such another world
	Of one entire and perfect chrysolite,
	I'd not have sold her for it.
EMILIA	My husband?	145
OTHELLO	Ay, 'twas he that told me on her first;
	An honest man he is, and hates the slime
	That sticks on filthy deeds.
EMILIA	My husband?
OTHELLO	What needs this iterance, woman? I say thy husband.
EMILIA	O mistress, villainy hath made mocks with love!	150
	My husband say that she was false?
OTHELLO	He, woman;
	I say thy husband. Dost understand the word?
	My friend, thy husband, honest, honest Iago.
EMILIA	If he say so, may his pernicious soul
	Rot half a grain a day! He lies to th'heart.	155
	She was too fond of her most filthy bargain.
OTHELLO	Ha!
EMILIA	Do thy worst.
	This deed of thine is no more worthy heaven
	Than thou wast worthy her.
OTHELLO	Peace, you were best.	160
EMILIA	Thou has not half that power to do me harm
	As I have to be hurt. O gull! O dolt!
	As ignorant as dirt. Thou hast done a deed –
	I care not for thy sword – I'll make thee known,
	Though I lost twenty lives. Help! help! ho, help!	165
	The Moor hath killed my mistress. Murder, murder!

Montano, Gratiano and Iago come to investigate Emilia's cries of murder. She challenges Iago about what he has told Othello about Desdemona. Iago orders her home.

1 Four key moments (in sixes)

Imagine freezing the action on stage at four key moments:

- 'Disprove this villain, if thou be'st a man.' (line 171)
- 'O monstrous act!' (line 189)
- 'What, are you mad?' (line 193)
- 'thou hast killed the sweetest innocent / That e'er did lift up eye' (lines 198–9).

Take roles, and for each 'moment' create a still picture that you can hold for at least thirty seconds. Within each tableau, select a key character who can step out and describe their thoughts or fears at that precise moment. Present your four moments to the rest of the class in a sequence.

Language in the play

Repetition: dramatic effect (in pairs)

Throughout this part of the script, characters have a tendency to repeat certain words or phrases (for example, 'lie' and 'villainy').

a Talk together about the dramatic effect of each repetition.

b The interjection, 'O', is used eight times in the script opposite (uttered by Emilia, Montano, Othello – and even chorused by everyone on stage at one point). Find all these instances and experiment with how it might be said on each occasion. Look in particular at Othello's 'O! O! O!' at line 197. What might 'O' mean here? Does each 'O' mean the same thing?

Characters

Emilia's rebellion

''Tis proper I obey him, but not now', declares Emilia at line 195. Increasingly in this scene, Emilia takes centre stage.

a Using the knowledge you've gained about acceptable wifely behaviour, what social and financial repercussions would this act of rebellion carry for Emilia?

b Not only does Emilia show great courage (for example, 'I care not for thy sword', line 164), but she is also the one character who has worked out what's been going on. What does this episode add to your understanding of her character?

---

lay their murders … neck blame you for their murders

false unfaithful

apt reasonable

charm hold still

set the murder on caused the murder

strange unbelievable

'Tis proper it is right that

roar howl

Enter MONTANO, GRATIANO *and* IAGO.

MONTANO	What is the matter? How now, general?
EMILIA	O, are you come, Iago? You have done well,
	That men must lay their murders on your neck.
GRATIANO	What is the matter?
EMILIA	Disprove this villain, if thou be'st a man.
	He says thou told'st him that his wife was false.
	I know thou didst not, thou'rt not such a villain.
	Speak, for my heart is full.
IAGO	I told him what I thought, and told no more
	Than what he found himself was apt and true.
EMILIA	But did you ever tell him she was false?
IAGO	I did.
EMILIA	You told a lie, an odious damnèd lie:
	Upon my soul, a lie, a wicked lie!
	She false with Cassio? Did you say with Cassio?
IAGO	With Cassio, mistress. Go to, charm your tongue.
EMILIA	I will not charm my tongue; I am bound to speak:
	My mistress here lies murdered in her bed.
ALL	O, heavens forfend!
EMILIA	And your reports have set the murder on.
OTHELLO	Nay, stare not, masters; it is true indeed.
GRATIANO	'Tis a strange truth.
MONTANO	O monstrous act!
EMILIA	Villainy, villainy, villainy!
	I think upon't, I think – I smell't – O villainy!
	I thought so then; I'll kill myself for grief.
	O villainy, villainy!
IAGO	What, are you mad? I charge you get you home.
EMILIA	Good gentlemen, let me have leave to speak.
	'Tis proper I obey him, but not now.
	Perchance, Iago, I will ne'er go home.
OTHELLO	O! O! O!
	Othello falls on the bed.
EMILIA	Nay, lay thee down and roar,
	For thou hast killed the sweetest innocent
	That e'er did lift up eye.

Line numbers: 170, 175, 180, 185, 190, 195

Othello confesses the murder to Gratiano, who says that Brabantio is dead. Emilia reveals that Iago persuaded her to steal Desdemona's handkerchief and give it to him. Iago tries to silence her.

Themes
Attitudes to women (in pairs)

What do you think of Gratiano's response at lines 203–5 on discovering that Desdemona has just been murdered (remember, Gratiano is a relative of Desdemona)? Some commentators have expressed surprise that he seems more preoccupied with Brabantio's death than Desdemona's. They interpret this as meaning that he blames Desdemona for Brabantio's death. How do you interpret his words?

Write about it
What was 'confessed'?

Othello claims that Desdemona committed 'the act of shame' many times with Cassio, and that 'Cassio confessed it'. Remind yourself exactly what Cassio 'confessed' to, and in what circumstances. There are three versions of this 'confession': Iago's, Othello's and Cassio's. Turn back to Act 4 Scene 1, lines 72–153, to remind yourself of the 'evidence' involved.

- Write three paragraphs – one each for Cassio, Othello and Iago. Each paragraph begins: 'This is what I believe happened in the eavesdropping episode in Act 4 Scene 1.'

1 Dramatic moment (whole class)

At line 221, the stage direction reads: 'Iago draws his sword and threatens Emilia.' Think about the action on stage at this precise moment. A group of five volunteers comes to the front of the class. All take roles, ready to create a tableau. A sixth volunteer steps forward as director and positions the actors. Consider the following:

- Who is looking at whom?
- What are their facial expressions?
- How much distance should there be between specific characters – and why?

New volunteer directors from the rest of the class may step forward in turn to alter positions and explain why they have done so.

I scarce did know you I barely recognised you

uncle (Gratiano is Desdemona's uncle)

shows appears

mortal fatal

Shore … twain tore him apart

Did he live now if he were alive now

turn deed

curse … side drive his guardian angel away

reprobance state of damnation

act of shame adultery

gratify reward

amorous works love-making

recognisance keepsake

'Twill out it (the truth) will come out

north either north wind, or people of the north

by fortune by chance

OTHELLO	[*Standing up.*] O, she was foul!
	I scarce did know you, uncle; there lies your niece, 200
	Whose breath indeed these hands have newly stopped.
	I know this act shows horrible and grim –
GRATIANO	Poor Desdemon, I am glad thy father's dead.
	Thy match was mortal to him, and pure grief
	Shore his old thread in twain. Did he live now, 205
	This sight would make him do a desperate turn,
	Yea, curse his better angel from his side
	And fall to reprobance.
OTHELLO	'Tis pitiful; but yet Iago knows
	That she with Cassio hath the act of shame 210
	A thousand times committed. Cassio confessed it,
	And she did gratify his amorous works
	With that recognisance and pledge of love
	Which I first gave her. I saw it in his hand:
	It was a handkerchief, an antique token 215
	My father gave my mother.
EMILIA	O God! O heavenly God!
IAGO	Zounds, hold your peace!
EMILIA	'Twill out, 'twill out. I peace!
	No, I will speak as liberal as the north;
	Let heaven, and men, and devils, let them all,
	All, all cry shame against me, yet I'll speak. 220
IAGO	Be wise and get you home.
EMILIA	I will not.
	[*Iago draws his sword and threatens Emilia.*]
GRATIANO	Fie,
	Your sword upon a woman!
EMILIA	O thou dull Moor, that handkerchief thou speak'st of
	I found by fortune and did give my husband,
	For often, with a solemn earnestness – 225
	More than indeed belonged to such a trifle –
	He begged of me to steal it.
IAGO	Villainous whore!

Stagecraft

Slow motion (in groups of five or six)

Iago's abuse of Emilia ('Filth, thou liest!') does not stop her telling the truth, and the scene erupts in a flurry of action.

a Act out the stage direction at line 233 in slow motion. Decide how to make the best use of the space you have available, and experiment with different ways of performing this intensely dramatic episode.

b Turn to the picture of an Elizabethan theatre on page 186 and plot the same action in that space. Make notes in your Director's Journal.

1 'honour outlive honesty' – what do you think?

Think about Othello's comment: 'why should honour outlive honesty?' (line 243).

- Write a paragraph explaining what you understand by these words and why they might be considered significant in the context of the whole play.

Themes

Attitudes to women (in pairs)

One commentator points out that the men on stage do nothing to save Emilia's life; indeed, when Montano disarms Othello, he inadvertently saves Iago at Emilia's expense. In her dying words Emilia asks to be laid next to Desdemona's body, but there is no stage direction to indicate whether this happens or not. No one mentions Emilia again.

- How significant do you think this is in light of the theme of attitudes to women? If you were directing the play, how would you want Emilia's final movements and her death to be staged? How would you instruct each of the men on stage to respond? Would Emilia get her final wish to be laid next to Desdemona? If so, how would this be effected (and by whom)?

coxcomb fool

stones thunderbolts
Precious (a term used to intensify abuse)

notorious absolute
recovered taken away from
without from the outside
pass get away

whipster whippersnapper, youngster
honour outlive honesty reputation for honour outlast possession of it
bode foretell
play the swan sing on the point of death
come … to bliss may my soul be saved

of Spain made in Spain (i.e. a high- quality sword)
ice-brook's temper steel strengthened by being plunged into an icy stream
perforce therefore
suffer get hurt
naked unarmed

EMILIA   She give it Cassio! No, alas, I found it
            And I did give't my husband.

IAGO   Filth, thou liest!

EMILIA   By heaven, I do not, I do not, gentlemen.   230
            O murderous coxcomb, what should such a fool
            Do with so good a wife?

OTHELLO   Are there no stones in heaven
            But what serves for the thunder? Precious villain!

            [*Othello runs at Iago; Montano disarms him; Iago stabs Emilia from
            behind and exit.*]

GRATIANO   The woman falls; sure he hath killed his wife.

EMILIA   Ay, ay; O, lay me by my mistress' side.   235

GRATIANO   He's gone, but his wife's killed.

MONTANO   'Tis a notorious villain. Take you this weapon,
            Which I have here recovered from the Moor.
            Come guard the door without; let him not pass,
            But kill him rather. I'll after the same villain,   240
            For 'tis a damnèd slave.

                                    Exeunt Montano and Gratiano

OTHELLO   I am not valiant neither,
            But every puny whipster gets my sword.
            But why should honour outlive honesty?
            Let it go all.

EMILIA   What did thy song bode, lady?
            Hark, canst thou hear me? I will play the swan   245
            And die in music: [*Sings*] 'Willow, willow, willow.'
            Moor, she was chaste; she loved thee, cruel Moor;
            So come my soul to bliss, as I speak true;
            So speaking as I think, I die, I die.   *She dies*

OTHELLO   I have another weapon in this chamber;   250
            It was a sword of Spain, the ice-brook's temper.
            O, here it is. – Uncle, I must come forth.

GRATIANO   (*Within*) If thou attempt it, it will cost thee dear;
            Thou hast no weapon, and perforce must suffer.

OTHELLO   Look in upon me then, and speak with me,   255
            Or naked as I am, I will assault thee.

Othello, now fully realising that he has murdered an innocent woman, expects the punishments of hell. Lodovico and the others return with Iago, and Othello attacks him.

Language in the play
Othello's speech

Some commentators have said that the broken Othello is here attempting to use language to reclaim his former glory as a renowned military leader. This is reflected in his use of:

- metaphor
- hyperbole (exaggeration)
- simple, powerful monosyllables
- grand, poetic language.

a Identify examples of each of these features in lines 257–79. Make notes on the dramatic effectiveness of each. Consider which of these features link to other parts of the play, and make notes explaining these thematic and verbal connections.

b Othello's speech is structured in three parts, corresponding with the three stages of his life: Othello the great warrior; Othello the murderer at his life's end; and Othello tortured in hell. His life's journey is imagined as a sea voyage. Choose one of the following:

- Devise a group presentation, exploring the structure of the speech and its images. Employ whatever dramatic method of presentation seems appropriate to you (words and movement, tableaux, mime or some other form).
- Produce a poster or collage based on the speech, using a sea voyage as the organisational frame.

sustain support

your stop your force as a guard

weaponed armed
butt goal, target
sea-mark beacon
utmost sail last voyage
'Tis a lost fear there's nothing to be afraid of
Man but a rush aim just a reed
ill-starred ill-fated
smock undergarment
compt the Day of Judgement

steep-down gulfs rushing waterfalls

1 Lodovico's entrance: Venetian law restored

With the entrance of Lodovico and Cassio, the controlling force of Venetian law is reintroduced. Lodovico calls on the two defendants as if in a court of law, and presides as if he is a high court judge. But Othello's violence towards Iago momentarily disturbs that order.

- Work out how you would stage the entrance of Lodovico and the others in a way that suggests this return to Venetian authority, following the script in lines 275–84. Block the moves and positioning, either as a class or on your own, using the picture of an Elizabethan theatre on page 186. Write a paragraph justifying your choices in your Director's Journal.

his feet ... fable (the devil was supposed to have cloven feet)

[*Enter Gratiano.*]

GRATIANO   What is the matter?

OTHELLO   Behold, I have a weapon:
A better never did itself sustain
Upon a soldier's thigh. I have seen the day
That with this little arm and this good sword   260
I have made my way through more impediments
Than twenty times your stop. But, O vain boast!
Who can control his fate? 'Tis not so now.
Be not afraid, though you do see me weaponed:
Here is my journey's end, here is my butt   265
And very sea-mark of my utmost sail.
Do you go back dismayed? 'Tis a lost fear:
Man but a rush against Othello's breast,
And he retires. Where should Othello go?
        [*He goes to the bed.*]
Now, how dost thou look now? O ill-starred wench!   270
Pale as thy smock! When we shall meet at compt
This look of thine will hurl my soul from heaven
And fiends will snatch at it. Cold, cold, my girl,
Even like thy chastity.
O cursèd, cursèd slave! Whip me, ye devils,   275
From the possession of this heavenly sight!
Blow me about in winds! Roast me in sulphur!
Wash me in steep-down gulfs of liquid fire!
O Desdemon! Dead Desdemon! Dead! O! O!

Enter LODOVICO, *Montano,* CASSIO *in a chair, Iago in the charge of*
OFFICERS.

LODOVICO   Where is this rash and most unfortunate man?   280

OTHELLO   That's he that was Othello: here I am.

LODOVICO   Where is that viper? Bring the villain forth.

OTHELLO   I look down towards his feet; but that's a fable.
If that thou be'st a devil, I cannot kill thee.
        [*He wounds Iago.*]

Lodovico takes control and investigates the case. Othello asks Cassio's pardon. Letters found in Roderigo's pockets tell of Iago's plot to kill Cassio and of Roderigo's threat to expose Iago. Iago refuses to give any explanation of his conduct.

Characters
Iago: 'I bleed, sir, but not killed'

a Iago's line could be uttered in a variety of ways. How would you advise an actor to say those words? Consider the following suggestions to help in your decision:

- Iago is playing for sympathy.
- He is bitterly sarcastic.
- He is resigned to his fate.
- He is detached and neutral.
- He is utterly defeated, in pain and wants to die.
- He is triumphant, taunting Othello.
- He is chillingly inhuman, hinting at his own indestructibility.

b Watch at least two movie versions of this scene and discuss how each actor cast as Iago plays this line.

c As an additional challenge, discuss why Iago refuses to speak further. Write a paragraph explaining possible reasons for his silence.

1 'An honourable murderer' (in pairs)

Othello claims that he is 'An honourable murderer … For naught did I in hate, but all in honour.' (lines 291–2). What do you make of this paradox – can a murderer be honourable?

- Role-play an imaginary interview between Lodovico and Othello, in which Othello is asked to defend this statement.

Write about it
Two letters

Ludovico reports that two letters have been found in Roderigo's pocket, both helping to explain Iago's plotting. The first is probably written by Iago and 'imports / The death of Cassio' (in other words, laying out instructions and reminding Roderigo why the murder needs to happen). The second is a 'discontented paper' written by Roderigo, probably to Iago or Othello, complaining about the way he has been treated, and wanting to recover the money he has lost.

- Write the two letters.

in my sense the way I feel

practice trap

Torments torture
thou dost best you know best

imports concerns

discontented paper letter of complaint

belike probably
in the nick in the nick of time
Came in intervened
satisfied him stopped his complaints
caitiff wretch, villain

214

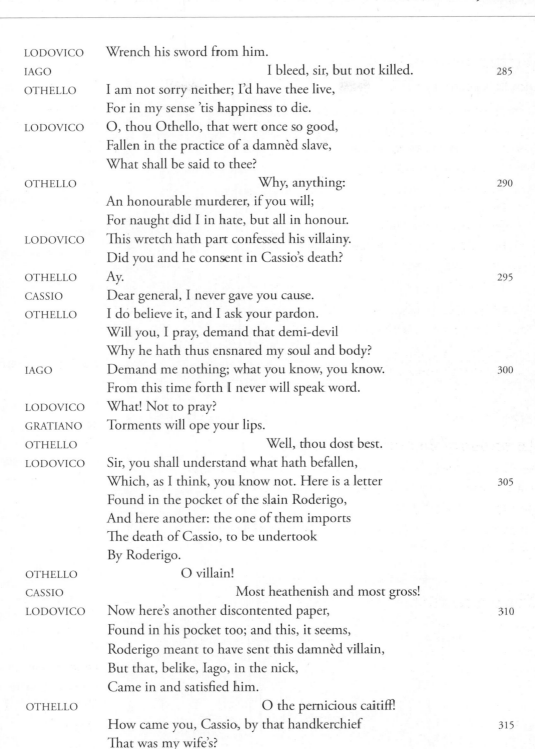

LODOVICO	Wrench his sword from him.	
IAGO	I bleed, sir, but not killed.	285
OTHELLO	I am not sorry neither; I'd have thee live,	
	For in my sense 'tis happiness to die.	
LODOVICO	O, thou Othello, that wert once so good,	
	Fallen in the practice of a damnèd slave,	
	What shall be said to thee?	
OTHELLO	Why, anything:	290
	An honourable murderer, if you will;	
	For naught did I in hate, but all in honour.	
LODOVICO	This wretch hath part confessed his villainy.	
	Did you and he consent in Cassio's death?	
OTHELLO	Ay.	295
CASSIO	Dear general, I never gave you cause.	
OTHELLO	I do believe it, and I ask your pardon.	
	Will you, I pray, demand that demi-devil	
	Why he hath thus ensnared my soul and body?	
IAGO	Demand me nothing; what you know, you know.	300
	From this time forth I never will speak word.	
LODOVICO	What! Not to pray?	
GRATIANO	Torments will ope your lips.	
OTHELLO	Well, thou dost best.	
LODOVICO	Sir, you shall understand what hath befallen,	
	Which, as I think, you know not. Here is a letter	305
	Found in the pocket of the slain Roderigo,	
	And here another: the one of them imports	
	The death of Cassio, to be undertook	
	By Roderigo.	
OTHELLO	O villain!	
CASSIO	Most heathenish and most gross!	
LODOVICO	Now here's another discontented paper,	310
	Found in his pocket too; and this, it seems,	
	Roderigo meant to have sent this damnèd villain,	
	But that, belike, Iago, in the nick,	
	Came in and satisfied him.	
OTHELLO	O the pernicious caitiff!	
	How came you, Cassio, by that handkerchief	315
	That was my wife's?	

Cassio tells how he found the handkerchief, and how Iago used Roderigo. Lodovico pronounces Othello's arrest and Cassio's instatement as governor. Othello asks that his whole story should be truthfully told. He stabs himself.

Write about it
Othello's obituary

Othello's last major speech in the play is in resonant, controlled verse, and amounts to his own obituary (a biographical account celebrating someone's life soon after they have died). He follows the conventions of obituary writers and includes the following elements:

- his service in Venetian colonial exploits (line 335)
- his emotional/love life (line 340)
- his downfall (lines 341–4)
- his last moments (lines 344–7)
- a past great deed (lines 348–52).

Some readers find it difficult to accept all aspects of Othello's own interpretation of his life. He claims he 'loved not wisely, but too well' and that he was 'one not easily jealous but, being wrought, / Perplexed in the extreme'. Both are contentious remarks, open to challenge. And while his claim to have served the state well may be true, that 'truth' is from the point of view of Venetians rather than their foreign subjects.

a Speak lines 334–52 aloud. Familiarise yourself with the language, and experiment with how it might be acted, depending how you interpret Othello's mood and tone at this point.

b Make some brief notes summarising what Othello says about each of the key areas of his life.

c Find published examples of obituaries of famous people in newspapers. Using these as models, write Othello's obituary. Remember, it should celebrate the great general's achievements. Decide which aspects of his life you would emphasise, and which aspects you might choose not to mention. As an additional challenge, try to embed some short quotations from the play in your writing (for example, complimentary comments other characters say about Othello, particularly earlier in the play).

d If you want a further challenge, write an *alternative* obituary. Follow the conventions of obituary writers, but write from the point of view of a Turk (Othello's 'enemy'). Where would it be critical of Othello, and how might the Turkish writer deal with Othello's attitudes: e.g. 'circumcisèd dog'?

but even now only just now

wrought to his desire worked in accordance with his wishes

upbraids tells off
Brave insult
upon the watch while I was on guard
cast dismissed
set him on incited him
forsake leave

hold him long make him suffer for a long time
close prisoner rest be kept under lock and key

Soft you just a moment

unlucky unfortunate
nothing extenuate do not make excuses
set down write
wisely moderately
wrought provoked
Perplexed in the extreme completely bewildered
base Indian (Native Americans were famed for their 'ignorance' about the value of precious gems)
subdued overcome
the melting mood weeping
medicinal gum myrrh (sap much prized for its healing properties, from particular species of Arabian tree)
traduced insulted
circumcisèd dog (i.e. Muslim soldier)
smote stabbed

CASSIO	I found it in my chamber;	
	And he himself confessed but even now	
	That there he dropped it for a special purpose	
	Which wrought to his desire.	
OTHELLO	O fool, fool, fool!	
CASSIO	There is besides in Roderigo's letter	320
	How he upbraids Iago, that he made him	
	Brave me upon the watch, whereon it came	
	That I was cast; and even but now he spake –	
	After long seeming dead – Iago hurt him,	
	Iago set him on.	325
LODOVICO	You must forsake this room and go with us.	
	Your power and your command is taken off	
	And Cassio rules in Cyprus. For this slave,	
	If there be any cunning cruelty	
	That can torment him much and hold him long	330
	It shall be his. You shall close prisoner rest	
	Till that the nature of your fault be known	
	To the Venetian state. Come, bring him away.	
OTHELLO	Soft you; a word or two before you go.	
	I have done the state some service and they know't:	335
	No more of that. I pray you, in your letters	
	When you shall these unlucky deeds relate,	
	Speak of me as I am; nothing extenuate,	
	Nor set down aught in malice. Then must you speak	
	Of one that loved not wisely, but too well;	340
	Of one not easily jealous but, being wrought,	
	Perplexed in the extreme; of one whose hand,	
	Like the base Indian, threw a pearl away	
	Richer than all his tribe; of one whose subdued eyes,	
	Albeit unusèd to the melting mood,	345
	Drops tears as fast as the Arabian trees	
	Their medicinable gum. Set you down this;	
	And say besides that in Aleppo once	
	Where a malignant and a turbaned Turk	
	Beat a Venetian and traduced the state,	350
	I took by th'throat the circumcisèd dog	
	And smote him thus.	

He stabs himself.

217

Othello dies beside Desdemona. Lodovico awards Othello's possessions to Gratiano, and orders Cassio to decide Iago's punishment. Lodovico leaves to report in full to the Venetian state.

Write about it
Lodovico's report

Lodovico states his intention of going immediately to Venice to make his formal report of events to the Senate. Write his report.

1 'he was great of heart' (in pairs)

In lines 334–52, Othello imagined what his obituary would be like. Here, Cassio's words about the dead Othello are the closest anyone comes to a real obituary or eulogy. Othello is hardly mentioned in the closing lines of the play and attention is drawn to Iago.

- Talk together about the dramatic effect of this decision to focus on Iago.

Stagecraft
A final image (in large groups)

What last image would you want an audience to be left with in a production of *Othello*? The final stage direction ('*Exeunt*') is for all the remaining actors to go off, but there are important choices for a director to make. For example, would you have them all leaving together? Would you want the bodies on the bed to be spot-lit or obscured by curtains – and where does Emilia's corpse lie? Might you wish to end with a tableau involving all or some of the remaining characters? Should there be some music or other sound effects, or complete silence? Discuss, and stage your final image.

▼ How does this staging of the final moments of the play compare with your own interpretation?

period conclusion

great of heart of great courage
Spartan dog (the legendary hounds of Sparta in Greece were extremely savage)
fell cruel
object spectacle

keep stay in
seize upon take legal possession of
they succeed on you you inherit them
censure judgement
Myself … abroad I'll head straight back to Venice

LODOVICO	O bloody period!
GRATIANO	All that's spoke is marred!
OTHELLO	I kissed thee ere I killed thee: no way but this,
	Killing myself, to die upon a kiss.

355

He [falls on the bed and] dies

CASSIO	This did I fear, but thought he had no weapon,
	For he was great of heart.
LODOVICO	[*To Iago*] O Spartan dog,
	More fell than anguish, hunger, or the sea,
	Look on the tragic loading of this bed:
	This is thy work. The object poisons sight;
	Let it be hid.

360

[*The bed-curtains are drawn.*]

      Gratiano, keep the house
And seize upon the fortunes of the Moor,
For they succeed on you. To you, lord governor,
Remains the censure of this hellish villain:
The time, the place, the torture, O, enforce it!

365

Myself will straight aboard, and to the state
This heavy act with heavy heart relate.

Exeunt

Looking back at the play
Activities for groups or individuals

1 Fifteen-minute version

Split into five groups, with each group taking one act of the play. Produce a three-minute version of your chosen act, using only words from the script. When you are ready, put each of the five acts together in turn to create a fifteen-minute version of the whole play. As a variation, you could try performing each act in a different style (soap opera, documentary, slapstick comedy, melodrama).

2 Production matters

Imagine you are planning a production of *Othello*.
In groups, discuss and then execute the following tasks:

- At what point in the play would you have the interval? Explain your decision.
- What music will you play as the audience settles in at the start, or as people leave at the end of the play? Justify your choices.
- Design a poster, publicity material (flyers) and a programme cover.
- Write the programme notes for your production.
- Draw up a cast list, indicating which characters could 'double up' their parts.

3 Coroner's investigation (written version)

Three or four corpses – one suicide and three suspected murders – all in the space of one evening! The coroner in Cyprus would be kept busy investigating the full circumstances of each of the deaths.

- Compile the coroner's dossier. It includes eye-witness statements, psychiatric reports, post-mortem reports, and any other relevant documentation about the deceased. Include mock-ups of army personnel files, newspaper cuttings and personal letters. Use your imagination! Work in small groups and produce a large display of the various examples of written 'evidence'. (See also pp. 228–9.)

4 Production photographs

Look through all the photographs in this edition, including those in the photo gallery at the start. Choose three or four images that most appeal to you. Consider costume, style and colour. Use them as inspiration for a piece of analytical writing, explaining what you find interesting about their interpretations of characters or particular moments of the play. Include key quotations from the script to support your points.

5 The myth of the handkerchief

a How significant is Desdemona's 'napkin', which Emilia finds and gives to Iago in Act 3 Scene 3? Trace its history and meaning as it is passed from person to person in the course of the play. (See Act 3 Scene 3, lines 288–330; Act 3 Scene 4, lines 48–96; Act 4 Scene 1, lines 142–91.)

b Each person takes one of the following roles:

- Bianca
- Egyptian charmer
- Iago
- Cassio
- Othello
- Othello's mother
- Desdemona
- Emilia.

Pass an appropriately decorated handkerchief or tissue from person to person in the correct order; when the 'napkin' is passed to you, state who you are, how you got it and what you believe to be its significance.

c Discuss how far the napkin serves merely as a plot device, or whether it becomes richly symbolic as the play progresses. Also, discuss how it links the female characters in the play.

OTHELLO

Perspectives and themes

What is the play about?

Traditionally, answers to this question have focused on characters or themes. Themes are ideas or concerns that are dramatically explored or presented in different ways as the play develops. In *Othello*, such themes include: jealousy; appearance versus reality; reputation; public versus private concerns; and racism. In recent years, developments in literary theory have led to several different ways of approaching Shakespeare, and each of these provides different answers to the question 'What is *Othello* about?'

Cultural materialist criticism – this argues that the play offers a subversive critique of the social and political beliefs of Shakespeare's time (and shows how changing beliefs have shaped subsequent readings). For example, racism and sexism in *Othello* are seen as inherent in the way early (and late) capitalist society is structured, rather than simply located in individuals.

Feminist criticism – this emphasises the importance of the three female characters, and explores the limits imposed on their freedom to act. It shows how gender has constructed traditional (male) readings of the play, accusing it of having a 'domestic' focus. So, traditional criticism tends to idealise Desdemona as a submissive wife, whilst diminishing the roles of Emilia and Bianca.

New historicist criticism – this places the play firmly in its historical context, and explores ideas about society and power that were current in Shakespeare's time. New historicists may be interested in apparent acts of subversion, and the way these moments of disorder are contained within the action of the play. One focus, therefore, might be on Othello as a self-made man, who represents a move away from the medieval belief in humans' fixed place in society.

Performance criticism – this explores *Othello* as performance text, analysing past and present theatrical productions. Through the centuries, different productions have reflected changing interpretations of *Othello*. In more recent years, this also encompasses film and other moving-image performances.

Post-colonial criticism – this exposes European colonial attitudes towards race and difference as reflected in literary texts. It explores cultural assumptions of superiority and what it is to be 'civilised', highlighting, for example, the way Othello is presented as both intriguingly exotic and threateningly savage.

Post-modernist criticism – here, the focus is on the script itself, rather than on its context. Post-modernist criticism stresses how meaning is hard to pin down, as in the concepts of 'honesty' and 'justice', for example.

Psychoanalytical criticism – this focuses on undercurrents of desire, and repressed sexuality. For example, Iago's attitudes to sex and women offer a productive starting point for analysis, with some commentators suggesting latent homosexuality as an explanation of his behaviour towards Othello.

At the heart of modern forms of criticism is the belief that all interpretation carries certain assumptions (for example, about society, literature, political issues in the play). No interpretation is the 'correct one', and in each case, evidence must be sought to illustrate the reading.

◆ Choose a critical approach from the list above, then pick at least two scenes or dramatic moments from *Othello* and explain how they can be interpreted in a way that supports your selected reading. Write five paragraphs arguing why the play should be read in this way.

Characters

This section offers a number of activities that will help you explore different views of 'character'. These combine more traditional ideas about characterisation with broader considerations of the thematic, dramatic and political functions of the characters in *Othello*.

Traditional approaches to 'character'

Character analysis has traditionally been regarded as the key to understanding any Shakespeare play. One of the most influential writers about Shakespearean tragedy, A. C. Bradley, said that the plays told universal truths about human existence.

Early twentieth-century criticism therefore tended to focus on Othello as a tragic hero. Critics have applied ancient Greek ideas on tragedy (notably those of Aristotle), and assumed that the tragic hero is a mixture of admirable qualities and a fatal tragic flaw. Much twentieth-century criticism was dominated by debates about whether Othello's 'flaw' is jealousy (triggered by the malevolent Iago) or his inherent egotism and self-centredness. This approach usually treats characters as if they were living people, with real feelings, thoughts and lives that go beyond the confines of the play.

However, there are problems with such readings. It has been argued that Elizabethan and Jacobean playwrights were not concerned with constructing psychologically consistent 'characters'. Indeed, there is evidence that certain 'character traits' would be conveyed to audiences on Shakespeare's stage through 'stock' gestures and signalled by types of costume, so when it came to dramatic roles, 'realism' was highly unlikely. It may be that the fascination with tragic heroes emerged some time during the nineteenth century – the time of the great Victorian actor-managers, famed for their starring roles – and further influenced by the kind of characterisation developed in the novels of the time. Some critics and historians have suggested that Victorian moralists were interested in using Shakespeare's characters as examples for moral guidance.

◆ In small groups, discuss how you might apply the idea of the tragically flawed noble hero to Othello. Give examples of things Othello says and does that might be termed 'noble' or 'heroic', then describe what goes wrong for him. How far can his downfall be ascribed to external factors (such as a hostile society or Iago's hatred), and how far should it be blamed on a 'flaw' in his own character?

◆ In 1693, Thomas Rymer (the earliest recorded critic of *Othello*) suggested that the play's central lesson was that 'maidens of quality' should not 'run away with Blackamoors'. What 'moral lesson' could you draw from the play today?

Alternative approaches to character

Shakespeare was writing at a time of rapid change – socially, politically and economically. Today, many critics argue that his audiences were more concerned with the interplay between characters and the exchange of ideas in the plays.

Much recent literary theory assumes that the most important aspect of a character is his or her dramatic function within the social and political context of the play. As such, characters embody the themes and wider concerns of the play, and they exist only while on stage, within a dramatically created world. (See the activity on Roderigo's role on p. 227 for a further exploration of this idea.)

Themes most commonly identified in *Othello* include:
appearance and reality; opposites (such as loyalty
and disloyalty, honesty and dishonesty, light and dark);
the position of women; the importance of reputation;
alienation/belonging; justice.

◆ Consider which characters most contribute to
an understanding of each of the themes above
and in what way. In pairs, create a poster for a
classroom display.

The representation of women

*Nowhere in Shakespeare are relations between males
and females more searchingly, painfully probed.*
                                    Marilyn French, 1982

There are only three women in the play, and each of
them is bound up in a relationship with a man. Only
one survives.

◆ In small groups, consider the roles of the three
women. Discuss the following list of statements in
turn, deciding which you agree or disagree with:

a All three women are presented according to
   men's interpretations.

b The women are completely passive.

c Each woman is defined in terms of her
   male partner.

d Women are fully emancipated in the play.

e Each woman stands for an aspect of
   'womanhood' – romantic idealist, practical
   realist and sex object.

f Each relationship provokes jealousy in
   one partner.

g Women's roles in the play are ambiguous.

h The women are all portrayed as stupid.

i Men hold all the power in Venetian society.

j Each woman comes from a different social class,
   and that is significant.

k Women talk the most sense in the play.

l The women are bonded by a notion of
   'sisterhood'.

m The women are more trusting than the men.

n The men use abusive terms to refer to women;
   women don't use abusive terms back.

o All three women have identical attitudes to men
   and relationships.

◆ Select the three statements you most agree with
and write a short paragraph for each, explaining
your reasons. Then choose the statement you most
disagree with, and write a further paragraph giving
your arguments.

◆ Choose two or three quotations from the play
that seem to say something important about the
presentation of one or all of the women characters.
Put the lines together into a short oral, dramatic
or written presentation that sums up your
conclusions. Think about the way language
'normalises' gender roles.

◆ In the UK there is a long-running BBC radio programme called *Woman's Hour*, in which all sorts of women's issues are discussed, including current news events. Imagine that Emilia, Desdemona and Bianca have been invited on to the Venetian version of *Woman's Hour* to discuss their views on marriage, immediately after the announcement that society beauty Desdemona has independently arranged her own marriage to Othello. Find all the key scenes where the three women air their contrasting views. The table below will help you locate some of these.

Character	Scene
Desdemona	Act 1 Scene 3, lines 244–55; Act 2 Scene 1, lines 100–60; Act 3 Scene 3, lines 45–89
Emilia	Act 2 Scene 1, lines 100–60; Act 3 Scene 4, lines 97–100; Act 3 Scene 4, lines 153–6
Bianca	Act 3 Scene 4, lines 163–95

◆ In groups of four, improvise the studio discussion. Try to incorporate some of each woman's actual words from the play, and aim to bring out their contrasting views. For example, how might Desdemona and Emilia relate to Bianca?

◆ Some critics believe that each woman's love for their man is much stronger than the love or loyalty they feel for each other as women. All three are underestimated and abused by the men they love. Use your experience of *Othello* to write an essay on the claim that: 'The real tragedy for Desdemona, Emilia and Bianca is that their marital and emotional bonds take precedence over their common cause as women.'

225

How Othello changes

In the course of the play, Othello apparently changes from the 'noble Moor' to a 'devil' and a 'murderous coxcomb'. In Act 1 Scene 2, he speaks with calm authority: 'Keep up your bright swords, for the dew will rust them' (line 59). By the start of Act 4, he is suffering from tortured confusion: 'Pish! Noses, / ears, and lips. Is't possible? – Confess? Handkerchief? O devil!' (lines 40–1).

◆ In groups of five, each person takes one act of the play and researches Othello's role by completing the activities below:

  a Briefly summarise Othello's actions during the course of the act.

  b Note down any significant descriptions of Othello made by other characters.

  c Describe how Othello relates to one other character – pick out a short piece of dialogue that seems significant, and explain why. Look carefully at the language used.

  d Pick out one or two of Othello's speeches that you consider to be particularly dramatic. Are they in verse or prose? What effect does this have?

◆ When each person has completed their individual investigation, pool your research. Discuss any changes you see in Othello in terms of action, relationships and language. Present your findings as graphs, flow diagrams or a storyboard.

◆ Consider whether this research provides all the evidence that you need to show how Othello changes over the course of the play. Does it tell the 'full story'? What other aspects of Othello's development might you have investigated?

Iago – the malcontent

Iago is a malcontent, a man with a grudge. He puts on the outward appearance of a bluff, honest soldier, but behind that false exterior he manipulates, mentally tortures and betrays Othello. Yet for over four hundred years this deeply malicious figure has fascinated audiences. The following activities invite you to think about him in today's world.

◆ In groups, play around with the character of Iago. If he was a real person, what:

  a would be his favourite movie?

  b would be his favourite book?

  c would be his favourite TV programme?

  d would be his favourite type of music?

  e daily newspaper would he read?

  f football (or other sports) team would he support?

  g would he do for a living?

  h would his leisure activities be?

  i political party might he support?

  j would be his views of key current affairs?

Present your group's ideas to the rest of the class. Be prepared to explain why you made those choices for Iago.

◆ In pairs, create a 'photograph' of Iago with one other character (like the one on the right). The second person's identity should be obvious from their posture, position and facial expression. Show your 'photograph'. The rest of the class guesses who Iago's companion is.

◆ When all pairs have shown their 'photographs', hold a class discussion on why some characters were easier to guess than others, and what all the photographs reveal about Iago (e.g. whether there were differences in the way he was portrayed by each pair).

Cassio – a press conference

◆ One student takes the part of Cassio; others play government advisers (perhaps Montano and Lodovico) and at least one spin-doctor. Prepare a formal statement for Cassio to read out at a press conference, following the deaths of Othello and Desdemona. Prepare answers to questions that journalists are likely to ask. (Which questions might Cassio refuse to answer?)

◆ Other students take on the roles of newspaper and television reporters. Prepare questions about recent events, Cassio's view of Othello and others, his military career, his motivation, interests, feelings, private life and so on. What kind of information will your readers/viewers be interested in? Organise the press conference and role-play the event as a whole class. You could even video it.

Roderigo's role

Shakespeare based *Othello* on a story by a sixteenth-century Italian writer, Giraldo Cinthio, in which a wicked ensign falls in love with a Moorish captain's wife, Disdemona. The ensign grows bitter when she refuses to return his advances, so he tells lies to make the captain believe his wife has been unfaithful. Cinthio's story is much longer and more complicated than Shakespeare's taut, focused version, but the character of Roderigo is entirely Shakespeare's invention and does not exist in the original source.

◆ Write at least three paragraphs exploring what dramatic function Roderigo serves in the play. Think about:

• the various things Iago asks Roderigo to do. Which of these help further the plot, and in what ways?
• what sense you gain of Roderigo from his manner of speaking and how he relates to others
• the ways in which Roderigo provides a contrast to Iago, Othello and Cassio
• the points in the play when Roderigo appears – for example, does each appearance raise or lower the dramatic tension?

The characters – a summary

◆ Make a list of all the 'main' characters in the play (first, you should agree who you would include or exclude in this category). Look back over all the production photographs in this edition, including the photo gallery at the beginning of the book.

◆ When you have made your list, take each character in turn and say what characteristics are emphasised in the various images, making sure you consider age, ethnicity, physical features, facial expressions, clothes and props as appropriate.

◆ For each character, decide which photo best fits your idea of how the role should be portrayed and defend your choice. Feed back to the rest of the class.

▼ Who do you think is the other person with Iago in the production photograph below?

Coroner's investigation

A role-play activity for the whole class

Time: a month after Othello's death.
Place: a coroner's court in Venice.

Create a whole-class role-play around an imaginary coroner's investigation. It provides plenty of scope for getting everyone imaginatively involved in an active investigation of characters' relationships, motivations and the public and private aspects of the play.

The following notes will help focus each participant's preparation for the role-play. Take time to prepare your character and their side of the story, then set the room out as a court. The coroner presides over the hearing and assesses the evidence at the end of the role-play.

Coroner

- Work in a small group with the assistant/usher(s), etc.
- What questions will you put to each character?
- What concrete evidence exists? Any exhibits to use in court (e.g. weapons/letters)?
- Consider how you will shape your questions to elicit full answers (as opposed to 'yes'/'no' replies).

Coroner's assistant

- Assist coroner in running the proceedings.
- Establish an order of events and present it on paper.
- Keep a record of the proceedings of the court..

Montano

- What contact did you have with Othello/Cassio/ Iago? What impressions did you get of them?
- Did you witness any important/significant events at first hand?
- Did Othello live up to his reputation?.

Duke of Venice

- How will you behave in court?
- Which characters did you know well?
- What relevant evidence do you have for the court?
- How do you now see your position in relation to the whole Cyprus venture?
- Do you feel any sense of responsibility for what has happened?

Iago

- Will you offer any defence? Why might you be persuaded to talk?
- What motivation exists for your acts? (Look up your major speeches and soliloquies.)
- Why do you think Cassio got the job of Othello's second-in-command instead of you?
- What do you think of other characters?

Bianca

- What contact did you have with any of the main characters?
- Were there any significant events you witnessed at first hand?
- How do you regard your position in this society?

Lodovico

- What is your considered opinion about the cause of the deaths?
- What do you think of Othello's behaviour in the time you knew him?
- What relevant events were you present at?
- How do you see your position in relation to the whole Cyprus venture?

Roderigo

- Yes – you live! (See Act 5 Scene 2, lines 323–4 – you might be walking with difficulty.)
- What happened at your meetings with Iago?
- What was your part in his plots?
- What do you now think of Iago, Desdemona, Cassio, Othello?
- What did you say to Cassio before the brawl?
- Where have you been for the past month?

Cassio

- What is your version of events?
- Who seems to blame?
- What is your opinion of Othello now?
- What was Othello like to serve under?
- Why did you get promoted over Iago?
- What do you look forward to?

A Gentleman of Cyprus

- At what important event were you present?
- Why were you there?
- Give your version of the occasion.
- What is your reaction to the tragic deaths, and how do you feel about the continuation of Venetian rule?

Clown

- Who employed you?
- What messages were you given and to whom were you sent?
- What was your impression of the people you came into contact with?
- How would you describe their changing moods?
- Consider how you might act/speak in court (terrible puns, for instance).

Gratiano

- How do you feel about the deaths of your brother and niece?
- How has your family in Venice reacted?
- Could you have done anything to prevent the tragedy?
- What eye-witness accounts can you offer the court?

Other roles (if needed)

Jury members, court ushers – could be involved in helping others to prepare their roles, or be responsible for creating exhibits (letters, etc.)

The language of *Othello*

Dramatic language

Shakespeare was writing for theatre conditions that were very different from those common today – open-air stages with no electric light. There was little in the way of scenery, and few props. Playwrights therefore had to create atmosphere, mood and setting almost entirely through language.

◆ Below are some examples of this kind of language in *Othello*. In each case, identify where the quotation comes from and who is speaking. Then find other examples of each feature in the script:

   a Embedded stage directions: 'Look where she comes!'; 'Iago beckons me'.

   b Setting the scene: 'What from the cape can you discern at sea?'; 'on the brow o'the sea / Stand ranks of people'; 'Strike on the tinder, ho!'; 'Light, I say, light!' (indicating it's night-time).

   c Voicing a character's 'thoughts': this could be done through asides or soliloquies. For examples of how a soliloquy might be staged see pages 44 and 88. A number of asides reveal inner thoughts and sometimes emphasise dramatic irony: 'I am not merry, but I do beguile / The thing I am by seeming otherwise'; 'He takes her by the palm'; 'By heaven, that should be my handkerchief!'.

Verse and prose

Like most playwrights at the time, Shakespeare wrote poetic drama, mostly in **iambic pentameter** – lines that are made up of a basic five-beat rhythm. This rhythm is thought to be the one that most closely echoes everyday speech patterns (da DUM, da DUM, da DUM, da DUM, da DUM), and when spoken aloud a line is said to last as long as a normal human breath. However, Shakespeare also varied the way he wrote lines of his scripts, playing around with the five beats, sometimes using **rhyming couplets**, sometimes using prose, depending on the effect he wanted to create.

Verse

Shakespeare traditionally gave verse to his high-status characters. Othello's early speeches are in iambic pentameter. Lines are often run on (**enjambement**) as ideas are developed in a coherent and confident way (e.g. Act 1 Scene 3, lines 76–94). In contrast, Iago's speeches are often **end-stopped** or have a mid-line **caesura** (pause). This suggests he is a plain-speaking man.

Prose

Prose is commonly used by comic or low-status characters – for example, the Clown and the Musician speak in prose. (Surprisingly, the Herald's announcement at the beginning of Act 2 Scene 2 is not in prose.)

However, Shakespeare sometimes alternates between verse and prose in order to change the mood and tone of a scene. An example is when Othello and Cassio speak in verse together at the beginning of Act 2 Scene 3, but as the scene progresses and Cassio becomes more drunk, he switches to prose. Iago, of course, skilfully switches between the two. His use of prose gives the impression of informal talk, taking others into his confidence, whereas his soliloquies are in verse.

◆ Trace Othello's speeches through the course of the play. Where does his syntax (sentence structure) begin to fall apart? How is his state of mind reflected in his language? To help you, look at two or three of his major speeches. For example: his first full speech in front of the Senate (Act 1 Scene 3, lines 76–94); his 'general camp' speech to Iago (Act 3 Scene 3, lines 346–58); his speech directly before he falls into a trance (Act 4 Scene 1, lines 35–41). As an extension, go on to consider what happens to Othello's language right at the end of the play, once he has realised the truth and has – too late – shaken off Iago's influence (Act 5 Scene 2, lines 334–52).

◆ Look carefully at two scenes in which Iago speaks in prose. At what point does he switch to verse? Present your ideas about the effect of this.

Imagery

Imagery conjures up vivid pictures or associations in the mind and adds a symbolic and visual dimension to the play. Shakespeare's language is rich in imagery, and he particularly makes repeated use of **similes** and **metaphors**. In *Othello*, certain image clusters recur, which are outlined below.

Animals

- Usually insulting, especially when used by Iago: 'an old black ram / Is tupping your white ewe'; 'Plague him with flies'.
- As Othello comes under Iago's influence, he echoes Iago's choice of image: 'I had rather be a toad / And live upon the vapour of a dungeon'; 'as prime as goats, as hot as monkeys'.
- Exposed as a villain, Iago is called 'inhuman dog' and 'viper'.

Poison and disease

Disease reflects the supposed corruption of Venetian society, and becomes a metaphor for the corruption of Othello's mind.

- Iago's words act as poison in the play: 'poison his delight'; 'pour this pestilence into his ear'.
- Othello's jealousy acts like poison: 'If there be cords or knives, / Poison or fire … I'll not endure it.'
- Othello asks Iago for real poison: 'Get me some poison, Iago, this night'.
- Ironically, in Act 1 Othello is falsely accused by Brabantio of drugging Desdemona: 'corrupted / By spells and medicines'.

Hell and the devil

The play resonates with numerous references to hell and damnation.

- Iago to Brabantio: 'the devil will make a grandsire of you'.
- Brabantio to Othello: 'Damned as thou art, thou hast enchanted her'.
- Iago about himself: 'Divinity of hell! / When devils will the blackest sins put on, / They do suggest at first with heavenly shows / As I do now.'
- Othello on vengeance: 'Arise, black vengeance, from thy hollow cell'.
- Othello on Desdemona: 'the fair devil'.
- Emilia to Othello: 'thou art a devil'.
- Iago is revealed to be 'that demi-devil'; 'this hellish villain'.

Seeing and not seeing

Sight, or seeing things as they really are, works on an increasingly metaphorical level throughout the play, infusing the language and driving the plot.

- At the beginning of the play, Desdemona is very clear about what she sees in Othello: 'I saw Othello's visage in his mind, / And to his honours and his valiant parts / Did I my soul and fortunes consecrate'. She disregards outward appearances, for example his black skin.
- Act 2 begins with people staring out to sea, waiting to see the arrival of ships.
- Othello, though he demands 'ocular proof', is frequently convinced by things he does not see.
- After Othello has killed himself, Lodovico says to Iago: 'Look on the tragic loading of this bed. / This is thy work. The object poisons sight. / Let it be hid'.
- Even at a public level, seeing is portrayed as a very misleading sense: in Act 1 Scene 3, a senator suggests that the Turkish retreat to Rhodes is 'a pageant / To keep us in false gaze'.

◆ In small groups, create a collage that captures key images in the play. You can use any found pictures that you think are appropriate, or combine images and words. Be prepared to explain and/or analyse your collage to other groups, with close reference to the text.

Images: is Othello avoiding reality?

Othello's 'cause' speech, uttered as he enters Desdemona's bedchamber, about to kill her (Act 5 Scene 2, lines 1–22), is rich in visually striking images. One writer has suggested that Othello cannot face the reality of his own role, the living woman before him and his intended act, so he finds symbols for each in an attempt to idealise his situation.

◆ Explore this interpretation by locating the following images and explaining briefly the effect of each one.

Image	How it is being used
A carved alabaster effigy on a tomb	
Light	Metaphor for life. 'Snuff out' = killing. Desdemona is personified as light – opposite to hell.
A rose	
The figure of Justice (usually depicted with sword and scales)	

◆ Create a series of tableaux that visually capture the speech.

◆ Look again at Othello's final speech (Act 5 Scene 2, lines 334–55). Identify the images he uses and explain their effect. Talk together about whether you think his imagery here may be another example of avoiding the reality of his situation.

◆ Using Othello's 'cause' speech and one other speech of your choice, write an analysis of Othello's language in the play. Pay close attention to verse and imagery, providing quotations to support your comments. How does the language reflect the themes of the play, suggest something about the 'character' speaking, and provide dramatic moments which might move an audience emotionally?
Aim to write at least five paragraphs, including an introduction and conclusion.

Race and culture in *Othello*

Is *Othello* a racist play?

The central character of this play could be said to be:

- mentally unstable
- physically aggressive
- sensual
- insanely jealous
- highly gullible.

His main action in the play is to strangle a white woman. He is black.

A clear example of offensive racial stereotyping?

Certainly, there is some historical evidence of racial stereotyping in Shakespeare's England. There were enough black residents (mainly from Africa) to prompt Elizabeth I to express her discontent at the great numbers of 'Negars and blackamoors which are crept into the realm', and to proceed to expel some from the country. Popular travel books portrayed the natives of Africa as barbarous, lawless and 'a people of beastly lyvinge'. One contemporary writer on the history and people of Africa claimed that:

> Whomsoever they finde but talking with their wives they presently go about to murther them … by reason of jealousie you may see them daily one to be the death and destruction of another.

One source Shakespeare appears to have used when composing *Othello* is Leo Africanus's *A Geographical History of Africa*, published around 1600. It is typical of the contemporary attitudes and assumptions:

> Those which we named the inhabitants of the cities of Barbarie are somewhat needie and covetous, being also very proud and high-minded, and woonderfullly addicted unto wrath; insomuch that (according to the proverbe) they will deeply engrave in marble any injurie be it never so small, & will in no wise blot it out of their remembrance … Their wits are but meane, and they are so credulous, that they will beleeve matters impossible, which are told them.

▲ The Moorish ambassador to Queen Elizabeth I, 1600–01.

'The Moor'

The word 'Moor' has its roots in the name of a people originating from North Africa (roughly what is now Morocco and Algeria). In Shakespeare's time, however, it could also be used as a generic term to describe anyone from the African continent. Othello is variously described as 'a Barbary horse' (suggesting he is Arabic), or 'black' and 'thick-lips', indicating he is darker skinned from sub-Saharan Africa. Critics have argued for centuries over Othello's precise ethnicity, but why should this matter?

What some critics have said

In *A Short View of Tragedy* (published in 1693), Thomas Rymer drew comparisons between the imagined Venetian society of the play and seventeenth-century England:

> With us a Blackamoor might rise to be a trumpeter … With us a Moor might marry some little drab, or Small-coal Wench … certaynly never was any Play fraught like this of Othello with improbabilities.

Just over a century later, Samuel Taylor Coleridge expresses a similar view:

> It would be something monstrous to conceive this beautiful Venetian girl falling in love with a veritable negro.

Such attitudes continued to be expressed even in the twentieth century. Several influential writers on *Othello* concentrated on debating Othello's precise ethnic origins, taking great pains to prove that he would have been Arabic in appearance (see the illustration on p. 233). A. C. Bradley (*Shakespearean Tragedy*, 1904) explains why he considered this to be a particularly important point:

> Perhaps if we saw Othello coal-black with the bodily eye, the aversion of our blood … would overpower our imagination.

It was assumed that it would be less uncomfortable for white audiences to watch a lighter-skinned Othello having physical contact with Desdemona than an actor portrayed as black.

F. R. Leavis (*The Common Pursuit*, 1952) echoes some of the early Renaissance attitudes towards men of African descent when he ascribes 'voluptuous sensuality' and 'sensual possessiveness, appetite' to the central character, and comments that 'the stuff of which he is made begins … to deteriorate and show itself unfit'. In other words, there is something inherently unstable about Othello, a man who is naturally prone to uncontrollable sexual urges and jealousies. Leavis's view was highly influential during the latter half of the last century, and dominated ways of thinking about *Othello* until serious challenges were mounted by critics coming from more politically aware traditions from the 1980s onwards (see pages 238–9 for some examples).

Is the play about 'race'?

When Shakespeare wrote the play, it is unlikely that this concept was at the forefront of people's consciousness. However, this question has fascinated critics over the past fifty years.

The Caribbean writer C. L. R. James famously asserted that *Othello* was not a play about 'race', and that if all racist references were removed the basic plot would remain the same. Instead, he said, it is a play about jealousy, and the ethnic origins of the leading characters are irrelevant.

In contrast – and having originally agreed with this view – the Nigerian poet and novelist Ben Okri wrote that he changed his mind after watching a live performance in a London theatre as 'practically the only Black person in the audience'. Okri draws a parallel between his own feeling of isolation in the audience with Othello's visible isolation as a black man on stage. Okri goes on to say:

> *Any Black man who has gone out with a white woman knows that there are a lot of Iagos around … If it did not begin as a play about race, then its history has made it one.*

◆ Make a list of all the elements in the play that you would argue are directly linked to issues of race and racism. Divide them up into: verbal references (what characters actually say); implied references; and what are likely to be visual references (for example, on stage the visible contrast between black and white characters is strongly marked at all times, whereas on the page it is less noticeable).

◆ Discuss with a partner whether you agree that the play would not be changed very much if all direct verbal references to race/ethnicity were removed. Could Othello then be played by a white actor?

'Far more fair than black'

On page 12, you were asked to explore the way that language carries and reinforces the prejudices of the dominant social group. It is easy to recognise the blatant and intentional racist abuse in much of Iago's and Roderigo's dialogue, but language often works more subtly in carrying meaning. The activities that follow explore more fully how language can be culturally loaded.

Definitions

◆ Working in pairs, look up the word 'black' in a dictionary. Note down how many different uses there are of the word. Now do the same for 'white' and 'fair'. Divide the definitions into positive and negative uses. See if you can find the earliest recorded dates of particular usages. Discuss your findings in class, making links and comparisons between the three sets of definitions and, if possible, constructing a timeline of historical usage.

◆ Compile a list of sayings that use the various meanings of the words 'black', 'fair' or 'white'. For example, a 'whitewash' can refer to glossing over negative associations in a report; giving someone a 'black look' means looking at someone in an unfriendly way; 'black Wednesday' is a term used to refer to the day the stock markets crashed … and so on. Discuss how the various meanings of these words informs the way we use everyday language, then move on to a consideration of the ways language works in *Othello*.

Meanings

◆ In groups of three, discuss in what sense the Duke is using the word 'black' when he says: 'If virtue no delighted beauty lack, / Your son-in-law is far more fair than black.' (Act 1 Scene 3, lines 285–6).

◆ Identify other uses of 'black' in the play and discuss their meanings in the context of who uses the word and when.

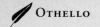

Portrayals

The conventional image of hell is of a place of evil, torture and darkness. In early Christian church paintings, devils were always portrayed as black (see the picture below). The connotation of evil is very evident in Emilia's raging at Othello for killing Desdemona: 'O, the more angel she, / And you the blacker devil!' (Act 5 Scene 2, lines 131–2). Iago also explicitly links blackness with sinfulness: 'When devils will the blackest sins put on' (Act 2 Scene 3, line 318).

In Shakespeare's *Macbeth* there are other examples of the way blackness is linked with evil. The three witches are called 'secret, black, and midnight hags', and the tyrant Macbeth himself is referred to as 'black Macbeth'.

◆ In pairs, make a collection of similar references in *Othello* that link blackness with the devil. Which characters make these references most?

◆ Now find references to 'fair', 'angels' and 'heaven'. Who uses theses terms and when? How often are fair and dark terms set up in opposition to each other?

Black and white imagery

At the heart of the play is the marriage of a black man and a white woman, seen by many of the play's characters to be 'against all rules of nature'. Black and white imagery emphasises this opposition throughout the fabric of the play's language. In the cultural and historical context of the play, black and white can be equated with dark and light, hell and heaven, good and bad. The contrast between black and white is further intensified by Shakespeare's use of **antithesis**: the setting of word against word, or phrase against phrase (as in 'fair' against 'black', 'black ram' against 'white ewe'). Shakespeare uses this device frequently in all his plays, probably because antitheses express conflict, and conflict is usually at the heart of all drama. It is used in different ways throughout *Othello* (as when 'hand' is set against 'heart' and in Othello's 'sweet revenge grows harsh'). But it is the insistent opposition of black against white that powerfully pervades the whole play.

In Shakespeare's day, black characters were not usually cast as the 'hero' and it is likely, therefore, that his audiences would automatically make negative associations. Black-skinned Othello is often referred to by his colour or ethnicity ('the Moor', 'sooty bosom') and linked to evil, yet expectations are reversed within the actions of the play in that it is white-skinned Iago who turns out to be evil, and who immerses himself in images of hell and night. In contrast, Desdemona's fairness is emphasised and, even at the end of the play, Othello refers to her as a 'pearl' and as 'light'.

The first scene of the play, where Iago's plan is first hatched, takes place at night. The play moves through storm into daylight, then moves back to night for the final tragic events. The drunken barracks party, where Iago's scheming really begins to take off, occurs at night, drawing Othello and Desdemona from their bed-chamber on what should be their wedding night.

Some commentators have suggested that Othello's inherent bravery and virtue mean that at the beginning of the play he is able to overcome colour prejudice. Then, he is comfortable in his position as a general, and speaks with calm authority, even when challenged by Brabantio in front of the Senate. But away from the civilised confines of Venice, he is corrupted by Iago. As his relationship with Desdemona is 'blackened' by lies, Othello becomes more conscious of himself as black, and begins to conform to racist stereotypes. He, too, comes to regard 'black' as a negative term: 'Her name, that was as fresh / As Dian's visage, is now begrimed and black / As mine own face.'

◆ Using only black-and-white illustrations, photos, display paper and other resources, create a collage out of words, quotations and pictures that explores the central opposition between black and white in the play. Mount a display of your collages on the wall and compare your interpretations. Pick out the key differences and discuss the reasons for these.

◆ Using the information in this section, and your collages, write an analytical essay entitled, *Othello: 'Far more fair than black'*, exploring the ways in which black and white are set in opposition to each other on both a literal and a metaphorical level.

Venice and Venetian culture

Shakespeare's choice of as a setting is significant. For an English audience in 1604, Venice was a byword for thriving capitalism. It was a republic where the wealthier merchant classes controlled the state, buying powerful military forces to protect their colonial exploits. In contrast, England had only just started increasing overseas trade in Africa, India and elsewhere, and was on the brink of massive colonial enterprise in the New World. It is likely that English merchants would recognise in Venice the mercantile and colonial force that they wanted to see England become.

The Venetian state employed mercenary soldiers. It was a cosmopolitan state, so a black military leader is quite a believable figure. Othello, an ex-slave, is revered by the Venetian Senate simply because he very effectively defends their interests. He is, however, not entirely 'one of them', especially not when it comes to marrying one of their daughters. Desdemona is described as a stolen jewel because Brabantio feels he has been robbed by someone who was employed to protect his possessions! The non-feudal society of Venice confers power on Othello – but not status. This provides a rich source of dramatic tension.

Critics' forum

On these two pages are extracts from influential Shakespeare critics, writing about *Othello*. You will discover that the readings offered are very different, and in some cases quite contradictory.

Working in small groups, read through each extract and summarise the main points. Then think about what evidence from the play the writer in each case might go on to use in support of their view. Try to suggest what assumptions underpin the readings, what other influences each reader brings to their interpretation of the play (for example, Christianity, empire) and what theoretical perspective they might be adopting (see p. 222).

Imagine *Critics' Forum* is a late-evening television arts programme, chaired by Melanie Bookworm. In it, a group of professional critics with very differing views is brought together for a discussion on a particular work of literature. Tonight it is *Othello*. One student (as Ms Bookworm) chairs the debate, the rest choose a critical stance from the extracts given, and each argues their case. Remember, you'll have to know the play really well and do thorough preparation beforehand.

Focus on character (and Othello's exoticism)

[Othello] does not belong to our world, and he seems to enter it we know not whence – almost as if from wonderland. There is something mysterious in his descent from men of royal siege; in his wanderings in vast deserts and among marvellous peoples; in his tales of magic handkerchiefs and prophetic Sibyls; in the sudden vague glimpses we get of numberless battles and sieges in which he has played the hero and has borne a charmed life; even in chance references to his baptism, his being sold to slavery, his sojourn in Aleppo. And he is not merely a romantic figure; his own nature is romantic. So he comes before us, dark and grand, with a light upon him from the sun where he was born.

A. C. Bradley, 1904

Focus on character and his language

Othello, in his magnanimous way, is egotistic. He really is, beyond any question, the nobly massive man of action, the captain of men, he sees himself as being … In short, a habit of self-approving, self-dramatisation is an essential element in Othello's make-up, and remains so at the very end. It is, at the best, the impressive manifestation of a noble egotism … This self-centredness doesn't mean self-knowledge: that is a virtue which Othello, as soldier of fortune, hasn't had much need of.

F. R. Leavis, 1952

Focus on the poetry

Among the tragedies of Shakespeare Othello *is supreme in one quality: beauty. Much of its poetry, in imagery, perfection of phrase, and steadiness of rhythm, soaring yet firm, enchants the sensuous imagination. Othello is like a hero of the ancient world in that he is not a man like us, but a man recognised as extraordinary. He seems born to do great deeds and live in legend. He has the heroic capacity for passion. But the thing which most sets him apart is his solitariness. He is a stranger, a man of alien race, without ties of nature or natural duties.*

Helen Gardner, 1955

Focus on the message *Othello* carries for us today

The action of Othello opens out to include the audience, and their perception of the struggle of good and evil. They do not go home hoping they will never meet an Iago, but rather understanding something of the nature of evil and how soon bright things come to confusion ... We no longer feel, as Shakespeare's contemporaries did, the ubiquity of Satan, but Iago is still serviceable to us, as an objective correlative of the mindless inventiveness of racist aggression. Iago is still alive and kicking and filling migrants' letterboxes with excrement.

Germaine Greer, 1986

Focus on society and culture

In loving and marrying each other, Othello and Desdemona instinctively act according to principles of racial equality and sexual freedom which are still not normative, still far from generally accepted and practised even in our own day, let alone in Shakespeare's. Shakespeare's tragic protagonists are all overpowered by the prevailing social and ideological tides which sweep them unawares out of their depth, rather than by some metaphysically predestined misfortune or by some flaw, whether culpable, haphazard or innate, in the composition of their characters.

Kiernan Ryan, 1989

Focus on attitudes to 'race' and culture

From the opening scenes of the play, we quickly note how Othello experiences his identity in contradictory terms set by the Venetians ... Generations of western critics largely ignored these ideological underpinnings of Othello's identity and focused instead on the Moor's character in terms of psychological realism. However, as the literary history of the play testifies, they had difficulty in reconciling Othello's role as a tragic hero

with his blackness ... Othello self-destructively internalizes the prevailing racism, while Desdemona ... remains an idealized, virtuous woman – keeping alive the image of a besieged, white femininity so crucial to the production of the black man as a 'savage'.

Jyotsna Singh, 2004

Focus on ideology – then and now

The relation between violence and the ideological power of the state may be glimpsed in the way Othello justifies himself, in his last speech, as a good Venetian: he boasts of killing someone. Not Desdemona ... but a 'malignant and a turban'd Turk' who 'Beat a Venetian and traduc'd the state'. Othello says he 'took by the throat the circumcised dog / And smote him thus'. And so, upon this recollection, Othello stabs himself, recognizing himself, for the last time, as an outsider, a discredit to the social order he has been persuaded to respect.

Alan Sinfield, 2004

Focus on carnival and burlesque elements

The abusive language, the noisy clamour under Brabantio's window, and the menace of violence of the opening scene of Othello link the improvisations of Iago with the codes of a carnivalesque disturbance or charivari organized in protest over the marriage of the play's central characters ... In staging the play as a ceremony of broken nuptials, Iago assumes the function of a popular festive ringleader whose task is the unmaking of a transgressive marriage. As the action of Othello unfolds, the audience is constrained to witness a protracted and diabolical parody of courtship leading to a final, grotesquely distorted consummation in the marriage bed.

Michael D. Bristol, 2004

Othello in performance

There is no substitute for seeing a live performance of the play at the theatre, as well as watching different movie versions, in order to gain an appreciation of the living play as opposed to simply reading the script.

Since its first recorded performance in 1604, *Othello* has remained a popular stage play, gripping in its focused intensity. During the 1700s, for example, *Othello* was performed on a London stage for all but seven years of the whole century. However, one of the earliest critics of the play, Thomas Rymer (1693), dismissed it as 'a Bloody Farce' because he thought that too much hinged upon 'so remote a trifle as a handkerchief'.

Key critical discussion in the twentieth century tended to focus upon whether it is Iago or Othello who commands the greatest stage presence. Largely, this debate was bound up with competing interpretations of *Othello*, shaped by the critical writings of A. C. Bradley (1904) and F. R. Leavis (1937). In brief, Bradley argued that Othello was essentially noble and was brought down by Iago's villainy. In contrast, Leavis saw Othello as self-centred and self-dramatising, all too ready to believe Iago's hints and lies. Bradley viewed Iago as the more complex, fascinating character, but Leavis asserted that Iago 'is not much more than a necessary piece of dramatic mechanism'. In reality, Iago has nearly one-third of the lines of the play – many more than Othello. The success or otherwise of productions is often measured by a director's ability to attain a dramatic balance between these two characters.

Since the late twentieth century, critical attention has been increasingly directed towards cultural, post-colonial and feminist/gendered readings of the play influenced by developments in literary theory (see pp. 222, 238 and 239).

Shakespeare's stage

Open-air playhouses in Shakespeare's day meant that the experience of going to see a play was very different from today. There were no stage lights, so performances took place in daylight. The large audience surrounded the stage on three sides, with those standing on the ground floor pressed against the edge of the stage itself (see p. 6 for a photograph of the modern Shakespeare's Globe, which was built on the site of the original theatre in 1997). With three tiers of seating, open-air acoustics, noisy bustling audiences and a lack of lights, it is likely that actors adopted an exaggerated acting style, with big gestures and 'stock' ways of standing to suggest certain moods or character types. Costumes would carry vital clues about the wearer (and don't forget that women's parts were played by boys because women were not allowed to act on stage until much later in the seventeenth century). Movements and facial expressions had to be visible from three floors up.

Theatre companies like The King's Men (Shakespeare's company) were expected to perform a range of plays from a repertoire at any one time, presenting a different play each day of the week. This would mean little rehearsal time and the necessity of learning lines very quickly. Actors would not get a copy of the whole play – just their own lines (literally, their 'part') with the addition of preceding cues. Embedded stage directions would therefore contain vital clues to each actor about what was going on and where it was happening. To make this process even more complicated, plays often included more speaking parts than actors in the company. Therefore actors doubled up and played more than one role.

◆ In small groups, choose any key scene from *Othello* and talk about how it might have been staged at the Globe. Have a go at acting the parts, using grand gestures and stylised ways of speaking the lines.

◆ What would be the major challenges for boys playing the parts of Emilia, Desdemona and Bianca?

Casting

From Shakespeare's day right up to the 1980s, Othello was played on the London stage by white actors 'blacked up'. Perhaps the most famous example was Laurence Olivier's performance in 1964 (below left), which is still regarded by many critics as the definitive Othello.

Heavily influenced by F. R. Leavis's reading of the play, Olivier portrayed Othello as a sensuous and barely civilised egotist. However, this view has been challenged in recent times. Modern understandings of 'race' and cultural politics have led to less favourable criticisms of Olivier's performance, which is now regarded by many as relying on racist stereotypes.

Two famous black actors challenged the tradition of white actors taking the role, one in the nineteenth century and one in the twentieth. Ira Aldridge, an African-American actor, was the first black actor to play major Shakespeare roles. Aldridge's performances in the 1850s could not help but carry political resonance, coming as they did at a time when the anti-slavery movement was gathering pace.

The African-American actor Paul Robeson's performance as Othello in the 1930s and 1940s (below right) has come to be regarded as the antithesis of Olivier's, in that it emphasised 'noble', sympathetic aspects of Othello. Robeson, the son of a former slave, was a singer and political activist. A campaigner for civil rights in the United States, he interpreted the role of Othello as an outsider who takes a fierce pride in his culture. Robeson was at first wary of being cast as Othello, in case he was perceived in a stereotypical way. He did not receive a wholly positive reception on the London stage, but in a later production he took Broadway (New York) by storm.

Nowadays, audiences expect to see a black actor playing Othello, and it would be regarded as potentially racist to cast a white actor in the role, given the struggle experienced by black actors to gain equal access to leading roles in the professional theatre. Blacking up carries memories of racist 'minstrel' routines and it is unlikely that a director would contemplate this now. An interesting experiment, however, was the 'photonegative' staging by the Washington Shakespeare Theatre (1997), where Othello was played by a white actor and all other parts by black actors, deliberately reversing the construction of 'outsider'.

◆ In small groups, discuss what effect you think different casting decisions might have on the way a modern audience 'reads' a performance of *Othello*. For example, in the last two decades the part of Bianca has often been played by a black actor (see p. 225). Why do you think several directors have done this? What difference would it make if Emilia was black (see the image on p. 178)? Could you envisage a black Iago? Increasingly, a 'colour-blind' approach is taken to casting professional Shakespeare productions (for example, a black actor played Henry V at the National Theatre in London in 2003). Could Othello be played successfully by a white actor or is the play too specific about 'race' for that to work?

◆ Search the Internet for images of Othello taken from recent productions. Also look again at the photographs in this edition of black and white actors playing Othello and other characters. Summarise your discussion, make some notes, then compare your ideas with other groups.

Openings

As a skilled playwright, Shakespeare knew he had to catch the interest of his audience right at the start of each play. Therefore in most plays we find vigorous dialogue, intriguing situations and conflict introduced in the first scene. Scene 1 of *Othello* is no exception, opening as it does in the middle of a heated argument.

◆ Consider how the opening moments are portrayed in three different screen versions of *Othello*. For example:

- Trevor Nunn's 1990 RSC production starts briefly with an empty stage in half-light; a striking visual contrast is immediately established with Iago in dark military uniform and Roderigo dressed in a light-coloured linen suit and panama hat.
- Oliver Parker's 1995 Hollywood film opens with a lengthy title sequence, the camera tracking a gondola's journey through night-time Venice, establishing time and place. A shrouded pair of figures is seated close together; the woman's face is occasionally glimpsed, but the man is masked. The scene cuts to the Senate where war is being discussed. Cut back to a secret wedding scene, Iago and Roderigo as two surreptitious onlookers. It is only now that some of Iago's opening dialogue is introduced.
- Orson Welles chose to begin his 1952 black-and-white film version with Othello's funeral procession, overlooked by a caged Iago; in this version, the play is visually framed by its tragic outcome, the main action becoming a kind of flashback.

◆ Imagine you are making a new movie of *Othello*. How will your film begin? Where (and when) will it be set? What music or sound effects will you use? What atmosphere are you seeking to create? Will you want to reorder/cut the script? Storyboard the opening of the play. If you have access to cameras, film the opening three or four minutes of the play and share with other groups in your class. Which is the most successful and why?

Adaptations

In the eighteenth century, it became popular to rewrite certain of Shakespeare's tragedies in order to give them a happy ending.

◆ Imagine you are a stage adapter and have been asked to give Othello a happy ending. How will you do it? Which characters need to survive for it to be regarded as 'happy'? Which characters do not need to survive – why not? At what point in the play do you have to begin to make changes? Does a happy ending demand that Iago is punished or not? Make notes outlining your alterations, including some examples of your new script.

A number of modern writers and directors have taken the core elements of the *Othello* story and created a modern drama out of it. Tim B. Nelson's 2001 film version, *O*, transferred the action to a modern American high school. Othello becomes OJ, star of the basketball team and the only black student in the school. He has a relationship with Desi, the principal's daughter.

In a made-for-television adaptation (first screened in the UK in 2001), scriptwriter Andrew Davis transposed the story to modern London. Ben Jago, deputy Metropolitan Police Commissioner, is passed over for promotion in favour of his black colleague, John Othello. Michael Cass is assigned bodyguard duties when Othello and his beautiful wife, Dessie, are racially harassed.

▲ The movie *O* gave the Othello story a modern setting, in which jealous teenager Hugo deliberately drives a wedge between high-school couple OJ and Desi.

◆ Compile a file of ideas for a made-for-television drama based upon the *Othello* story.

• Summarise the new storyline in approximately 500 words and include a list of characters.
• Describe the setting and time (the present, the past or the future); suggest a series of locations, matched to specific scenes.
• Cast your production with known actors, film stars or other celebrities. Explain your choices.
• Take the key 'temptation' scene (Act 3 Scene 3) and explain how you will adapt this to fit your own version.
• Draw some costume designs, or use pictures taken from magazines or the Internet.

Silent Othello, triplicate Iago

The Russian-American company Synetic Theater specialise in silent adaptations of Shakespeare plays, which rely on choreographed dance, athletic physical movement, vividly designed costumes and screen projections to convey the drama. In their production of *Othello* three performers simultaneously took the role of Iago, creating the effect that he is everywhere whispering, listening or interfering in the action (see picture below).

◆ Choose one scene from Act 3 and decide how you could make a 'triple Iago' enhance the tension.

Political *Othello*

Othello challenges apartheid

Although some critics have argued that *Othello* is not a play primarily about race, in certain 'post-colonial' contexts this aspect of the play is unavoidably highlighted and the whole play becomes politically charged. One such production was directed by Janet Suzman in 1980s South Africa – in defiance of the apartheid regime there. The Market Theatre of Johannesburg production included a black actor as Othello, not only appearing alongside his white colleagues, but kissing a white woman on stage in a society where such conduct was punishable by imprisonment. The production drew international notice, and became a political weapon against the apartheid government.

Othello and the Metropolitan Police

On a smaller scale, Andrew Davies's modern adaptation (see picture opposite) was made in the context of accusations of racism against the London Metropolitan Police. Eammon Walker, who starred as police chief John Othello, emphasised the political context of the play when interviewed:

Andrew Davies … was dealing with a London problem: the Metropolitan Police and death within custody. This is a big issue for Britain … Now, I don't know if you can hope that something can be changed by this particular production, but what you can hope for is that you plant a seed in somebody's brain – maybe a person of power who is able to do something about it. You can hope that they can turn around and make a difference in the society that we are living in. That's basically what we do as playwrights, as directors, as actors: We shine a mirror on to society for them to look into. If they see something they don't like, then it's up to them to change it.

Othello in postcolonial India

In the late 1990s, *Othello* was adapted for a Kathakali style of production in India. Kathakali is a traditional form of Indian theatre, using masks, dance moves and formalised gestures. Arjun Raina, who played Othello, said in an interview that for him there were clear parallels

◀ The three Iagos in Synetic Theater's 2010 production.

between Othello's situation and that of Indians searching for their identity in the context of their colonial past under British rule.

◆ Debate with others in your class whether it is ever possible to read a Shakespeare play without filtering its meaning through our own current cultural and political understandings.

Othello on stage and on film

Seeing a performance of any play you are studying is vitally important in helping you to understand the way it works as a drama. A good way to develop ideas about different ways in which *Othello* might be interpreted is to watch more than one production. A live performance will provide you with a very different experience than watching a movie version. However, you are most likely to have access to a film version. A number of activities in this book have suggested that you look at key scenes in different film versions.

▼ Andrew Davis's television adaptation was released at a time when the police force was being accused of racism.

There are a number of ways in which you might work with a movie:

a Look at the date it was made and consider how the film is a reflection of its social and cultural history (e.g. fashions in hair styles, clothes; attitudes to women, to 'race'; style of acting; sophistication of editing technology, and so on).

b Watch the whole movie and see if you can identify any changes the screenwriter has made (cutting the original script, omitting minor characters, changing the order of any scenes).

c Take a key scene and examine the way it has been constructed. For instance, look at:
  • camerawork (shot type, movement, camera angles)
  • editing (the way shots are cut)
  • sound (dialogue, music, sound effects)
  • lighting (light, dark, sources of light)
  • costumes, props, setting and locations; use of colour.

d Press the pause button and freeze the action at a key moment. Analyse the *mise en scene* (in other words, whatever you can see in the frame including many of the items listed above).

e Compare two or more movie versions at the same point in the plot. How do they differ and which do you find the most effective? Explain your reasons.

Write a review

◆ Look at full-length film or theatre reviews in a newspaper or online. Familiarise yourself with the style of writing and the way each critic analyses aspects of the production. Write a review of a live theatre production if you are lucky enough to be able to see one; or write a review of one of the movie versions you have viewed. How has the director approached the play? How is the relationship between Othello and Iago presented? What kind of a woman is Desdemona? Is the turning of Othello by Iago convincing?

Writing about Shakespeare

The play as text

Shakespeare's plays have always been studied as literary works – as words on a page that need clarification, appreciation and discussion. When you write about the plays, you will be asked to compose short pieces and also longer, more reflective pieces like controlled assessments, examination scripts and coursework – often in the form of essays on themes and/or imagery, character studies, analyses of the structure of the play and on stagecraft. Imagery, stagecraft and character are dealt with elsewhere in this edition. Here, we concentrate on themes and structure. You might find it helpful to look at the 'Write about it' boxes on the left-hand pages throughout the play.

Themes

It is often tempting to say that the theme of a play is a single idea, like 'death' in *Hamlet*, or 'the supernatural' in *Macbeth*, or 'love' in *Romeo and Juliet*. The problem with such a simple approach is that you will miss the complexity of the plays. In *Romeo and Juliet*, for example, the play is about the relationship between love, family loyalty and constraint; it is also about the relationship of youth to age and experience; and the relationship between Romeo and Juliet is also played out against a background of enmity between two families. Between each of these ideas or concepts there are tensions. The tensions are the main focus of attention for Shakespeare and the audience; this is also how the best drama operates – by the presentation of and resolution of tension.

Look back at the 'Themes' boxes throughout the play to see if any of the activities there have given rise to information that you could use as a starting point for further writing about the themes of the specific play you are studying.

Structure

Most Shakespeare plays are in five acts, divided into scenes. These acts were not in the original scripts, but have been included in later editions to make the action more manageable, clearer and more like 'classical' structures. One way to get a sense of the structure of the whole play is to take a printed version (not this one!) and cut it up into scenes and acts, then display each scene and act, in sequence, on a wall, like this:

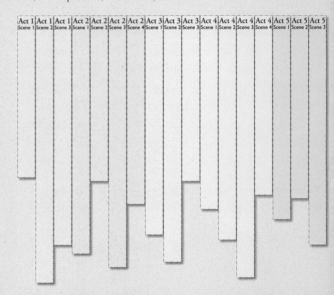

As you set out the whole play, you will be able to see the 'shape' of each act, the relative length of the scenes, and how the acts relate to each other (such as whether one act is shorter, and why that might be). You can annotate the text with comments, observations and questions. You can use a highlighter pen to mark the recurrence of certain words, images or metaphors to see at a glance where and how frequently they appear. You can also follow a particular character's progress through the play.

Such an overview of the play gives you critical perspective: you will be able to see how the parts fit together, to stand back from the play and assess its shape, and to focus on particular parts within the context of the whole. Your writing will reflect a greater awareness of the overall context as a result.

The play as script

There are different, but related, categories when we think of the play as a script for performance. These include *stagecraft* (discussed elsewhere in this edition and throughout the left-hand pages), *lighting, focus* (who are we looking at? Where is the attention of the audience?), *music and sound, props and costumes, casting, make-up, pace and rhythm*, and other *spatial relationships* (e.g. how actors move around the stage in relation to each other). If you are writing about stagecraft or performance, use the notes you have made as a result of the 'Stagecraft' activities throughout this edition of the play, as well as any information you can find about the plays in performance.

What are the key points of dispute?

Shakespeare is brilliant at capturing a number of key points of dispute in each of his plays. These are the dramatic moments where he concentrates the focus of the audience on difficult (sometimes universal) problems that the characters are facing or embodying.

First, identify these key points in the play you are studying. You can do this as a class by brainstorming what you consider to be the key points in small groups, then debating the long-list as a whole class, and then coming up with a short-list of what the class thinks are the most significant. (This is a good opportunity for speaking and listening work.) They are likely to be places in the play where the action or reflection is at its most intense, and which capture the complexity of themes, character, structure and performance.

Second, drill down at one of the points of contention and tension. In other words, investigate the complexity of the problem that Shakespeare has presented. What is at stake? Why is it important? Is it a problem that can be resolved, or is it an insoluble one?

Key skills in writing about Shakespeare

Here are some suggestions to help you organise your notes and develop advanced writing skills when working on Shakespeare:

- Compose the title of your writing carefully to maximise your opportunities to be creative and critical about the play. Explore the key words in your title carefully. Decide which aspect of the play – or which combination of aspects – you are focusing on.
- Create a mind map of your ideas, making connections between them.
- If appropriate, arrange your ideas into a hierarchy that shows how some themes or features of the play are 'higher' than others and can incorporate other ideas.
- Sequence your ideas so that you have a plan for writing an essay, review, story – whichever genre you are using. You might like to think about whether to put your strongest points first, in the middle, or later.
- Collect key quotations (it might help to compile this list with a partner), which you can use as evidence to support your argument.
- Compose your first draft, embedding quotations in your text as you go along.
- Revise your draft in the light of your own critical reflections and/or those of others.

The following pages focus on writing about *Othello* in particular.

Writing about *Othello*

As you will have seen from the pages dealing with *Othello* in performance, directors have interpreted the play in a number of different ways. It is likely that the specific versions you have watched either on the stage or on film will shape the way you respond to the play. Reading any piece of literature is an active process on the part of the reader, in which your own experiences, values and beliefs help you to make sense of the text. That is one of the reasons why we all read texts in different ways (and why critics argue about what each play 'means'). When you come to write about *Othello*, it is important that you think carefully about what the play means to you personally.

Conventional essays

You may have to write an essay about *Othello* that will be formally assessed. These essays often follow a set structure and need to fulfil the specific requirements of the examination syllabus you are studying. You will need to decide what your opinion is, then plan out a carefully constructed argument that lays out your points in a logical order, supporting each point with reference to the text, sometimes giving precise quotations. Make sure you do not just retell the story of the play.

The following titles are typical examination essays based on *Othello*:

a Choose two or three central themes and explain how each is developed linguistically and dramatically through the play.

b Discuss Othello's relationship with Desdemona. Do you believe he truly loves her?

c Write a detailed character study of Desdemona that is sympathetic to her; now write a second version that is unsympathetic. Write approximately one page for each. The first part will argue that she is a completely innocent participant in the tragedy; the second part will argue that she makes a number of

wrong decisions and is partly responsible for what happens.

d In the story on which Shakespeare based *Othello*, the characters sailed to Cyprus on a calm sea. Why do you think Shakespeare adds a mighty storm at the beginning of Act 2 Scene 1?

e How far is Othello's tragic downfall brought about because he is an outsider?

f Within the world of the play, is Othello's love for Desdemona 'against all rules of nature', as Brabantio says?

g Some commentators have said that the focus of *Othello* is not the title character, as is the case with Shakespeare's other great tragedies. Instead, the play should have been called *Iago*. Do you agree?

h Comment on the time-scheme of the play, where realistically not enough time could have elapsed on Cyprus for Desdemona to have committed adultery. Examine the problem of time in *Othello* and the possible dramatic reasons behind this 'double time-scheme'.

i Write about an aspect of language that interests you in *Othello*.

Pick at least two of these essay titles and sketch out an essay plan for each. Find between five and ten relevant quotations from the script that you can match to specific points on each plan. Swap plans with two other students in your class and give constructive feedback. Make suggestions for improvements.

Select the two essay titles that you think are the most difficult to answer. Try to pinpoint what aspects of the questions you find most challenging. Talk together with a partner and share ideas. Based on your selected essay titles, draw up some revision notes on each topic.

Research projects

The better you understand Shakespeare's times and the social context in which he was writing, the better you will understand *Othello*. Choose one of the following topics and undertake some detailed research, using library resources and the Internet. Make sure you select information carefully from your sources (don't just copy) and always check that as far as you can tell you are using a reliable source. Present your information in as clear a manner as you can – the exact written format is up to you.

a Venice in the seventeenth century

b Shakespeare's London

c playhouses and Shakespeare's acting companies

d attitudes to women in Shakespeare's time (you might like to look for examples of seventeenth-century sermons that outline how to be a good wife)

e overseas exploration, travel writing and the beginning of colonial expansion

f the main sources Shakespeare used when composing *Othello*.

Creative responses

Throughout the left-hand pages of this book, you have been encouraged to be creative in your responses to *Othello*, particularly through drama-based activities and visual display work. Sometimes for school assessments you are asked to write creatively, for example, by creating missing scenes, or by composing stories inspired by events, characters or themes. Here are some ideas for creative writing (feel free to think of some alternative activities yourself):

a Roderigo claims to be hopelessly in love with Desdemona. We learn that Brabantio had banned him from the house. Imagine that Roderigo writes two love letters to Desdemona – one delivered to her house before the news of her marriage to Othello, and one following their arrival on Cyprus that remains undelivered. Write the letters.

b Othello and Desdemona's marriage takes place off stage, before the play opens. Decide who would have been present in addition to the couple themselves, then write the missing scene.

c Write the scene where Othello tells Desdemona what has just happened in the barracks and why he has had to dismiss Cassio.

d What happens to Cassio and Bianca after the play ends? Write Bianca's story.

e Who owns the handkerchief at the end of the play? Compose a story that focuses on the new owner and what happens to him or her.

f Recast the murder scene in Desdemona's bedchamber (Act 5 Scene 2, lines 22–107) as an extract from a novel. Use third-person narrative, decide what action will be described by the narrator and what dialogue you want to keep. End on a cliff-hanger as Emilia comes into the room.

And finally …

Write a reflective account of your time spent studying *Othello*. What did you initially expect the experience of studying Shakespeare to be like? (Try to pinpoint where those assumptions came from.) Were your expectations fulfilled – or challenged? What aspects of studying the play did you find most difficult and what helped you overcome them? What did you like best about the play? What was your favourite activity from this book and how did it transform your understanding of an aspect of the play?

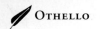

William Shakespeare
1564–1616

1564	Born Stratford-upon-Avon, eldest son of John and Mary Shakespeare.
1582	Marries Anne Hathaway of Shottery, near Stratford.
1583	Daughter Susanna born.
1585	Twins, son and daughter Hamnet and Judith, born.
1592	First mention of Shakespeare in London. Robert Greene, another playwright, described Shakespeare as 'an upstart crow beautified with our feathers'. Greene seems to have been jealous of Shakespeare. He mocked Shakespeare's name, calling him 'the only Shake-scene in a country' (presumably because Shakespeare was writing successful plays).
1595	Becomes a shareholder in The Lord Chamberlain's Men, an acting company that became extremely popular.
1596	Son, Hamnet, dies aged eleven. Father, John, granted arms (acknowledged as a gentleman).
1597	Buys New Place, the grandest house in Stratford.
1598	Acts in Ben Jonson's *Every Man in His Humour*.
1599	Globe Theatre opens on Bankside. Performances in the open air.
1601	Father, John, dies.
1603	James I grants Shakespeare's company a royal patent: The Lord Chamberlain's Men become The King's Men and play about twelve performances each year at court.
1607	Daughter Susanna marries Dr John Hall.
1608	Mother, Mary, dies.
1609	The King's Men begin performing indoors at Blackfriars Theatre.
1610	Probably returns from London to live in Stratford.
1616	Daughter Judith marries Thomas Quiney. Dies. Buried in Holy Trinity Church, Stratford-upon-Avon.

The plays and poems

(no one knows exactly when he wrote each play)

1589–95	*The Two Gentlemen of Verona, The Taming of the Shrew, First, Second* and *Third Parts* of *King Henry VI, Titus Andronicus, King Richard III, The Comedy of Errors, Love's Labour's Lost, A Midsummer Night's Dream, Romeo and Juliet, King Richard II* (and the long poems *Venus and Adonis* and *The Rape of Lucrece*).
1596–99	*King John, The Merchant of Venice, First* and *Second Parts* of *King Henry IV, The Merry Wives of Windsor, Much Ado About Nothing, King Henry V, Julius Caesar* (and probably the Sonnets).
1600–05	*As You Like It, Hamlet, Twelfth Night, Troilus and Cressida, Measure for Measure,* **Othello***, All's Well That Ends Well, Timon of Athens, King Lear.*
1606–11	*Macbeth, Antony and Cleopatra, Pericles, Coriolanus, The Winter's Tale, Cymbeline, The Tempest.*
1613	*King Henry VIII, The Two Noble Kinsmen* (both probably with John Fletcher).
1623	Shakespeare's plays published as a collection (now called the First Folio).

Acknowledgements

Cambridge University Press would like to acknowledge the contributions made to this work by Rex Gibson.

Picture Credits

p. iii Donmar Theatre 2007, Johan Persson/ArenaPAL; p. v: Shakespeare's Globe 2007, © Marilyn Kingwill/ArenaPAL; p. vi left: Theatre Royal, Northampton 2003, © Donald Cooper/Photostage; p. vi right: RSC/Barbican Theatre, London 2000, © Donald Cooper/Photostage; p. vii top: The Royal Opera/Royal Albert Hall, London 1997, © Donald Cooper/Photostage; p. vii bottom: RSC, Stratford-upon-Avon 1999, © Ben Christopher/ArenaPAL; p. viii top: RSC/Barbican Theatre, London 2000, © Donald Cooper/Photostage; p. viii bottom: Crucible Theatre, Sheffield 2011, © Johan Persson/ArenaPAL; p. ix top: Young Vic Theatre, London 1984, © Donald Cooper/Photostage; p. ix bottom: Northern Broadsides and West Yorkshire Playhouse/Trafalgar Studios 2009, © Donald Cooper/Photostage; p. x top: Northern Broadsides and West Yorkshire Playhouse/Leeds 2009, © Nobby Clarke/ArenaPAL; p. x bottom: RSC/The Other Place, Stratford-upon-Avon 1989, © Donald Cooper/Photostage; p. xi top: RSC/Barbican Theatre, London 2000, © Donald Cooper/Photostage; p. xi bottom: Northern Broadsides and West Yorkshire Playhouse, Leeds 2009, © Donald Cooper/Photostage; p. xii: Donmar Theatre 2007, Johan Persson/ArenaPAL; p. 6: Chicago Shakespeare Theater/Shakespeare's Globe 2012, © Donald Cooper/Photostage; Shakespeare's Globe 2007, © Johan Persson/ArenaPAL; p. 16: Pennsylvania Shakespeare Festival 2006, © Pennsylvania Shakespeare Festival; p. 18: RSC/Royal Shakespeare Theatre 1985, © Donald Cooper/Photostage; p. 20: 'Grand Procession of the Doge, Venice' (16th century illustration), © Lifestyle Pictures/Alamy; p. 24: Birmingham Repertory Theatre 1993, © Donald Cooper/Photostage; p. 36: RSC/Barbican Theatre, London 2000, © Donald Cooper/Photostage; p. 42: Donmar Theatre 2007, Johan Persson/ArenaPAL; p. 44: Crucible Theatre, Sheffield 2011, © Geraint Lewis; p. 47 The Doge's Palace, Venice, © Dmitri Ometsinsky/Shutterstock; p. 52: Donmar Theatre 2007, Johan Persson/ArenaPAL; p. 56: RSC/Barbican Theatre, London 2000, © Donald Cooper/Photostage; p. 58: Northern Broadsides and West Yorkshire Playhouse, Leeds 2009, © Donald Cooper/Photostage; p. 62: RSC/Barbican Theatre,

London 2000, © Donald Cooper/Photostage; p. 64: Ludlow Festival 2010, © Donald Cooper/Photostage; p. 68: Synetic Theater 2011, © Graeme Shaw/GBS Photography; p. 70: RSC/Royal Shakespeare Theatre 1985, © Donald Cooper/Photostage; p. 72: RSC/Barbican Theatre, London 2000, © Donald Cooper/Photostage; p. 86: Synetic Theater 2011, © Graeme Shaw/GBS Photography; p. 91 top: Regent's Park Open Air Theatre 1979, © John Timbers/ArenaPAL; p. 91 bottom: Ludlow Festival 2010, © Donald Cooper/Photostage; p. 102: Donmar Theatre 2007, © Donald Cooper/Photostage; p. 108: Crucible Theatre, Sheffield 2011, © Donald Cooper/Photostage; p. 112: RSC/The Other Place, Stratford-upon-Avon 1989, © Donald Cooper/Photostage; p.114: Northern Broadsides and West Yorkshire Playhouse Leeds 2009, © Donald Cooper/Photostage; p. 116 RSC/Swan Theatre 2004, © Donald Cooper/Photostage; p. 122; RSC Tour/Warwick Arts Centre 2009, © Donald Cooper/Photostage; p. 132: Synetic Theater 2011, © Graeme Shaw/GBS Photography; p. 134: Birmingham Repertory Theatre 1993, © Donald Cooper/Photostage; p. 143 top: Crucible Theatre, Sheffield 2011, © Donald Cooper/Photostage; p. 143 middle left: RSC/Royal Shakespeare Theatre 1979, © Donald Cooper/Photostage; p. 43 middle right: Paul Robeson and Peggy Ashcroft in Othello 1930, Bettmann/Corbis; p. 143 bottom: Northern Broadsides and West Yorkshire Playhouse Leeds 2009, © Donald Cooper/Photostage; p. 148: RSC/Swan Theatre 2004, © Geraint Lewis; p. 150: Ludlow Festival 2010, © Donald Cooper/Photostage; p. 152: RSC/Barbican Theatre, London 2000, © Donald Cooper/Photostage; p. 158: RSC Tour/Warwick Arts Centre 2009, © Geraint Lewis; p. 170: RSC/Barbican Theatre, London 1986, © Donald Cooper/Photostage; p. 174: Crucible Theatre, Sheffield 2011, © Johan Persson/ArenaPAL; p. 178: Cheek by Jowl/Riverside Studios, London 2004, © Donald Cooper/Photostage; p. 180: Ludlow Festival 2010, © Donald Cooper/Photostage; p. 183 top: RSC/Royal Shakespeare Theatre 1985, © Donald Cooper/Photostage; p. 183 bottom: Donmar Theatre 2007, © Geraint Lewis; p. 196: Synetic Theater 2011, © Graeme Shaw/GBS Photography; p. 200 left: Northern Broadsides and West Yorkshire Playhouse Leeds 2009, © Donald Cooper/Photostage; p. 200 right: Cheek by Jowl/Riverside Studios, London 2004, © Donald Cooper/Photostage; p. 204: Ludlow

Festival 2010, © Donald Cooper/Photostage;
p. 218: RSC/Barbican Theatre, London 2000, © Donald
Cooper/Photostage; p. 221: RSC/Swan Theatre 2004,
© Donald Cooper/Photostage; p. 224: RSC/Barbican Theatre,
London 1986, © Donald Cooper/Photostage; p. 225 top:
Shakespeare's Globe 2007, © Johan Persson/ArenaPAL;
p. 225 bottom: RSC/Barbican Theatre, London 2000,
© Donald Cooper/Photostage; p. 227: Northern Broadsides
and West Yorkshire Playhouse Leeds 2009, © Donald
Cooper/Photostage; p. 232: Donmar Theatre 2007, Johan
Persson/ArenaPAL; p. 233: Moorish ambassador, © University
of Birmingham Collections; p. 234: Glyndebourne Festival
Opera 2001, © Donald Cooper/Photostage; p. 236: 'Descent
of Christ into Limbo' by Jacopo Bellini, © DEA/A. Dagli Orti/
Getty Images; p. 237: Crucible Theatre, Sheffield 2011,
© Johan Persson/ArenaPAL; p. 241 left: Laurence Olivier
and Maggie Smith in Othello 1964, © Topfoto/ArenaPAL;
p. 241 right: Paul Robeson in Othello 2006, © Topfoto;
p. 242: Patrick Stewart as Othello with Patrice Johnson as
Desdemona in the Shakespeare Theatre Company's Othello
(1997). Photo by Carol Rosegg. P. 243: Still from the film O
2001, © Miramax/Dimension Films/The Kobal Collection/
Bob Basha; p. 244: Synetic Theater 2011, © Graeme Shaw/
GBS Photography; p. 245: Keeley Hawes and Eamonn Walker
in Othello 2001, © AF Archive/Alamy.

Sources

The quotations in the Critics' forum section are from the
following sources:

Extract from 'Lecture V: Othello' from Shakespearean Tragedy
by A. C. Bradley, 1904, Macmillan and Co.; extract from
'Diabolic intellect and the noble hero' from The Common
Pursuit by F. R. Leavis, 1952, Chatto & Windus; extract from
The Noble Moor by Helen Gardner, Proceedings of the British
Academy, volume LXI, 1955; extract from Shakespeare by
Germaine Greer, 1986, Oxford University Press; extract
from Shakespeare by Kiernan Ryan, 1989, Pearson Education
Ltd; extract from 'Othello's identity, postcolonial theory
and contemporary African rewritings of Othello' by Jyotsna
Singh and from 'Cultural materialism, Othello and the politics
of plausibility' by Alan Sinfield in Lena Cowen Orlin (ed.),
Othello, New Casebook series, 2004, Palgrave Macmillan;
extract from 'The pathos of Western modernity: Charivari' in
Big-time Shakespeare by Michael D. Bristol, 1996, Routledge.

 Produced for Cambridge University Press by
White-Thomson Publishing
+44 (0)843 208 7460
www.wtpub.co.uk

Managing editor: Sonya Newland
Designer: Clare Nicholas
Concept design: Jackie Hill